P9-CBP-171

Books That Don't Bore 'Em

Young Adult Books That Speak to This Generation

James Blasingame

New York • Toronto • London • Auckland • Sydney
Mexico City • New Delhi • Hong Kong • Buenos Aires

Teaching *Resources*

To Margaret Blasingame (1928–1986), who believed that
all children are special and all children can learn, and to
Virginia Dooley, who patiently coaxed this book out of me.

Cover design by Maria Lilja
Interior design by Holly Grundon
Interior photos courtesy of the author

"I Never Said I Wasn't Difficult" by Sara Holbrook from I Never Said I Wasn't Difficult
by Sara Holbrook. Copyright © 1997. Published by Boyd's Mills Press.

ISBN-13 978-0-439-91963-0
ISBN-10 0-439-91963-0
Copyright © 2007 by James Blasingame
All rights reserved. Published by Scholastic Inc.
Printed in the U.S.A.

1 2 3 4 5 6 7 8 9 10   40   14 13 12 11 10 09 08 07

Table of Contents

Foreword
by Gary Soto

Several years ago I received a complimentary textbook in which a story of mine was presented with zealous illustrations adorning the borders (textbook companies are of the mind that the louder the artwork, the more fun the literature is). I glanced at my story and, at the end, read the questions posed to provoke thought or ignite debate about my intentions. There was, for instance, a question that went something like this: "Soto employs sensory language in juxtaposition to the lyric expression of the boy's uncertain new relationship, emphasizing the dilemma of a character's situation and his personal assessment in context. How do you think the author solved this problem?" I reread the question and looked up, mystified—no, terrified. What if a bright high school student posed this question to me in public? What would I do? Rake sweat from my pleated brow? Cup a hairy ear and say, "Eh, young fella?" Change the question around and answer, "Yes, I'm from Fresno, California"?

I make light of this moment and confess my shortcomings. Most writers—and in the section of this book called "In the Authors' Words" this will be evident—wrestle with the writing part and couldn't provide answers without stirring up a tornado of confusion. Most of us wordsmiths are plagued with other kinds of worry, such as the pace of a story, fresh phrasing, true and convincing dialogue, heartfelt moments, the self-censoring apparatus within us, succinctness, and so on. Sure, we read a lot (at my bedside this day are the collected stories of Elizabeth Bowen and a novel in Spanish by Paul Coelho). Wisely, however, we leave our impressions about books to scholars, such as James Blasingame. Scholars are trained thinkers who read literary text better than writers do.

I have written critical essays, and understand this sort of intellectual exploration. But for me, writing criticism has always been a sort of Fred Flintstone experience in that it feels like chiseling rocks; my literary prose has a forced feeling. This is why I appreciate Blasingame, whose voice is natural, confident, erudite, and speaks volumes of his obvious dedication to and love for his material. He is a champion of adolescent literature and flexes his mental gifts here. He begins by defining young adult literature and even suggests its therapeutic nature when he writes, "Young adult literature may just be the lifeboat teachers and students alike need to stay afloat." I believe this true, but it wasn't until Professor Blasingame put it this way that I recognized what I had been doing for a long time. If we debate within ourselves the purpose of our craft, we writers shed our egos and stand shoulder-to-shoulder with our readers. We recognize that young adult literature wants to speak to youth, or, perhaps, speak for youth—on those occasions when young people doubt themselves, doubt the adult world with its lies and distortions, and doubt the very future of the planet.

I recall my high school years. Time was slow, as if a magnet inside the school's clock pulled the sweeping hand in the other direction. My three years there felt like an eternity. My grades were anemic, but I knew I'd get out eventually! I was moody, I was a non-joiner, and I was a loner (as a good many writers are). Though I never saw young adult literature— a small wave then, but now a tsunami in the publishing world —it wasn't because my teachers were unkind. No, the problem was that there were no guides; they weren't sure where to look for suggested reading. Now, Blasingame has provided this much needed guide. His tome is thick as a medical dictionary. In fact, it may be taken as medicine. It's scholarly; this much is certain. It's also friendly and generous as it delves into young adult literature on every topic—animal stories, biography, graphic novels, intolerance, outdoor adventures, and so on. It tells us about the publishing world and offers lists of awards.

Better yet, we also get to hear from the writers themselves in the form of mini-interviews. Reading the interviews reaffirms our impressions that we are flesh and bone. Sure, we may have photos on the backs of our books, smiley sorts of portraits, but when we read these interviews (many of them done by e-mail), we are able to feel the personalities of our own favorite writers and learn from them. I'm thinking of Laurie Halse Anderson, author of *Prom*, who in her interview says that proms are celebrations of youth; they are also grotesque when she realizes "the money spent on proms is truly obscene and stupid." This is a wonderful interview—and not because I agree with Ms. Anderson—but because the voice caught is accurate, full of passion, and even oddly contradictory (she's in favor of proms, but wait, she's not!). In short, she has the writer's mind; we just can't be reined in!

Writers are not in search of readers. No, that may not be true, either. I think what is paramount is our stubborn desire to work language well, whether it's in a novel, short story, play, or poetry. We're obsessed. We rise early to write, or we stay up late to write. Dark circles show up under our eyes. Pencils are chewed. Our printers spit out manuscript pages, which are then read by friends, relatives, editors—anyone who is willing to comment on our productivity.

I believe it's the same with scholars. They fret, too. They worry about the exactness of their writing and, moreover, their critical meaning. Blasingame set out to produce a book about young adult literature that would mean something. He is a source of energy and pleasure; he is friend of writers.

Introduction

I have always loved books. As a boy, growing up outside of Cedar Rapids, Iowa, I waited all week for Friday, the day our mother would load all four kids into the station wagon and head to town for groceries and books. There in the parking lot of Witwer's Grocery Store, she would park right next to the Cedar Rapids Public Library bookmobile, and the four of us (Jeff, Mike, Terri, and I) would hit the bookmobile steps at a sprint, bouncing off the walls and each other until we stood in front of the rows of books, all carefully selected by the folks at the downtown library.

No Brinks armored car ever carried more precious treasure than that bookmobile. We always checked out our limit, read all the way home, and finished every book by Thursday. And every Friday we would once again race up the bookmobile steps and gaze in wonder at the new titles that hadn't been there the week before: *Have Spacesuit, Will Travel*; *Mike Mulligan and his Steam Shovel*; and *Little House on the Prairie*.

Our house was full of books. Our mother, like her mother, had filled spare hours of rural life with reading and was learned well beyond her formal education. She read to us every night: *The Story About Ping, Bartholomew and the Oobleck*, and many more, all of which were lovingly saved through the years and now reside in my brother Mike's home where he and his wife, Renée, keep a veritable library for Katelin, Alex, and Nick.

Years went by, and after graduating from the University of Northern Iowa, I landed the job of my dreams as a high school English teacher and wrestling coach in central Iowa. Every day was filled with books. My favorite days were at the beginning of each semester when I introduced the independent reading unit. Working from a list obtained from the American Library Association, I talked about the books I liked and let the students tell about the books they liked. Most students shared my love of reading and went way beyond the required one book per quarter. I was in heaven.

Then everything changed.

I was assigned to teach a literature class for students who did not fit neatly into either a remedial reading or college preparatory class. The curriculum consisted of the teacher's choice of books from boxes in a store room, some of which were not too bad; outside selections were fine, too.

The first month was a disaster. The students turned up their noses at everything. I tried some of the easier books from the canon, recent popular adult fiction, various genres from mystery to science fiction, but nothing piqued their interest. The principal even gave us a little money to visit a popular bookstore and go out for lunch. The students filled out questionnaires about their interests, and I created individualized lists of novels, nonfiction books, and magazines for them to investigate at the bookstore. They had fun, but very few came away with anything to read that they liked. Class was only marginally better.

Then one day, in a box of 30 paperbacks, Louie Banks came to class, and nothing would be the same again. Louie, the protagonist in Chris Crutcher's *Running Loose*, is a teenager whose problems range from an unethical high school coach to his first sexual experience. I read the first 10 pages out loud in class and assigned 20 more for the following day.

That next day I wondered if I might be in the wrong class. The students were all there on time—a rarity. Not only were they on time, but as the bell rang, they had their books out and were looking at me expectantly, obviously waiting for something.

They were waiting to talk about the book. They *loved* this book.

I opened class with a question about Louie Banks's conflict with his football coach, and a sea of hands shot up. They were dying to share their thoughts and feelings about the story! They genuinely hated Louie's football coach, Lednecky, and they were disgusted by the win-at-any-cost attitude toward sports in Louie's hometown, something many of them had witnessed in real life. Conversation was so lively that, at some point, I abandoned my prepared questions and concentrated on making sure that everyone got a turn. And this wasn't an anomaly; lively discussion became the daily norm. They roared through *Running Loose*, many of them reading it in a single day. At one point, I asked the last student out the door how this book differed from our previous reads. "It isn't boring," she told me.

Suddenly we were sprinting up those bookmobile steps together, and I was back in heaven.

Deathwatch by Robb White was next. They loved that one, too. Years later, I would learn about reader-response theory, adolescent developmental phases, and instructional approaches such as literature circles, and pre-/during/post-reading strategies, but at the time I wasn't employing any theories or strategies. I was simply witnessing the power of a good book.

Good young adult literature is powerful. It grabs kids' interest and speaks to them in language they can understand about the very issues they worry about on a daily basis.

Much has happened since that baptismal experience with young adult literature. I spent twenty-something years as a high school teacher and principal before joining the folks in higher education, where I was fortunate enough to come under the tutelage of John (Jack) Bushman and Alleen Pace Nilsen. I have been blessed with the opportunity to make thousands of friends among young readers, parents, teachers, librarians, authors, agents, editors, and publishers, and to read hundreds of fabulous new books.

Thank goodness for that day many years ago when the students and I got our hands on *Running Loose*, a book that wasn't boring. In the following pages, you will find hundreds of books that I hope will enable you and your students to have that same powerful experience.

CHAPTER 1

WHAT IS YOUNG ADULT LITERATURE?

I NEVER SAID I WASN'T DIFFICULT

By Sara Holbrook

I never said I wasn't difficult,
I mostly want my way.
Sometimes I talk back
or pout
and don't have much to say.
I've been known to yell, "so what,"
when I'm stepping out of bounds.
I want you there for me
and yet,
I don't want you around.
I wish I had more privacy
and never had to be alone.
I want to run away,
I'm scared to leave my home.
I'm too tired to be responsible.
I wish that I were boss.

I want to blaze new trails.
I'm terrified
that I'll get lost.
I wish an answer came
every time I asked you, "why."
I wish you weren't a know-it-all.
Why do you question when I'm
bored?
I won't be cross examined.
I hate to be ignored.
I know
I shuffle messages like cards,
some to show and some to hide.
But,
if you think I'm hard to live with
you should try me on inside.

The dilemma of the first-person narrator in Sara Holbrook's poem humorously, sympathetically, and—as most of us who work with adolescents would agree—accurately captures the constant tension that seems to exist in the teenage psyche. Holbrook (*Chicks Up Front, Nothing's the End of the World, Isn't She Ladylike?, The Dog Ate My Homework*), a popular poet with middle school students and teachers, is remarkably adept at reflecting the essence of the adolescent experience. In fact, as you will see later in this chapter, her poem sounds very much like the set of opposite choices or conflicts that noted theorist of adolescent psychology, Erik Erikson, claims young people face. According to the Academy of Child and Adolescent Psychiatry (ACAP, 2004), not only do polar opposites of behavior plague this age, but also a number of other elements, such as "focus on self, alternating between high expectations and low self-esteem," "worries about being normal," "development of ideals and selection of role models," and much more (2004).

If the emotional and psychological urges of adolescence are such powerful forces, then harnessing them for the purposes of reading and writing instruction, as well as meeting the developmental needs of students, seems much more logical than attempting to swim against the tide. Well-chosen young adult literature may be just the lifeboat teachers and students alike need to stay afloat. It can help young people with a number of developmental needs, as well as help teachers to meet learning outcomes or standards for literacy.

In this chapter we will attempt to define young adult literature and briefly explore the nature of adolescence. Specific recommendations for choosing authors and books and using them in the classroom will be covered in greater detail in later chapters.

Out in the Real World of Reading

The power of well-chosen young adult literature was brought home to me on a recent visit to Catalina Ventura School, a K–8 school in central Phoenix, Arizona, where I spent a day with eighth graders. Since the majority of students at the school are of Mexican-American heritage, for a read-aloud I chose a book by an acclaimed Chicana writer. I love this book for its artful use of language and subtle yet deep thematic content about the complexities of life for a young person growing up in a Chicano neighborhood. I've also watched as high school students were entranced by the story and used it as a springboard for reflecting and writing about their own lives.

As I read aloud to the first eighth-grade class of the day, however, I was no more than two paragraphs into the chapter I had chosen when I had that sinking feeling that the lesson was failing. Notes were passed, eyes glazed over, and shoulder-punching contests erupted. I slogged through the chapter anyway. When we launched into the writing part of the lesson and the kids could discuss and write about their own lives, the majority were soon engaged in brainstorming the memorable events in their lives, detailing the sights, sounds, and smells of those events, and expressing some emotion over the people they had loved or lost. I had intended to keep referring to the story I had read during the writing lesson, but any references to that narrative seemed to fall on deaf ears. Hardly any of the kids could recall interesting and meaningful moments in the story, moments that hit home for them.

A teacher who will not change horses in the middle of the stream is a teacher who will drown both herself and her horse. I knew I needed to make a change fast or face a miserable day for me, for the entire eighth grade, and for the eighth-grade teachers who were patiently giving up their English classes so that a university "expert" could interlope. I had brought other books with me, just in case, so I grabbed a different one out of my briefcase. As I began reading this second book to the second-period eighth-grade English class, I knew immediately I had a winner. In fact, the difference between the two books was so huge that the second book would actually effect a change in the reading offerings at the school.

The second book was *The Bully* by Paul Langan (Scholastic's Bluford Series), and it took the next six periods of eighth-grade classes by storm. I was no more than two paragraphs into reading my chosen chapter when I could tell from the absolute silence that the audience was hooked. Silence gave way to the choral groans and laughter before a tense moment resulted in silence again and finally cheers when the protagonist, a small, bullied ninth grader named Darrell, confronted the school bully, Tyrae, unexpectedly in the school cafeteria and sent him sprawling in a pool of spilled spaghetti.

At the end of the chapter, I asked that second-period class if anyone would like me to leave one of my copies with the teacher; three fourths of the hands shot up.

Not only was the novel a huge success, but it also enabled the students to make a reading/writing connection and launched them into their own personal narratives and poetry. After reading that one chapter from *The Bully*, we had grand success in writing workshop for the remainder of each period because we had a good model to refer to. In attempting to facilitate the brainstorming that would enhance setting and word choice in the kids' writing, I asked, "Did the Bluford High School cafeteria feel real to you? How do you think the author accomplished that?" "Was Darrell's problem with Tyrae a typical one for kids at school or one you've never seen before?" Students were soon re-creating memorable events from their own lives and making word choices that would appeal to the senses to make the events seem real.

Students besieged their teacher with requests for *The Bully*. Soon he was exploring the whole Bluford Series and discovering that Townsend Press made classroom sets available very inexpensively. *The Bully* has become common reading at Catalina Ventura.

A Definition of Young Adult Literature

So what was it about *The Bully* that those eighth graders connected with? *The Bully* has many of the qualities of successful young adult literature, so it provides a starting point for constructing a good definition.

I propose a working definition of young adult literature with the four characteristics listed in Figure 1.1. We'll take an in-depth look at each of these characteristics.

Characteristics of Young Adult Literature

Young adult literature

1) has characters and issues young readers can identify with; those issues and characters are treated in a way that does not invalidate, minimize, or devalue them.

2) is framed in language that young readers can understand.

3) emphasizes plot above everything else.

4) is written for an audience of young adults.

Figure 1.1

IDENTIFICATION

Young adult literature has characters and issues young readers can identify with, treated in a way that does not invalidate, minimize, or devalue them.

Whether you call them archetypes or stereotypes, there are certain experiences and certain kinds of people that are common to adolescence. Although it may seem old hat to an adult reader, the first bully that a kid meets on the street or at school is the first bully in his or her life—it's a new and powerful encounter for that youngster. The first day in a new school or a new neighborhood is an unaccustomed and unnerving experience for a young person, as is a family divorce or loss of a loved one, regardless of how many people have endured it before. A broken heart is a broken heart. Reading about it may help a young person validate his or her own experience and make some kind of meaning out of it.

When Chris Crutcher, one of young adult literature's most accomplished authors, addressed high school students at an Arizona English Teachers' Association state convention, he opened with a statement of great import in understanding what young adult literature is and what makes it succeed. Chris said, "You and I have a lot in common even though I am 53 and you are probably 18 or so. We're both as old as we have ever been, and we both have our whole lives ahead of us." The significance of this statement lies in understanding that for a young reader the issues of adolescence are the most serious he or she has ever faced, and knowing how to handle these issues does not seem as clear as it will with an adult's hindsight.

Young adult literature addresses not only the after-school-special variety of adolescent problems, (e.g., getting a date for the prom, making an athletic team, developing new friendships after a move across the country), but it can also deal with some very disturbing aspects of life that a vulnerable adolescent may

> **1** YOUNG ADULT LITERATURE HAS CHARACTERS AND ISSUES YOUNG READERS CAN **IDENTIFY** WITH, AND THOSE ISSUES AND CHARACTERS ARE TREATED IN A WAY THAT DOES NOT INVALIDATE, MINIMIZE, OR DEVALUE THEM.

feel powerless to combat (e.g., rape [Speak], child molestation [Uncle Vampire], and AIDS [Night Kites]). Whatever the issues, young people are better off first confronting them and examining strategies for coping with them in the fictional world than in real life, although this may sometimes be unavoidable. Reading about characters who have the same problems that they do can provide affirmation for adolescents, most of whom tend to think that they are different and that no one could possibly face the same horrendous challenges.

According to Laurie Halse Anderson (*Speak, Catalyst, Fever 1793, Prom*), there are many more young adults who face serious problems than most people are willing to admit, as evidenced by the mail she gets from readers:

> *The letters that I get are heart wrenching. . . . [T]here is a whole lot more of sexual assault going on in the middle schools and the high schools of America than even the experts are willing to admit. It's appalling. But they also write to me about harassment, about bullying, about feeling powerless, and about feeling voiceless.*
>
> *(Anderson, 2005, p. 55)*

Anderson goes on to describe the letters she has received from young people about her novel *Speak*, the story of a ninth-grade girl who is raped at a high school beer party and the emotional anguish and clinical-level depression she suffers in secret through her first year of high school. It is not just young women who have shared the horrid experience who relate to the book, as Anderson explains:

> *Speak is a book about depression. Pretty much every kid in America has gotten to that ugly, gloomy, dark hole that they can't find a way out of. I've gotten letters that say, "OK, like, I'm the biggest jock of the school and if you ever tell anybody this I'll kill you, but I know exactly what that girl feels like." That's something we need to pay attention to.*
>
> *(Anderson, in press)*

Even young people who haven't yet faced serious problems know classmates who have, and they fear that one day these problems will knock on their own doors. Teens can see themselves and their friends in these stories of young people with difficult lives, which makes this *their* literature in a way that *Moby Dick* or *Of Mice and Men* can never be.

Mel Glenn (*Split Image, The Taking of Room 114, Who Killed Mr. Chippendale?, Class Dismissed, My Friend's Got This Problem, Mr. Chandler*, and more), who spent 31 years as a masterful teacher at his alma mater, Abraham Lincoln High School in Brooklyn, has this to say about the young adult reader's need to find characters to identify with:

> It may be too simple to say, but I think a major key for good young adult literature is one word—identification. Even if the setting is foreign, the characters alien, the plot weird, when a reader can say, "Hey, I feel what that character is going through" a tangible connection has been made between printed word and human recipient, or in other words, what is that character to me or me to that character that I should care so; the reader and the protagonist intertwine.
>
> (Glenn, interview, 11/9/04)

In the case of *The Bully*, 99.9 percent of readers will see themselves or someone close to them in the main character's (Darrell) woes, from the lunchroom to the wrestling mat. When his single-parent mother decides to move from Maryland to California, Darrell must leave his friends in Baltimore behind and go to an environment completely foreign to him. He loses the support system he had built up over years in his old neighborhood and finds himself at the mercy of bullies who test his courage and teachers who don't know that he is a good and honest person but instead suspect him of being a troublemaker. Darrell has to navigate his way through a new family organization with an uncle he doesn't like and cousins he can't stand. Slowly Darrell makes and earns new friends, including members of the high school wrestling team, who will eventually help him out with the bully problem (or at least even the odds for him), and an attractive female classmate who has a romantic interest in him.

ACCESSIBLE LANGUAGE

Specifically, this often means vocabulary is accessible to young readers without much explanation. Defining a few unfamiliar or new words is fine, but if lecturing or note-taking is required to translate most of the text into language the readers can understand (a practice which denotes the learner is being asked to memorize an adult's interpretation of text or events), then this text is not really young adult literature. For example, *The Outsiders* is about two rival social groups vying for dominance in a city, and so is *Romeo and Juliet*. Both texts have content that is appropriate for eighth- or ninth-grade readers, but one has language that will not be accessible to most of them without considerable help from an expert (the teacher). *Romeo and Juliet* is great literature and is appropriate for young readers (some of whom can understand a great deal, but not all, of the language), but it would not be appropriately called "young adult literature" because of its language challenges.

I contend that if young readers cannot read a book because the language is unfamiliar to the point of being indecipherable to them, it is not a true reading experience, and their reading skill development will plateau rather than climb. Rather than experience literature in this way for years, young readers will be far better served through a means of engaging with literature called reader-response. The concept of reader-response theory as first espoused by Louise Rosenblatt (1938) will be discussed in depth in Chapter 2, but the basic concept as applied to young adult readers is this: We need to facilitate our students' intense engagement with their reading and help them make their own meaning of the text rather than memorizing what someone else tells them a book means. They can't make connections to their own lives and the nature of the human experience, nor can they look for universal truths or evaluate the quality of a work or find comfort or entertainment in it if they can't read and understand it.

> **2** YOUNG ADULT LITERATURE IS TYPICALLY FRAMED IN LANGUAGE THAT YOUNG READERS CAN **UNDERSTAND**, AND ITS COMPLEXITY IS COMMENSURATE WITH THE READING SKILLS OF THE INTENDED AUDIENCE.

Again, in the case of *The Bully*, the language sounds familiar and authentic to a middle school reader. Paul Langan's skillful narration is in the voice of a ninth grader, and it reflects the feelings, hopes and fears, frustrations and insecurities that monopolize a 15-year-old's thoughts. There are no suspect words or concerns to remind the reader that an adult writer created this text. And even though the slang and regional vernacular of young people varies somewhat with time and place, S. E. Hinton's classic young adult novel, *The Outsiders*, has shown that dialogue, if not made too timely or place-specific, can stay fresh for 37 years and longer. Both *The Outsiders* and *The Bully* also show that obscene language is not necessary for authenticity, although some young adult authors do at times use this kind of language in developing believable characters.

IMPORTANCE OF PLOT

Plot drives the story in young adult literature. Both Gordon Korman (*Son of the Mob, No More Dead Dogs, A Day in the Life of a Garbage Bag*) and Rodman Philbrick (*The Last Book in the Universe, Freak the Mighty, The Young Man and the Sea*) have made the point that good young adult literature will generally emphasize story over literary artistry. Young adult literature works best if it is not encumbered with so many literary devices that the reader has to pick through the allusions, metaphors, and symbols to find the actual story (Blasingame, 2004, p. 519). In an interview, Philbrick writes

> [A]n overly developed style—which calls attention to the author—can actually detract from the power of the narrative, and thereby diminish the story. And I do believe in the general rule that a good story indifferently written will trump a poor story well-written. All of which is not to say that I don't spend many hours rewriting my prose, trying to get it just right. In my case that means taking out all the extra words.
>
> (Blasingame, 2004, p. 519)

This doesn't mean, of course, that one of the qualifying characteristics of good young adult literature is that it's "indifferently written" but rather that it will not resonate with young readers if it does not have a good story. Kevin Brooks (*Martyn Pig, Lucas, Kissing the Rain, Candy*) explains that quality writing for young adults should find a happy medium: "I've always loved really good writing, especially good writing that includes a good story; that's the ideal—when great writing doesn't get too much in the way of the story" (Blasingame, 2003, p. 76). Brooks goes on to explain that even if he likes the literary quality of a passage he has written, he has learned to edit out "passages that . . . get in the way of the story."

> 3 YOUNG ADULT
> LITERATURE IS
> **PLOT DRIVEN**.

By comparison, consider Carson McCullers' novel *Member of the Wedding*, a masterful work of literary artistry. *Member of the Wedding* should not be considered young adult literature by virtue of the fact that is *does not* emphasize story over literary artistry. Literary masterpiece though it is, with a protagonist who is clearly an adolescent, *Member of the Wedding* contains a conflict and resolution subtly nuanced over the course of the whole book, making it appropriate for a high school class in American literature but not qualifying it as young adult literature.

As recognized author, editor, and former president of ALAN Michael Cart points out, "The traditional *New Yorker* story that is essentially an actionless mood piece or moment-of-truth story simply doesn't cut it with young adult readers" (Cart, interview, 2004). In young adult literature something needs to happen; a conflict, minor or major, needs to come to its resolution fairly frequently to match the attention span of an adolescent audience. In *The Bully*, the climax comes in the school cafeteria when Darrell is initially humiliated by the bully Tyrae, who spills Darrell's tray of food. But when Darrell faces off with Tyrae, and the older boys on the wrestling team stand behind him, Darrell sends a bawling Tyrae to the hospital with a broken wrist. The scene is almost pure narration, pure story.

<table>
<tr>
<td>

4   YOUNG ADULT LITERATURE IS **WRITTEN FOR** AN AUDIENCE OF **YOUNG ADULTS.**

</td>
</tr>
</table>

WRITTEN FOR YOUNG ADULTS

My initial attempt at choosing a passage that would grab the Catalina Ventura eighth graders' attention failed because although the book had an 11-year-old protagonist, the language and perspective of the narrator were those of an adult looking back, with adult eyes, words, and sensibilities. This was a book *about* adolescence but the intended audience was an adult audience. Award-winning author Jack Gantos (*Joey Pigza Swallowed the Key, Heads or Tails, Hole in My Life*), on the other hand, modifies voice and perspective to fit the intended young audience. Read a Gantos book about fifth grade, and you'll get a fifth grader's sense of humor and perspective, and the same is true of Gantos's sixth- and seventh-grade books, as well as his book about his life from age 19 to 22 (*Hole in My Life*). Likewise, Paul Langan succeeds with *The Bully* because he writes with an audience of young adults in mind.

The Nature of Adolescence

Young adult literature should logically deal with the issues of adolescence. To understand the basics of these issues, we need to have some understanding of the "emotional, psychological, developmental forces" mentioned earlier, especially if we are going to "harness them" (also suggested earlier). What issues of growing up are common to the young adult experience? What aspects of their development will adolescents potentially identify with in their reading? Young readers will not name a developmental level as if they were psychologists, but they will recognize events that resonate with them and be motivated to discuss them.

The ideas of Erik Erikson are especially useful in attempting to understand adolescence for the purpose of selecting meaningful literature for young readers. Erikson is most frequently credited with coining the phrase "identity crisis," and he believed that without successfully resolving conflicts in each stage of development, human beings would have difficulty moving on in their development.

Erikson posited human life as having eight developmental stages, including the fifth stage, adolescence (from puberty to roughly 18 years of age). Like Sara

Holbrook's poem, "I Never Said I Wasn't Difficult" (page 7), Erikson described this stage as a time of conflict between polar opposites that he called "ego identity" and "role confusion." Ideally, a healthy tension eventually develops between these opposites and results in a happy medium: a person who neither rejects all roles or identities suggested by society, nor identifies completely with the values of one group (in the worst-case scenario, a cult or gang, both of which will provide the individual with a ready-made and complete system of values and beliefs). This happy (and healthy) medium that an adolescent should reach (a desirable state of mental health) is one in which he or she has a firm idea of who he or she is and what values, beliefs, and behaviors that entails. A healthy adolescent should not become so entrenched in a belief system as to have zero tolerance for any other system of beliefs, nor so inflexible as to be incapable of self-reflection or change. According to Erikson, healthy adolescence involves experimenting with roles in life, arriving at the ability to accept deferred gratification when working toward desired goals, developing clear gender identity, and building a sense of competence and confidence for future success.

If we accept the premise that young adults vicariously experience the events as characters do in the books they read, then the benefits of reading widely in helping them resolve the issue of identity should be obvious. We surely prefer that our students be spared the kinds of experiences that can be physically or emotionally harmful. Given the limits of time and space, young people who read a lot will have a better understanding than those who know only what they have seen with their own eyes.

Closing Thoughts

In the final analysis, works of young adult literature might best be understood and appreciated for the purpose they serve in helping young readers through this crucial, formative time in their lives. As young people try on different identities, begin to strongly define their personal values and answer the question "Who am I?", literature in which they seem themselves, whether it is the person they are, the person they are becoming, or the person they want to be, can play an important role in facilitating healthy growth toward adulthood. In the next chapter, we'll explore how young adult literature can serve this purpose for young people from diverse walks of life, as well as how it can be an absolute gold mine for meeting benchmarks of academic achievement.

CHAPTER 2

WHY USE YOUNG ADULT LITERATURE?

ven armed with a definition of young adult literature and an understanding of the nature of adolescence, you may still wonder how to face questions and concerns from parents, the community, and others about the use of young adult literature. In this chapter, we'll look at some of the issues that surround the use of young adult literature and the compelling reasons for using it. We'll discuss how you can use young adult literature to meet national and state standards and motivate your students to become lifelong readers while incorporating the best research-supported instructional practices.

It's Not Either . . . Or; It's What . . . When

When it comes to young adult literature and the canon, we must not think of it as an *either . . . or* situation, but rather, a *what . . . when* situation: *what* books should we use *when* to move our students along a path to becoming lifelong readers whose interpretive skills continue to grow. Matching students with books that are appropriate to their reading skills, emotional maturity, and life experience will enable them to process what they read with success and satisfaction. Young adult literature also serves as a vehicle for helping young readers transition successfully into adult reading, including the classics, contemporary literature, and popular fiction and nonfiction. Recent evidence suggests, as we will see later in this chapter, that failure to provide for this transition may have the effect of stunting the growth of readers' interest in reading and their skills for interpreting it, resulting in adults who simply do not read literature.

We give our children Dr. Seuss as early readers, with the hope that they will one day be ready for *Dr. Zhivago.* We recommend *Charlotte's Web*, fully believing they will one day be capable of interpreting the political meaning of another barnyard in *Animal Farm.* But would it make sense to *start* with Pasternak and Orwell rather than Seuss and White? Not really. I remember my father putting me on a 28-inch adult bicycle in my last summer before kindergarten and giving me a big, rolling shove down the street, ignoring my mother's worried plea for installation of the training wheels. When the bike bounced off the curb and toppled, I left the majority of skin from my elbows and knees in a bloody trail along the pavement. That night my father put the training wheels on my bike. The next summer I learned to swim, but first I had to endure a brush with drowning. Can you guess how that happened? Teaching and learning happen best in thoughtfully prepared increments, not sink-or-swim absolutes.

Zone of Proximal Development

Riding a bike without training wheels at age 4 was way outside my "zone of proximal development." Zone of proximal development (ZPD) is a term first used by noted psychologist Lev Vygotsky (1896–1934) to define "the distance between the actual development level as determined by independent problem solving and the level of potential development as determined through problem solving under adult guidance or in collaboration with more capable peers" (Vygotsky, 1978). (See Figure 2.1.) Vygotsky theorized that tasks a child could accomplish with assistance would eventually become tasks the child could accomplish alone. Vygotsky's idea of assistance has come to be called "scaffolding." When you provide scaffolding for students, you provide only enough assistance to enable the learner to complete a task and move to the next level of learning or mastery.

Young adult literature provides us with a wealth of texts to choose from in a wide range of readability levels and relevant subject matter that are within our students' ZPDs. Your role in determining what literature fits within a student's ZPD involves finding the right balance between the interest level a book holds for that student and the distance between the young reader's reading level and the book's reading level. The goal is to select or recommend books that are interesting enough to the individual reader so that a mild increase in reading level is not discouraging. Ideally, as the year progresses, the student will read books at higher and higher reading levels, thus stretching to learn new vocabulary and to comprehend increasingly complex sentence structures. The wealth of wonderful young adult books makes this possible. Relying solely on the classics would make this much more of a challenge. Chapter 3 provides many suggestions for finding just the right books for your students in terms of reading levels and interests.

What a learner cannot do, even with help.

Zone of Proximal Development (ZPD)

What a learner can do independently.

Figure 2.1

Diverse Students, Diverse Books

Although the diversity of our students is increasing dramatically, the cultural heritage and experience of our student population had never been reflected in their reading until young adult literature came along. The narrow range of the human experience covered in traditional, canonical literature has typically been limited to what the late Ted Hipple, longtime executive secretary of the Assembly on Literature for Adolescents of the National Council of Teachers of English, called "DOWM," or Dead Old White Men.

I have nothing against dead old white men; in fact, I plan to be one someday. But it is very possible that the issues teens find relevant to their lives may not deal with hunting down evil masquerading as a whale, explaining the levels of hell, or distinguishing between windmills and evil giants (somehow evil seems to loom large in most of these books).

When I was in high school in the 1960s, the canon was really all that was available for teachers to use. J. D. Salinger's *Catcher in the Rye* (1952) and John Knowles's *A Separate Peace* (1960) were the only books that could even be considered young adult literature. *The Outsiders* (1967) and other late '60s landmark young adult books hadn't had time to make their way into classrooms. But all that has changed.

Books for Today's Students and Their Issues

Young adult literature is now readily available and inexpensive, and it deals with every topic under the sun. As Laurie Halse Anderson points out:

> Young adult literature is multicultural literature. We have accepted, pretty much every place in America . . . the need for multicultural reading in the curriculum. And if you think about adolescence as its own unique culture, the language, music, artistic expression, you will realize that they deserve books that reflect their cultural experience and what is going on inside them. . . . We have Walter Dean Myers and Gary Soto and all these authors that speak to the conditions of our readers so we can finally, in America, produce a literate generation. We haven't done that yet.
>
> (Anderson, 2005, p. 57)

What are some of these issues? Let's take a closer look.

CHANGING FAMILY STRUCTURE

The structure of the families in which our students live continues to change dramatically. As Fred Rodriguez, author of *Affirming Equity: A Framework for Teachers and Schools* (1999) proclaims, "The 1950s family is gone. The family of today is different, maybe no better or no worse, but different" (4). The trend is away from the traditional family with two biological parents in the home and toward single-parent families or families in which adults in the role of parent are not the biological parents. As of 2001, only 53 percent of adolescents between 15 and 17 years of age lived with both of their married, biological parents (Federal Interagency Forum on Child and Family Statistics).

GENDER AND SEXUAL IDENTITY

The gender or sexual identity of our students is also a consideration when addressing diversity, an issue largely ignored until the 1960s and still not proportionately represented in literature. As Michael Cart, former president of NCTE's Assembly on Literature for Adolescents and author and editor of numerous successful books, points out, one of the greatest reasons for reading literature is the lifesaving necessity of seeing one's own face reflected in the pages of a good book and the corollary comfort that derives from the knowledge that one is not alone.

Yet one group of teenage outsiders—GLBTQ youth (gay, lesbian, bisexual, transgender, and questioning)—continues to be nearly invisible. Since the 1969 publication of John Donovan's *I'll Get There. It Better Be Worth the Trip* (Harper & Row), the first young adult novel to deal with the issue of homosexuality, no more than 150 other titles have followed, a woefully inadequate average of four or five per year to give faces to millions of teens. (Cart, 2004).

Many students, of course, maintain silence about their sexual identity. The effect in years past of the absence of GLBTQ literature for young adults has been harmful to young people. As Alex Sanchez (*Rainbow Boys, Rainbow High, So Hard to Say*) remembers from his own childhood:

Believe me, I knew that I was gay—as surely as many of
you knew you were straight. And I hated myself for it.
Why? Because growing up gay or lesbian means growing up
surrounded by homophobia. At 13 years old, I believed that
being gay was the worst thing in the world a boy could be.
("Crossing Two Bridges," p. 57)

When young readers with doubts about their value as human beings absolutely cannot find themselves in their reading, the results can be devastating.

PHYSICAL AND SEXUAL ABUSE

Just as many gay and lesbian students maintain silence about their sexual identity, so do many students who are the victims of sexual, physical, or emotional abuse. Shame, intimidation, and even love for their abusers may prevent kids from revealing their plight, however, and statistically we know that for every 1,000 kids in America, approximately 17 of them from the ages of 12 to 17 are the victims of some form of abuse. This never happened to Nancy Drew or the Hardy Boys but it's happening to many of our students, and even those who do not experience it firsthand are often aware of it happening to their friends or classmates. Teachers need to be aware, as well, that they are required by law to report to the appropriate government agency any evidence they see that a student under their care may have been harmed.

MENTAL ILLNESS

Increasing numbers of young people also wrestle with mental health issues such as depression, bipolar disorder, anxiety, and eating disorders. Although one in five children has a diagnosable mental, emotional, or behavioral disorder (Surgeon General's Report on Mental Health, 1999), with the exceptions of Sylvia Plath's *The Bell Jar* and Joanne Greenberg's *I Never Promised You a Rose Garden*, not many books were written with young protagonists experiencing mental health issues until the last ten years or so. More recently, books such as A. M. Jenkins' *Damage* (2003), the story of an all-American-type (handsome high school football star) young man who hides the fact that he is unhappy and even suicidal, and John Marsden's *Checkers* (1996), whose anonymous narrator is telling her story from inside a mental institution, are driven by characters whose mental health is their major problem. Jack Gantos has written a three-book series that captures the experience of not only a dysfunctional family but also the struggle of a young adolescent dealing with ADHD.

Mental health issues also include substance abuse, and alcohol and drugs are very real parts of many adolescents' experiences. As of 2004, according to the Monitoring the Future Study done by the University of Michigan, 16.1 percent of eighth, tenth, and twelfth graders combined reported using illicit drugs in the past month. Although this reflects a decline in drugs such as marijuana and cocaine, and an overall decline in drug use, the use of new drugs such as OxyContin and Vicodin has remained the same or increased. Anabolic steroids, drugs that are in the headlines on a regular basis now, weren't even on anyone's radar screen back when *The Outsiders* (1967), *The Chocolate War* (1974), or *Forever* (1975) first came out.

These are the facts about the lives of our students. This is who they are, these are the lives they lead, the families they face, and the issues that challenge them on a daily basis. To omit this from their reading is to make reading meaningless to them.

You Are Not a Psychologist, Psychiatrist, or Therapist— Nor Should You Have to Be

One landmine we need to avoid in the process of providing our students with literature they can relate to is misapplied bibliotherapy. The term *bibliotherapy* refers to a type of counseling in which the client (young reader) is diagnosed as having certain problems and issues and supplied with reading matter that has characters going through the same things. The intention of bibliotherapy is good and has validation in research:

> *The underlying premise of bibliotherapy is that clients identify with literary characters similar to themselves, an association that helps the clients release emotions, gain new directions in life, and explore new ways of interacting (Gladding & Gladding, 1991). Teenage readers, for example, may feel relief that they are not the only ones facing a specific problem. They learn vicariously how to solve their problems by reflecting on how the characters in the book solve theirs (Hebert & Kent, 2000).*
>
> *(Abdullah, 2002)*

Although trained therapists use bibliotherapy effectively, teachers are generally not qualified to diagnose the problems of young people and implement a plan for therapy. Like all human beings, teenage readers are incredibly complex, and their lives are not appropriately judged or analyzed by us as classroom teachers, nor have they volunteered, or sought such treatment. It is my job as a classroom teacher to ensure that the literature I provide both in class and as recommended reading on independent reading lists reflects the myriad ways of being human, and the range of issues that teenagers face. It is not my job to analyze a student and provide a book based on what I think that student's issues are.

What Does Research Say Is the Best Way to Teach Literature?

When the principal gets an inquiring phone call (read: "complaint") from a parent who found *The Chocolate War* in a student's backpack, along with a reader-response journal, how can you defend this pedagogy as more than just a "touchy-feely," diluted curriculum? Are theory and research on your side, or is it all just for fun? Actually, theory and research are very much on your side. Some of this theory has been around for a very long time, and there is also newer, substantive research to support using young adult literature. This research shows that the most effective means for helping your students become lifelong readers is to give them literature they can easily relate to and guide them through activities to process their thinking about their reading.

Let's take a look at the theory and research in more depth.

VYGOTSKY'S THEORIES OF SOCIAL CONSTRUCTIVISM AND INTERNALIZATION OF LANGUAGE

Lev Vygotsky theorized that language does much more than provide a means for communication. As a child grows older, language becomes a tool for thinking and acts to influence or define a child's reality. Interaction with others is crucial because the child's cognitive development does not follow a preprogrammed plan but is largely constructed within social contexts experienced as a child. As Ricardo Schütz notes,

> [C]ognitive skills and patterns of thinking are not primarily determined by innate factors, but are the products of the activities practiced in the social institutions of the culture in which the individual grows up. . . . According to Vygotsky (1978), an essential feature of learning is that it awakens a variety of internal developmental processes that are able to operate only when the child is in the action of interacting with people in his environment and in cooperation with his peers.
>
> (2004)

Vygotsky's theories suggest that if we want young people to develop critical, rational, analytical minds, as well as language equal to the tasks society sets before them, we need to place them in social interaction that involves a lot of thinking and speaking and not have them remain quiet, passive learners in a teacher-centered learning environment. What better literature for firing students up for social interaction than young adult literature?

READER-RESPONSE THEORY

Reader-response theory further supports the use of young adult literature. As mentioned in Chapter 1, Louise Rosenblatt first outlined reader-response theory in her 1938 seminal work, *Literature as Exploration*. Rosenblatt believed that there was no one correct interpretation of a literary work. Instead, every reader, because of differences in life experience and frames of reference, brings a different reading to a text than another reader. The basic teaching premise of reader-response theory is that readers need to learn to read and interpret literature for themselves and to make meaning of their reading themselves. Doing so results in true engagement.

In his influential work *Adolescent Literature: Response and Analysis* (1984), reader-response expert Robert Probst further explains, "When literature is *read*, rather than worked upon, it draws us into events and invites us to reflect upon our perceptions of them. . . . Literature . . . allows us both to experience and to reflect upon experience, and thus invites the self indulgence of those who seek to understand themselves and the world around them" (p. 4).

The typical scholarly analysis of literature as done by university professors is fine, according to Probst, but this group was never the writer's "primary or intended audience. . . . [Literature] is the reservoir of all mankind's concerns. Although it may be studied in scholarly and professional ways, that is not its primary function" (p. 7). Probst continues by saying that studying literary texts from a scholarly perspective may or may not add to the experience of reading them, but "the literary experience is fundamentally an unmediated, private exchange between the text and the reader" (p. 7). Probst set forth five necessities for teaching literature with a reader-response approach (24–27). (See Figure 2.2).

In his collection of essays on reader-response from 20 experts in young adult literature, *Reader Response in the Classroom: Evoking and Interpreting Meaning in Literature* (Longman, 1992), Nicholas Karolides captures most of the wisdom on the subject, including his own. In his essay, "The Transactional Theory of Literature," Karolides indirectly makes the case for young adult literature when he notes that using texts beyond young readers' skills can prove counterproductive:

Five Necessities for Teaching Literature with a Reader-Response Approach

Receptivity

Students must recognize the classroom as an environment where their ideas are valued and welcomed.

Tentativeness

Students must feel that they are not expected to be "right," and should express their ideas even when the ideas are only initial ones and may change as the reading or discussion goes forth.

Rigor

Students must be challenged to dig deeply into their own experiences, examine their own beliefs, and define their own interaction with the text. And they must find ambiguity acceptable.

Cooperation

Students must understand the art of interacting in a group, make room for the thoughts or opinions of others, and depend upon one other for a successful learning experience.

Suitable Literature

Books need to have adequate "substance—ideas, style, language, attitude, whatever—worthy of reflection" (p. 27). The literature needs to be such that it will provoke a response, positive or negative, from the readers.

Source: Probst (1984)

Figure 2.2

> The language of a text, the situation, characters, or the
> expressed issues can dissuade a reader from comprehension
> of the text and thus inhibit involvement with it. In effect,
> if the reader has insufficient linguistic or experiential
> background to allow participation, the reader cannot relate
> to the text, and the reading act will be short-circuited.
> (p. 23).

If language, situations, characters, and issues inappropriate to the reader's
"linguistic or experiential background" harm comprehension and "short-circuit"
the reading act, logic dictates that we choose books with language, situations,
characters, and issues appropriate to our students' skill and experience. By our
definition, young adult literature is exactly that.

Karolides goes on to describe approaches to teaching literature that attempt to
identify the author's intended meaning, ascertain one inherent meaning contained
within the text, or "objectively analyze" the formal structure and techniques, while
totally ignoring the role of the reader, as "*about*" literature (p. 28) (italics are mine).
Karolides points out that information about the author, the time period, or analysis
of the structure of the text are not invalid for developing "insights to literature. The
issue is *when* these should be introduced and *how* they should be projected" (p. 29).

Obviously, predisposing students to a particular reading of a text with this
background information before they even read it would inhibit their own personal
response. Students may also become dependent on the teacher or published expert
and abandon their own interpretation, Karolides tells us. Instead, he recommends
letting the students' initial responses provide the starting place, and facilitating
their exploration of those responses. He suggests oral activities in groups of varying
sizes from small, in which students can use one other as sounding boards for their
ideas, to whole-class discussion where small groups share their conclusions. "[R]ole
playing, situation expanding, dramatization," as well as writing activities such as
"journals, logs, free response," can help students to discover what they think about
a book. Interaction with one other is helpful in recognizing how people "might be
affected by the insights of others" (p. 30).

The Theory in Action

Vygotsky theorized about the nature of learning language, and Rosenblatt, Probst, and Karolides articulate theories of the best approach to teaching literature, but what happens when these theories are applied? Do they really work?

As professor of education at the State University of New York at Albany and director of the federally sponsored National Research Center on English Learning & Achievement, Arthur Applebee has been periodically reviewing and revisiting the bulk of research extant on the teaching of language arts, as well as conducting his own, since 1974. In 2003, Applebee synthesized the findings of significant research on teaching literature to secondary students, concluding that the old method of teaching, in which the students do not respond to literature themselves but, instead, repeat what they are told is not productive:

> The results converge to suggest that comprehension of difficult text can be significantly enhanced by replacing traditional I-R-E [teacher *initiates* question, student *responds*, teacher *evaluates* answer] patterns of instruction with discussion-based activities in which the students are invited to make predictions, summarize, link texts with one another and with background knowledge, generate and answer text-related questions, and interrelate reading, writing and discussion. (p. 693)

Not only did Applebee and his coauthors update his previous reviews of studies on the teaching of literature, but they also conducted a study of 974 students in 64 middle and high school English classrooms in 19 schools in 5 states in an attempt to determine which instructional approaches are most effective. The study examined the relationship between "classroom instruction and student performance" by chronicling the instructional approaches in a range of classroom environments and measuring students' growth from fall to spring in performing "complex literacy tasks." Applebee sums up his findings:

The approaches that contributed most to student performance on the complex literacy tasks that we administered were those that used discussion to develop comprehensive understanding, encouraging exploration and multiple perspectives rather than focusing on correct interpretations and predetermined conclusions. (p. 722)

Using the students' responses to the literature is more effective in increasing students' ability to perform complex literacy tasks, the experts said. But that's not all; another factor was "significantly related to literacy performance," and that was "high academic demands" (p. 722).

High academic standards, Applebee and associates found, were not a function of the kind of literature used in the classroom, but rather a function of how it was used. Lower-track high school classes tended to use young adult literature more often than honors or advanced classes, but time spent on discussion of students' responses to literature in lower-track classes was only a fraction of the time spent discussing students' responses to literature in honors classes. Middle school students might use *To Kill a Mockingbird*, while high school students used the *Iliad*, "but at both levels, high academic demands and discussion-based approaches were significantly related to literacy performance" (p. 722).

Young Adult Literature as a Bridge to the Classics

Young adult literature can actually improve the likelihood that students who are not ready to read the classics now will read and enjoy them later—at the point in their lives when they will be most meaningful. As Sarah Herz and Don Gallo suggest in the title of their important work centered on this technique, *From Hinton to Hamlet: Building Bridges Between Young Adult Literature and the Classics* (2005), it's a matter of instructional approaches that will help students "bridge" the difference in complexity, style, and subject matter of the two literatures by capitalizing on the thematic, topical, and archetypal ways they are similar. This bridging will allow students to make the transition into adult literature and the canon individually as they become developmentally ready, with the expectation that by the time they leave high school, for most of them (but not all, perhaps) the transition will be complete.

Notice that the following approaches are designed to provide meaningful reading experiences and growth for every student by providing a variety of levels within the same class rather than treating every student exactly the same.

1 PAIRING A YOUNG ADULT TEXT WITH A CLASSIC

Especially at the high school level, a teacher can pair a classic book with a young adult novel that has some similarity in theme. An excellent example of pairing comes from Judith Hayn and Brigid Patrizi, who have presented their unit "Deceit, Despair, Dejection: Connecting *Speak* and *The Scarlet Letter*" at numerous conferences around the country. Laurie Halse Anderson's *Speak* is a young adult novel about a ninth-grade girl who lives through almost an entire year carrying the secret that she was raped by another high school student at a party. Nathaniel Hawthorne's canonical work *The Scarlet Letter* is, as we all probably know, a novel from the nineteenth century about a Puritan woman who keeps a secret—the identity of her illegitimate child's father.

Hayn and Patrizi's rationale for pairing a work from the canon with a young adult novel is that students are often uninterested in canonical works, most of which were written between 200 and 50 years ago, and, as a result, adolescent readers fail to make connections between the characters, setting, and conflicts of these books and their own world. Young adult novels such as *Speak*, however, provide literary elements similar to those of the canonical works but with characters, settings, and conflicts that are familiar and relevant to the students, enabling them to easily make connections to their own world. Hayn and Patrizi also point out that when students create these links, difficulties with one text are addressed by understanding the other.

The unit linking *Speak* and *The Scarlet Letter* includes discussion questions, writing activities, and projects that make a natural bridge between the two books, especially between characters, setting, and conflict, thus linking the student's world (the same world Anderson's protagonist, Melinda, lives in) with the Puritan world of seventeenth-

Some Potential Pairings of Young Adult Literature and Works From the Canon

- Ernest Hemingway's *The Old Man and the Sea* with Rodman Philbrick's *The Young Man and the Sea*

- F. Scott Fitzgerald's *The Great Gatsby* with Gordon Korman's *Jake, Reinvented*

- John Steinbeck's *The Grapes of Wrath* with Pam Muñoz Ryan's *Esperanza Rising*

- William Shakespeare's *Romeo and Juliet* with Sharon Draper's *Romiette and Julio*

- Homer's *Odyssey* with Mildred Taylor's *The Land*

- Erich Maria Remarque's *All Quiet on the Western Front* with Walter Dean Myers' *Fallen Angels*

- Anne Frank's *The Diary of Anne Frank* with Lois Lowry's *Number the Stars*

- Nevil Shute's *On the Beach* with Karen Hesse's *Phoenix Rising*

- William Golding's *Lord of the Flies* with Robert Cormier's *The Chocolate War*

- William Shakespeare's *Julius Caesar* with S. E. Hinton's *Rumble Fish* or Walter Dean Myers' *Scorpions*

- Stephen Crane's *The Red Badge of Courage* with Gary Paulsen's *Soldier's Heart: Being the Story of the Enlistment and Due Service of the Boy Charley Goddard in the First Minnesota Volunteers*

- Robert Penn Warren's *All the King's Men* with Janet Tashjian's *Vote for Larry*

Figure 2.3

century Boston. The Puritans' ostracism of Hester is similar to Melinda's ostracism by the various teen cliques at her high school. Melinda wrestles with feelings of shame and wins, as did Hester, all the while suffering the community's scorn. And as in Hawthorne's book, the guilty male character in *Speak* is ultimately revealed. Figure 2.3 includes other possible pairings of young adult literature and works from the canon.

If a skeptical parent, administrator, or colleague looks askance at this technique of using both classic works and popular young adult literature at once, I suggest they consider the problems veteran teachers find in teaching nothing but the canon to kids before they're ready for it. In a 2001 issue of *English Journal* devoted entirely to young adult literature, Guy Bland, a veteran high school English teacher from Georgia, bluntly assessed teaching only the classics to all students:

> Let's face it: Most of the classics offer few of what John Steinbeck called "points of contact"—that is, tangible, meaningful experiences and themes that students can fit into their lives. These connections are crucial to getting students to read. Without them, teachers must try to sell literature that is essentially meaningless to students. (p. 21)

2 CREATING THEMATIC UNITS

A teacher might also create a thematic unit in which the readings include young adult literature along with other readings that are not categorized as young adult literature (some of which may be considered contemporary classics) and popular reading (some of which may be considered recreational pulp fiction by literature majors despite their appearance on the *New York Times* Best Seller list), as well as works from the Western canon, all dealing with the same theme.

For example, a theme such as "Darkness of the Heart" might include:

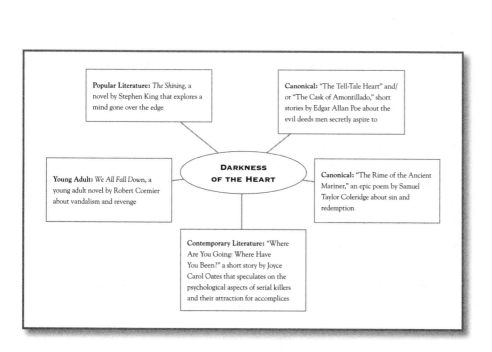

A thematic unit on "War: The Glory and the Horror" could include a variety of genres and reading levels, such as these:

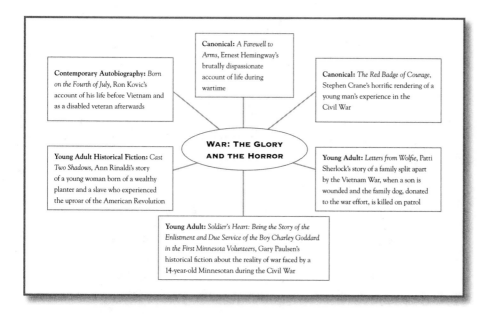

3 INCLUDING CLASSICS AND YOUNG ADULT BOOK CHOICES FOR LITERATURE CIRCLES

The literature circle approach is one in which students choose one book from several options and then participate in something like an adult book club to discuss the work with others who have read the same book. Before students make their choices, the teacher presents each book, not only summarizing the plot but also indicating the general level of reading difficulty. Then students have the opportunity to look through the book choices so that they can skim the reading for difficulty as well. As mentioned earlier, the teacher should provide a range of readability levels. In the best scenario, students will select the book which most interests them but does not exceed their reading level by much. A set of literature circle selections for a science fiction/fantasy unit that exhibit this might include the following:

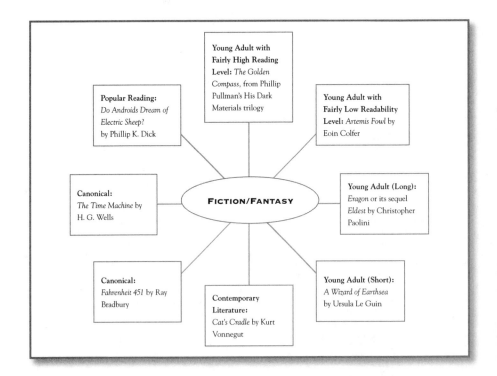

Young Adult with Fairly High Reading Level: *The Golden Compass,* from Phillip Pullman's His Dark Materials trilogy

Popular Reading: *Do Androids Dream of Electric Sheep?* by Phillip K. Dick

Young Adult with Fairly Low Readability Level: *Artemis Fowl* by Eoin Colfer

Canonical: *The Time Machine* by H. G. Wells

FICTION/FANTASY

Young Adult (Long): *Eragon* or its sequel *Eldest* by Christopher Paolini

Canonical: *Fahrenheit 451* by Ray Bradbury

Contemporary Literature: *Cat's Cradle* by Kurt Vonnegut

Young Adult (Short): *A Wizard of Earthsea* by Ursula Le Guin

4 "BOOK TALK" THE CLASSICS

The teacher or student volunteers can briefly "book talk" classics they have read for independent reading. In this situation, advanced students for whom these classics are appropriate reading (falling within their ZPDs) learn about additional titles they might find meaningful. For students who are not yet ready to read these books, a seed may be planted for future reading, as students learn that there are books for adult readers they can look forward to reading.

The book talk can address a work's strengths and weaknesses, but not give so much detail as to harm the reading experience. The book talker will want to describe the major characters, the setting, and major and minor conflicts; expound on the author's talents and any special strong points of the book; and then stop at a point that has whetted potential readers' appetites.

Can I Meet the National and State Standards with Young Adult Literature? Absolutely!

I believe that students stand a far greater chance of meeting the standards by using young adult literature and a reader-response approach, which puts students' responses to literature at the center of the curriculum, than by using the traditional approach of focusing on previous "correct" interpretations of the classics or canon. More simply put, students will better learn and sharpen their skills of literary analysis by exploring theme in *The Chocolate War* than by being asked to take notes on and memorize the theme of *The Scarlet Letter* as previously decided by literary scholars.

Language Arts Standard 6:

Uses reading skills and strategies to understand and interpret a variety of literary texts.

List of Benchmarks

1. Uses reading skills and strategies to understand a variety of literary passages and texts (e.g., fiction, nonfiction, myths, poems, fantasies, biographies, autobiographies, science fiction, tall tales, supernatural tales)

2. Knows the defining characteristics of a variety of literary forms and genres (e.g., fiction, nonfiction, myths, poems, fantasies, biographies, autobiographies, science fiction, tall tales, supernatural tales)

3. Understands complex elements of plot development (e.g., cause-and-effect relationships; use of subplots, parallel episodes, and climax; development of conflict and resolution)

4. Understands elements of character development (e.g., character traits and motivations; stereotypes; relationships between character and plot development; development of characters through their words, speech patterns, thoughts, actions, narrator's description, and interaction with other characters; how motivations are revealed)

5. Understands the use of specific literary devices (e.g., foreshadowing, flashback, progressive and digressive time, suspense)

6. Understands the use of language in literary works to convey mood, images, and meaning (e.g., dialect; dialogue; symbolism; irony; rhyme; voice; tone; sound; alliteration; assonance; consonance; onomatopoeia; figurative language such as similes, metaphors, personification, hyperbole, allusion; sentence structure; punctuation)

7. Understands the effects of an author's style (e.g., word choice, speaker, imagery, genre, perspective) on the reader

8. Understands point of view in a literary text (e.g., first and third person, limited and omniscient, subjective and objective)

9. Understands inferred and recurring themes in literary works (e.g., bravery; loyalty; friendship; good vs. evil; historical, cultural, and social themes)

10. Makes connections between the motives of characters or the causes for complex events in texts and those in his or her own life

Source: Content Knowledge: A Compendium of Standards and Benchmarks for K–12 Education (3rd ed.)

Figure 2.4

Teachers are under increasing pressure to meet both national and state standards; in fact, measurement of students' mastery of these standards is mandated by Congress's most recent reenactment of the Elementary and Secondary Education Act, more commonly known as No Child Left Behind. It would be difficult to list all the state reading standards for every state, and probably pointless, since most teachers know them by heart or can easily view them online. Instead, it should suffice to quickly examine one of the models for state standards.

Mid-Continent Research for Education and Learning (McREL), one of ten regional educational laboratories under contract with the federal government to provide research and training to teachers and schools, has compiled and evaluated national and state standards—and proposed what teachers should provide for their students to become proficient in the language arts (among other curriculum areas). Figure 2.4 shows the benchmarks that McREL has proposed for Standard 6 as it relates to grades 6–8.

Obviously, young adult literature contains all the very same elements contained in canonical literature, elements specifically named in the standards as summarized in figure 2.4, such as characterization, point of view, setting, plot structure (conflict, rising action, climax, denouement), theme, foreshadowing, irony, and mood. I've included book suggestions for exploring these literary elements in Chapter 3.

Closing Thoughts

Young adult literature may be our last hope for creating a generation of lifelong readers. *Reading at Risk*, the report from the National Endowment for the Arts based on 20 years of United States Census Bureau surveys, indicates that literary reading is declining at such a rapid and accelerating rate in the United States that it may be nonexistent in 50 years. Thomas W. Bean, widely published professor of reading and literacy at the University of Nevada at Las Vegas, takes us to task as professional educators charged to reverse the decline in reading:

> If educators are serious about developing students' lifelong love of reading, they need to incorporate in the curriculum literature that is captivating and issue-based. The extensive and evolving genre

of young adult literature offers an array of books that appeal to adolescents' interests and experiences. To exclude this literature from the classroom is to do a disservice to our youth . . . . Until educators stem the tide of adolescents' declining recreational reading, we will continue to produce a nation of people who can read but choose not to. (2004, p. 267)

Let me turn the issue of using young adult literature in our classrooms around and ask: What will happen if we don't? What will happen if students are never allowed to read anything but the classics, if they have never read a book that speaks to them, if they have never read a book with characters and a story to which they can connect? If they have never read a book that they can draw any meaning from, then I contend they will choose not to read when that choice is all theirs later in life as adults. The wrong books at the wrong time will set our students up for failure.

Kind of like that full-size bike my dad gave me when I was 4.

CHAPTER 3

CHOOSING THE BEST

Literature specialist and author Teri Lesesne distills the strategy perfectly in the title of her book *Making the Match: The Right Book for the Right Reader, at the Right Time (2003)*. The right book is out there for every reader; we just need to make the match. As a veteran teacher in Kansas once told me: "When kids say, 'I've never read a book I liked,' I always finish their sentence for them with 'YET! You haven't read a book you like yet, but we're going to find one you will love!'"

In this chapter we will take a look at how to make that match. We'll look at some of the criteria for judging and selecting books for quality and ways to make the best match between student and book.

Matching Students and Books

Like Dr. Lesesne, I believe there is a perfect book out there for every young reader, and as advocates for our students and proponents of reading and literature, it is our responsibility to make the match. A perfect example of this comes to mind from my experience as a high school principal at Interstate 35 High School, in rural Iowa.

The members of our school board, made up mostly of lifetime residents of

Madison, Warren, and Clarke counties (counties within our 1600 square miles of rolling hills covered with corn, soybeans, and timber), although very frugal about many things, had vowed that expense would never prevent students from having the books they needed to get the best education possible. No anonymous students fell through the cracks at our little school of 240 students, and we even produced a Rhodes Scholar in those years (1990s). We had the newest books and a full-time librarian—an unusual staffing for a school our size.

We also had a very structured study hall program. The study hall teacher was apprised of each student's homework and held him or her accountable for attending to it during the 50 minutes of study hall time. One day the conscientious study hall teacher came to my office to talk about a student who was not doing his reading homework in study hall.

"Clark is supposed to be doing his homework, but today for the third time I caught him with a magazine hidden in his reading book. I could give him Saturday school for this, but something isn't right about that because he is actually reading, but he's not getting his reading homework done. What should I do?" she asked.

"What are the magazines he sneaks into study hall?" Usually when kids got in trouble with magazines at school, the magazines were inappropriate for school (or anywhere else!), and I would have to inform parents and provide a punishment as school policy outlined. I waited for the answer.

"He reads those hunting dog magazines," came the reply.

Having spent many an evening poring over *Outdoor Life*, *Field & Stream*, *Sports Afield*, and similar magazines myself, I was not only relieved but also somewhat intrigued by this.

"I am going to talk to Mrs. McClure in the library about this. Let's send Clark to her next time study hall rolls around."

In those days, I liked to make a circuit through the lunchroom every day and say hello to every table of kids. It was a good way to stay on a positive footing with students (too often students only interact with the principal when something bad has happened) and also a good way to gauge what was going on with individuals who most often needed my attention. Two days after my conversation with the study hall moderator, Clark had obviously been to see Mrs. McClure. As I stopped at the table where he was eating with his friends, I saw that along with his math and equine science book, he had *Dogs, Puppies and Blue Northers* and *My Life in Dog*

Years, two books by renowned outdoorsman and author Gary Paulsen. I didn't ask about them (principal approval can be the kiss of death to appropriate behavior), but I stuck my head in study hall that day, and from the back of the room I could see that Clark was deep into a good dog story. A successful match had been made.

Choosing the Best:
How Do I Know a Book Is Good Quality?

As co-editor of *The ALAN Review* (published by the Assembly on Literature for Adolescents of the National Council of Teachers of English) and book reviewer for a number of journals, I receive hundreds of books yearly from publishers who make their books available for review to professionals charged with getting the word out to the young adult literature community about the newest and best books available. Since I can't read them all, I have developed a system by which I judge a book as it comes to me. Here follow the questions I ask myself, some of which can be answered simply by reading the book jacket, and the rest by going online, reading one of the major reviewing publications, and reading just a couple of pages of the book itself:

1) Has it been reviewed by one of the reputable review publications?
2) Has the book or the author won any awards?
3) Is the publisher established and well known?
4) Does the author have a proven reputation for quality work?
5) Will the topic be of interest to teens?
6) Do the characters represent the diversity of teen readers?
7) What is the book's reading level?

Now let's tease out and answer each of these questions in detail.

1 HAS IT BEEN REVIEWED BY ONE OF THE REPUTABLE REVIEW PUBLICATIONS?

Reviews of young adult books are readily available and easy to find, either in the library or online. For example, for most books, both Amazon.com and Barnesandnoble.com provide multiple reviews from reputable publications, such as *Publishers Weekly, Kirkus Reviews, Voice of Youth Advocates* (VOYA), *Booklist,* and *The ALAN Review.* In addition, the websites of these two major booksellers provide reader reviews, which can give insight into how young readers feel about a book and how appropriate its content is for an all-class read. The sheer volume of reviews sent in by readers may indicate how well received a book is. *Harry Potter and the Sorcerer's Stone,* for example, drew over 5,000 reviews from fans on Amazon.com in the first seven years since it appeared in the United States in 1998—surely testimony to how much young readers love it.

Another one of the best online resources for investigating young adult literature is Richie's Picks: Great Books for Children and Young Adults, which can be found at http://www.richiespicks.com/. Richie Partington is one of the most highly respected authorities on children's and young adult literature today and is or has been a member of the selection committee for many of the top awards given to children's and young adult literature. Richie's Picks is free, and subscribers are automatically emailed each new round of reviews. In addition to reviewing hundreds of books each year, Richie has his own Best of the Year list and all of his reviews are archived and available on the Internet.

Publications such as *Publishers Weekly, Kirkus Reviews,* and VOYA receive advanced reading copies of almost every book from a major publisher and have knowledgeable reviewers who summarize the plot, evaluate the quality, and make age recommendations for each book. Usually reviewers will indicate if a book contains questionable material, such as graphically depicted sex or violence, which may disqualify it from some uses (such as a required whole-class reading or a literature circle). Individuals can subscribe to these publications, but most are available at public or university libraries and some have online reviews that do not require a subscription at all. Some of the best-known publications for reviews are listed in Figure 3.1.

Publications With Reviews
of YA Literature

Kirkus Reviews, reviews 5,000 books of all kinds annually and comes out 24 times a year. It offers print, online, and combined subscriptions, as well as electronic archives of 250,000 reviews going back to 1933.

The Horn Book Magazine and *The Horn Book Guide* are publications evolved from the *Horn Book* organization, which has been in existence since the 1920s. the *Horn Book Magazine*, which contains articles and reviews of children's and young adult literature, is published six times a year. The *Horn Book Guide* publishes in the spring and fall and prints nearly 4,000 reviews of children's and young adult books each year. An online archive includes more than 35,000 book reviews.

The American Library Association publishes *Booklist* 22 times a year. In addition to 5,000 reviews of adult books, *Booklist* contains reviews of 2,500 books for children and young adults each year. Subscriptions are available for the print and online versions.

School Library Journal is a monthly magazine with articles of interest to anyone involved with libraries and/or books. A subscription includes electronic access to the journal and to archives of reviews going back to 1987. Each issue contains more than 100 reviews of books for young adults and adult books appropriate for young adults.

Voice of Youth Advocacy (*VOYA*) magazine contains roughly 150 reviews in each bimonthly issue, along with articles and columns on many different aspects of teen life and reading.

The *ALAN Review* is the publication of the Assembly on Literature for Adolescents of the National Council of Teachers of English. The *ALAN Review* is published three times a year and contains 32 reviews in each issue, in a "clip-and-file" section on index-card-stock pages in the center of it. The *ALAN*

Figure 3.1

Review archives contain past clip-and-file reviews at http://scholar.lib.vt.edu/ejournals/ALAN/ . ALAN subscriptions are comparatively inexpensive and include membership in the Assembly on Literature for Adolescents.

English Journal is a publication of the National Council of Teachers of English and comes out bimonthly. Each issue includes a column on young adult literature, which often includes reviews of books. Historically, *English Journal* has printed an Honor List of the best young adult books of the year and reviews of these books (between six and nine books generally make it). This Honor List is chosen each year by Alleen Nilsen, professor of English, Arizona State University, and Ken Donelson, Professor Emeritus, Arizona State University Department of English, and me (assistant professor of English, Arizona State University). Professors Nilsen and Donelson have been creating the Honor List since 1967, and the list is available in their book *Literature for Today's Young Adults* (2004).

Journal of Adolescent and Adult Literacy is a publication of the International Reading Association. The Books for Adolescents section has 7–10 in-depth reviews in each of the eight issues, including some reviews of books published in Spanish. The journal also publishes a list of best books each year.

 SIGNAL, the journal of the International Reading Association's Special Interest Group on Literature for the Adolescent Reader, comes out twice a year and contains articles of interest on authors, books, and the teaching of young adult literature.

A great resource for short reviews of books for children and adolescents written in or translated into Spanish is the Barahona Center for the Study of Books in Spanish for Children and Adolescents at the University of California, San Marcos. Their website (http://www.csusm.edu/csb/english/center.htm) has an easy-to-search database of thousands of book reviews.

Figure 3.1

2 HAS THE BOOK OR THE AUTHOR WON ANY AWARDS?

Many well-known organizations give awards for literature for adolescents. Although all awards merit note, the highest awards a young adult book can receive are the National Book Award, the Printz Award, and the Newbery Medal. There are also awards designed to give recognition to specific genres or cultures, which can be helpful if a certain kind of book is needed. For example, the Pura Belpré Award is given for literature accurately portraying and celebrating the Latino/Latina experience. Figure 3.2 lists some awards given to young adult literature. I have indicated when an award is for a category that involves more than just superior quality.

And let's not leave out awards for graphic novels and comic books:

♦ Academy of Comic Book Art Awards

♦ Harvey Awards

♦ LuLu Awards

♦ Reuben Awards

♦ Ignatz Awards

♦ Will Eisner Award

3 IS THE PUBLISHER ESTABLISHED AND WELL KNOWN?

By paying attention to who publishes the young adult books that engage us and our students, we soon begin to develop our own sense of which publishing houses and imprints best meet our needs as well as our standards. Once a publisher establishes trust by consistently delivering outstanding young adult literature, you can try an unknown author. Publishers find new and brilliant writers all the time, so a new talent might merit your consideration. In fact, you might find a gem and your students will feel like talent scouts. Please understand that there are many imprints within the house of a major publisher, so you may find that although you have not

Young Adult Literature Awards

1. American Library Association (ALA) Best Book for Young Adults
2. ALA Quick Pick for Reluctant Young Adult Readers
3. Before Columbus American Book Award (to acknowledge excellence and diversity in American writing)
4. Booklist Editors' Choice
5. Coretta Scott King Award (African-American authors representing an appreciation of the American dream)
6. Edgar Allan Poe Award (mystery)
7. The Heartland Award
8. Horn Book Fanfare Title
9. Hugo Award (science fiction)
10. International Reading Association (IRA) Teacher's Choice
11. IRA Children's Book Award, Young Adult Novel category
12. Jane Addams Book Award (promoting peace and social justice)
13. *Kirkus* Best Book
14. *Los Angeles Times* Book Prize
15. Margaret A. Edwards Award (ALA)
16. National Book Award
17. Nebula Award (science fiction/fantasy short story)
18. Newbery Medal
19. Printz Award
20. Publishers Weekly Best Book(s) of the Year
21. Pura Belpré Award (portraying and celebrating the Latino/Latina experience)
22. *School Library Journal* Best Books
23. Scott O'Dell Award for Historical Fiction for Children
24. *VOYA* Books in the Middle: Outstanding Books
25. YALSA Popular Paperback for Young Adults

Figure 3.2

Major Publishers of Young Adult Literature

- Amulet/Abrams

- Bloomsbury

- Boyds Mills

- Candlewick

- Clarion

- Farrar, Straus & Giroux

- Front Street

- Harcourt

- HarperCollins
  (Joanna Cotler, Greenwillow, Amistad, HarperTempest, Harper Festival, Harper Trophy, and more)

- Henry Holt

- Holiday House

- Houghton Mifflin

- Hyperion (Miramax)

- Image Comics

- Knopf
  (Alfred A. Knopf, Vintage, Anchor, Pantheon, and more)

- Little, Brown

- Peachtree

- Penguin
  (Berkley Books, Dutton, Grosset & Dunlap, New American Library, Penguin Putnam, Firebird Books, Ace Books, and more)

- Random House
  (Bantam Doubleday Dell, Delacorte, Dell Yearling, Dell Laurel-Leaf, Wendy Lamb Books, Ballantine, Del Rey, Crown Publishing Group, Doubleday Broadway Publishing Group)

- Roaring Brook

- Scholastic (Chicken House, Orchard, PUSH, Graphix)

- Simon & Schuster
  (Aladdin, Atheneum)

- Time Warner

- Tor Books

- Walker

Figure 3.3

heard of the publisher, closer examination of the copyright page reveals that this unknown publisher is actually the imprint of a major publishing house, possibly a new one with a special niche market that your students may find appealing. A partial list of the major publishing houses, divisions, and a few of their imprints is presented is Figure 3.3.

 ## 4 DOES THE AUTHOR HAVE A PROVEN REPUTATION FOR QUALITY WORK?

The authors listed in Chapter 4, In the Authors' Words, are some of the best, but space did not allow me to include all of my favorites. The list below includes young adult authors who are equally good. And remember, of course, that lucky for us, wonderful authors are being discovered all the time.

Adoff, Arnold	Cheripko, Jan
Alexander, Lloyd	Clements, Andrew
Alexie, Sherman	Cohn, Rachel
Anaya, Rudolfo	Colfer, Eoin
Angelou, Maya	Coman, Carolyn
Asher, Sandy	Cushman, Karen
Barker, Clive	Davis, Terry
Blackwood, Gary	Dessen, Sarah
Bloor, Edward	Frank, E. R.
Bradbury, Ray	Freymann-Weyr, Garret
Bridgers, Sue Ellen	Funke, Cornelia
Brown, Dee	Gaiman, Neil
Bruchac, Joseph	Garden, Nancy
Cabot, Meg	Giles, Gail
Cadnum, Michael	Going, K. L.
Card, Orson Scott	Gould, Stephen Jay
Carlson, Lori (editor)	Green, Bette
Chambers, Aidan	Greenberg, Jan

Grimes, Nikki

Gutman, Dan

Hale, Shannon

Hiaasen, Carl

Holt, Kimberly Willis

Horvath, Polly

Jackson, Helen Hunt

Jenkins, A. M.

Jiménez, Francisco

Jones, Diana Wynne

Klass, David

Koja, Kathe

L'Engle, Madeleine

Leitich Smith, Cynthia and Greg

Levithan, David

Lubar, David

Lynch, Chris

Marsden, John

Martin, Ann

Martinez, Victor

McCaffrey, Anne

McDonald, Janet

Morrison, Toni

Murphy, Jim

Myung-Ok Lee, Marie

Napoli, Donna Jo

Nixon, Joan Lowery

Nolan, Han

Oates, Joyce Carol

Paolini, Christopher

Pierce, Tamora

Plum-Ucci, Carol

Pratchett, Terry

Pullman, Philip

Rapp, Adam

Rowling, J. K.

Ryan, Pam Muñoz

Rylant, Cynthia

Seely, Deb

Shange, Ntozake

Shanower, Eric

Shusterman, Neal

Sleator, William

Sones, Sonya

Sonnenblick, Jordan

Spiegelman, Art

Stone, Jeff

Tan, Amy

Tolkien, J. R. R.

Trueman, Terry

Vizzini, Ned

Vonnegut, Kurt

White, Ruth

Williams-Garcia, Rita

Wittlinger, Ellen

Wolff, Virginia Euwer

Wynne-Jones, Tim

Yolen, Jane

5 WILL THE TOPIC BE OF INTEREST TO TEENS?

Unless the work is meant to be a parody or comedy, young readers expect authenticity in their reading. Certain literary weaknesses will turn them off immediately, such as an obvious moral tale in which the issues of sex, drugs, or any moral choices are simplified, used as a bludgeon, or trivialized. They will recognize the formulaic after-school-movie kind of plot immediately and respond to it with great gnashing of teeth and eye rolling. No worthwhile discussion or writing is likely to come from such a book. Kids' lives are not simple, and book plots need to recognize the complexity of the problems they face. Although sometimes graphic imagery is essential in creating a scene, young adult fiction often uses subtlety to great effect. In Laurie Halse Anderson's *Catalyst*, for example, the reader gradually begins to suspect that Teri Litch was the victim of incest. It is mostly implied rather than directly stated, and the reader and protagonist come to understand it for certain about three fourths of the way through the novel, thanks to the author's finesse.

Skimming for dialogue will quickly tell you how well the book re-creates the complexity of teen life, especially regarding problems, choice, and autonomy or the lack of it. If the dialogue has all the melodrama of a soap opera, kids are going to find it beneath them. The same is true of times when the character is thinking to him/herself. If that soliloquy seems too much of a caricature, students will reject it as phony.

For your own purposes you need to think about what kind of appeal the book will have: a broad, general appeal, making it appropriate for a whole-class read? Or a very narrow but strong appeal to one group, such as male reluctant reader males or the fantasy-book crowd? In the latter case it may be a good selection for one of the literature-circle book choices students can make.

6 DO THE CHARACTERS REPRESENT THE DIVERSITY OF TEEN READERS?

You need to ask this question not just as you look at an individual book, but as you consider the spectrum of books that you are making available to your students as required reading, as recommendations for independent reading assignments, or as suggestions for recreational reading. Is there something for everyone so that each person sees him/herself, sees characters he or she will care about?

As you evaluate an individual book, ask if it will add to the diversity of the total reading experience available to your students. If it is going to be one among many options for literature circles or independent reading, it may only have specific appeal to one group. A book such as any one in Ann Brashares' trilogy—*Sisterhood of the Traveling Pants, Second Summer of the Sisterhood,* and *Girls in Pants*—will be wildly popular and engaging for a majority of young women, and need not appeal to boys. Choosing a book like that for literature circles is a good idea but would need to be balanced with selections likely to appeal to readers who aren't drawn to the *Pants* books. *Brothers in Arms* by Paul Langan and Ben Alirez, for example, might appeal to young men. *Brothers in Arms* is about Martin Luna, a Latino youth, whose mother transfers him from a mostly Latino/a high school where gang violence has led to the death of his brother to Bluford High School, a mostly African-American high school, where he must deal with a whole new set of problems. If a book is to be used with the whole class, rather than self-selected by students, it will meet with more success if it has diverse characters and conflicts.

7 WHAT IS THE BOOK'S READING LEVEL?

You may want to ask a reading specialist in your school or district to help with the most modern methods for assessing reading level, but one widely used readability test is the Flesch-Kincaid. This is a formula that calculates the complexity of the writing in terms of numbers of words in sentences and numbers of syllables in words and arrives at a grade-level score meant to indicate that reading this passage would require this amount of education. See Figure 3.4 for information on how to find the readability of a passage.

Determining Readability Using the Flesch-Kincaid Method

Finding a readability score is actually one of the functions of Microsoft Word and can be easily accessed.

1. Click on Tools.

2. Click on Spelling and Grammar.

3. Click on Options.

4. Select Show Readability Statistics.

You will need to type in a passage of 200 words or more, and then run the test. After the Spelling and Grammar check runs, you will see a box containing all the statistics about the passage, including a Flesch-Kincaid readability grade level. You can also do the arithmetic yourself:

$$(.39 \times \text{average sentence length}) + (11.8 \times \text{average number of syllables per word}) - 15.59 = \text{grade level}$$

I used the Microsoft Word function on the manuscript of this book and found that it scored at the twelfth-grade level.

Figure 3.4

Reading scholars warn that the Flesch-Kincaid should be used as a rough guideline because it only addresses surface aspects of the reading. I recommend that you use your own judgment about the maturity level of the ideas and content of the book. A book that has a readability level of seventh grade but deals with complex adult issues that a senior in high school might face could be a good match for the right students, readers who need high-interest/low-reading difficulty books. A book with eleventh-grade readability that doesn't deal with conflicts any more adult than what a sixth grader normally faces might be a good match for students who read way above grade level but are not emotionally ready for adult conflicts.

Graphic Novels

Graphic novels and comic books (not necessarily the same thing) may appeal to readers who have not yet been drawn into books (and to advanced readers, as well). Stephen Krashen (1993), noted researcher in language acquisition, tells us about these illustrated forms and their readers:

- comic book readers are more often boys than girls

- proficient readers are just as likely to read them as struggling readers

- reading comics does not supplant other kinds of reading that the young readers would normally do

- reading comics provides a good bridge into other kinds of reading (1993)

Graphic novels have developed an underground mythology about their powers even though some libraries and schools resist buying them. According to three public librarians recognized as experts in this field, Kristin Fletcher-Spear, Merideth Jenson-Benjamin, and Teresa Copeland, the reputation, myth or not, is that:

> These books, which look like comic books on steroids, seem to
> have miraculous properties. They attract reluctant readers and
> bookworms. They lure teen boys, while retaining the qualities
> beloved by teen girls. They work for ESL students (Krashen, 54),
> teach visual literacy (Gorman, 9-10) and sequencing, and above
> all else, they are wildly popular with an adolescent audience
> (Fletcher-Spear et al. p. 37)

Graphic novels are not simplistic, low-level reading. In fact, they can be quite dense in text and highly researched. Eric Shanower's Age of Bronze series, for example, retells the story of the Trojan War in seven volumes, drawing upon Homer's *Iliad* and *Odyssey*, Virgil's *Aeneid*, Shakespeare's *Troilus and Cressida* (among others), opera, anthropology, architecture, and artifacts from those time periods. Shanower writes:

> Age of Bronze is not simply a graphic novel adaptation of Homer's
> Iliad. My goal is to retell the entire Trojan War story, which is
> at least 2,800 years old and likely much older, so it's had a lot

*of time to generate material. I've gathered different versions of the
story, while reconciling all the contradictions (2005, pp. 33–34).*

I suggest adding some graphic novels to your independent reading list and trying one or two as literature circle choices (if you can get the use of these books approved and funded at your school). Graphic novels encompass many favorite genres of adolescents, such as mystery, horror, short story, comedy, romance, and so on, but only some graphic novels are intended for a young adult audience. Some of the most popular titles are listed under Graphic Novels later in this chapter. To learn more about graphic novels, get some background, and stay abreast of new releases, Fletcher-Spear et al. recommend these websites:

* www.noflyingnotights.com (Librarians maintain this one, and it has reviews and definitions.)
* www.artbomb.net (Maintained by graphic novel artists and writers, this one has a great explanation of the genre, as well as reviews.)

Choosing Books for Specific Uses

It is important to note that not all books are best used in the same way. A book may contain content that an individual reader might be unprepared for emotionally, psychologically, or developmentally. For some readers, a particular book might trigger philosophical objections based on religious or political views. Some books may be too challenging for some students; others may not grab their interest. The suitability of a book will vary depending on its intended use—and its user. Some suggestions follow for specific uses, as well as lists of books that are particularly suited for those uses. These suggestions are just starting points, and I encourage you to add your own choices to these lists as you read and discover new young adult books.

1 REQUIRED READING FOR A WHOLE CLASS

This needs to be a book with broad appeal. That means setting, characters, and conflicts that will pique the curiosity of members of your class, even if these elements are unfamiliar. Remember the previous admonitions from Mel Glenn and others that in order to care about fictional characters and situations, young readers need to see themselves in the books they read? Identifying with a character makes them want to read on to see what happens next and to find out how the conflict is resolved.

A book for whole-class reading needs to be written at a level that is accessible to every student in the class. Sometimes a short story collection works best. Books should be chosen so that even the most reluctant reader can connect with the story. The best way to differentiate instruction is to pick books that can be interpreted on various levels, such as *The Giver* by Lois Lowry, which is so open to interpretation as to be meaningful to a reader of any age—the older the reader, the more mature the interpretation. This book is perfect for activities grounded in reader-response theory.

QUESTIONS TO ASK WHEN CHOOSING BOOKS FOR WHOLE-CLASS READING

- What is the reading level?
- Will this have broad appeal?
- Are the issues relevant to my students?
- Will they see themselves in the characters?
- Is it an interesting and engaging read?
- Does it allow for various levels of interpretation in line with the various levels of students' abilities?
- Can I use it to teach literary elements required by the standards?

Good Picks for Whole-Class Reading

47, Walter Mosley (Little, Brown, 2005) (middle school/high school)

Armageddon Summer, Bruce Coville and Jane Yolen (Harcourt, 1998) (middle school)

The Beast, Walter Dean Myers (Scholastic, 2003) (high school)

Bless Me, Ultima, Rudolfo Anaya (Tqs Pub, 1976) (middle school)

Bucking the Sarge, Christopher Paul Curtis, (Wendy Lamb Books, 2004) (middle school)

Buried Onions, Gary Soto (Harcourt, 1997) (middle school/ high school)

Bury My Heart at Wounded Knee: An Indian History of the American West, Dee Brown (Holt, 1971) (in an integrated unit with high school social studies)

California Blue, David Klass (Scholastic, 1994) (middle school)

The Canning Season, Polly Horvath (Farrar, Straus & Giroux, 2003) (middle school/high school)

Catalyst, Laurie Halse Anderson (Viking, 2000) (high school)

The Chocolate War, Robert Cormier (Pantheon, 1974) (middle school/high school)

Criss Cross, Lynne Rae Perkins (Greenwillow Books/HarperCollins, 2005) (middle school)

Eyes of the Emperor, Graham Salisbury (Wendy Lamb Books, 2005) (middle school/high school reluctant reader)

Farewell to Manzanar, Jeanne Wakatsuki (Houghton Mifflin, 1993) (high school)

Fat Kid Rules the World, K. L. Going (Penguin Putnam/G. P. Putnam's Sons, 2003) (middle school)

Freak the Mighty, Rodman Philbrick (Scholastic, 1993) (upper elementary/ middle school)

Good Picks for Whole-Class Reading *Continued*

Girls, Drums and Dangerous Pie, Jordan Sonnenblick (Scholastic, 2004) (middle school)

The Giver, Lois Lowry (Houghton Mifflin, 1993) (any level) (middle school)

The Gospel According to Larry, Janet Tashjian (Holt, 2001)

Holes, Louis Sachar (Farrar, Straus & Giroux, 1998) (middle school)

The Joy Luck Club, Amy Tan (Putnam, 1989) (high school)

The Last Book in the Universe, Rodman Philbrick (Blue Sky Press/Scholastic, 2000)

A Long Way from Chicago, Richard Peck (Penguin, 1998) (middle school)

Miracle's Boys, Jacqueline Woodson (Putnam, 2000) (middle school/high school)

Nothing but the Truth, Avi (Orchard, 1991) (middle school)

Number the Stars, Lois Lowry (Houghton Mifflin, 1989) (middle school)

The Outsiders, S. E. Hinton (Viking, 1967) (middle school)

Roll of Thunder, Hear My Cry, Mildred Taylor (Dial, 1976), or any one of the Cassie Logan books (middle school)

Shakespeare Stealer, Gary Blackwood (Dutton, 1998) (middle school, ninth-grade reluctant reader)

A Single Shard, Linda Sue Park (Clarion, 2001) (middle school)

Speak, Laurie Halse Anderson (Farrar, Straus & Giroux, 1999) (upper middle school/ high school)

When Zachary Beaver Came to Town, Kimberly Willis Holt (Holt, 1999) (middle school)

A Wizard of Earthsea, Ursula Le Guin (Houghton Mifflin, 1968) (middle school/ high school)

2 BOOKS FOR READ-ALOUD

We are never too old to enjoy a great story read aloud by a skilled reader. In addition to the community-building value of engaging read-alouds, they make more challenging material accessible to all. An experimental study by Warwick Elley found that reading aloud increased listeners' vocabulary significantly, even without explicit instruction of the vocabulary. Read-alouds also give students the opportunity to hear phrased, fluent reading that highlights and celebrates rich language and provides new models and inspiration for writing. If you're reading aloud an entire book, make sure that it's one you know well. If it's a tantalizing excerpt intended to entice readers, take time to practice, especially if the excerpt contains extensive dialogue that's not attributed to the speaker each time.

Great Books for Read-Aloud

47, Walter Mosley (Little, Brown, 2005) (middle school/high school)

The Amazing Life of Birds: The Twenty-Day Puberty Journal of Duane Homer Leech, Gary Paulsen (Wendy Lamb Books, 2006) (middle school)

Bronx Masquerade, Nikki Grimes (Dial, 2002) (middle school)

Bud, Not Buddy, Christopher Paul Curtis (Delacorte, 1999) (middle school)

Godless, Pete Hautman (Simon and Schuster, 2004) (middle school/high school)

The House on Mango Street, Sandra Cisneros (Random House, 1984) (middle school/high school)

How Angel Peterson Got His Name, Gary Paulsen (Wendy Lamb Books, 2003) (middle school)

Joey Pigza Swallowed the Key, Jack Gantos (Farrar, Straus & Giroux, 1998) (upper elementary/middle school)

Love that Dog, Sharon Creech (HarperCollins, 2001) (upper elementary/middle school)

Notes from the Midnight Driver, Jordan Sonnenblick (Scholastic, 2006) (high school)

Number the Stars, Lois Lowry (Houghton Mifflin 1989) (middle school)

Out of the Dust, Karen Hesse (Scholastic, 1996) (middle school)

Roll of Thunder, Hear My Cry, Mildred Taylor (Dial, 1976) or any one of the Cassie Logan books (middle school)

Rules of the Road, Joan Bauer (Putnam, 1998) (middle school)

Sing Down the Moon, Scott O'Dell (Houghton Mifflin, 1970) (middle school)

Soldier's Heart, Gary Paulsen (Delacorte, 1998) (high school)

Stargirl, Jerry Spinelli (Knopf, 2000) (middle school)

Stuck in Neutral, Terry Trueman (HarperCollins, 2000) (middle school/high school)

Vampires, A Collection of Original Stories, Jane Yolen (HarperCollins, 1991) (middle school)

The Watsons Go to Birmingham, 1963, Christopher Paul Curtis (Delacorte, 1995)

3 LITERATURE CIRCLE SELECTIONS

Since these books are summarized for students in advance and parental participation is encouraged, students can avoid books that are not appropriate for them. For this reason, some books in this group might have more adult content than those books suitable for whole-class reading. One key component of successful literature circles is choice, and your knowledge of your students and their talents and tastes will guide you in structuring a range of options to meet their diverse needs and interests. The books recommended below have the power to engage students as well as to invite and sustain rich discussion.

Great Books for Literature Circles

Always Running: La Vida Loca: Gang Days in L.A., Luis Rodriguez (Curbstone, 1993) (high school)

Artemis Fowl, Eoin Colfer (Hyperion, 2001) (upper elementary, middle school)

Bull Rider, Marilyn Halvorson (Orca, 2003) (middle school/reluctant readers)

A Corner of the Universe, Ann Martin (Scholastic, 2002) (high school)

Damage, A. M. Jenkins (HarperCollins, 2001) (middle school)

Dragonflight, Anne McCaffrey (Atheneum, 1976) (middle school/ high school)

Dreamland, Sarah Dessen (Viking, 2000) (middle school/high school)

The First Part Last, Angela Johnson (Simon & Schuster, 2003) (middle school/high school)

Forever, Judy Blume (Bradbury, 1975) (middle school)

Gingerbread, Rachel Cohn (Simon & Schuster, 2002) (middle school)

Godless, Pete Hautman (Simon & Schuster, 2004) (middle school/ high school)

The Golden Compass, Philip Pullman (Knopf, 1996) (high school)

Hatchet, Gary Paulsen (Bradbury, 1987) (upper elementary /middle school)

Hole in My Life, Jack Gantos (Farrar, Straus & Giroux, 2002) (high school, especially at-risk youth)

Hope Was Here, Joan Bauer (Putnam, 2000) (middle school)

House of the Scorpion, Nancy Farmer (Atheneum, 2002) (high school)

How Angel Peterson Got His Name, Gary Paulsen (Wendy Lamb Books, 2003) (high school)

Interstellar Pig, William Sleator (Dutton, 1984) (upper elementary/ middle school)

The Joy Luck Club, Amy Tan (Putnam, 1989) (high school)

Kira-Kira, Cynthia Kadohata, (Atheneum, 2004) (middle school)

The Last Mission, Harry Mazer Fox (Delacorte, 1979) (middle school)

Letting Go of Bobby James: Or How I Found My Self of Steam, Valerie Hobbs (Farrar, Straus, Giroux, 2004) (middle school)

The Man Who Loved Clowns, June Rae Wood (Putnam, 1992) (middle school)

Margaux with an X, Ron Koertge (Candlewick, 2004) (high school)

Miracle's Boys, Jacqueline Woodson (Putnam, 2000) (middle school/ high school)

4 INDEPENDENT READING
SELECTIONS

Since no one is required to select any of these books and parental participation is encouraged, there may be an even higher level of adult content in books for independent reading. Be aware that some books in this fourth group might be objectionable to some students and parents but popular choices for others.

The books listed in Themes, Genres, and Topics, as well as the books in Chapter 4: In the Authors' Words are all books that have won awards or have been reviewed by professionals in young adult literature. Because of their acclaim, you can easily find reviews online or in the archives of *VOYA* or any of the recommended professional review journals listed earlier in this chapter. In order to make kids passionate about reading, it's important that you provide as wide a variety of choices as possible for their independent/outside reading. Every student will need books at his or her independent reading level, and books that relate to their interests. The books recommended in Themes, Genres, and Topics are an attempt to suggest something for anyone and everyone.

A Note of Caution

Some books about adolescence focus on negative events (e.g., rape, incest, murder) and can be quite graphic, some to a degree that could be disturbing to an unprepared young reader experiencing the book alone. I believe that rather than censoring or banning books we should allow our young people to encounter as many of the problems and choices of life through their reading as possible before they encounter them in real life. Experiencing life vicariously through reading gives them a chance to process their thoughts, feelings, and values about the problems and choices they may face in life without suffering serious consequences (and possibly prevent them from encountering negative situations). As a teacher or librarian, however, I do not have the right to dictate what young people read, with no avenue for input from parents and guardians, whose values must be honored and respected. Required reading, whether it is whole-class or literature circle student selections, will be part of a published school curriculum, accessible to parents and already vetted through school policy for book adoption, but independent reading lists are a different matter. I recommend letting parents know about your independent reading requirements for class so that they are aware their sons and daughters will be making their own choices from a wide range of books. Encourage parents to talk to their children about what they're reading rather than holding you responsible for guaranteeing that any book on a list of suggested books will be appropriate by their standards—clearly an impossible task.

Themes, Genres, and Topics

Below you will find books organized by genre, topic, and possible thematic unit categories. Many books are cross-listed, meaning, for example, that Laurie Halse Anderson's *Speak* may be under A Girl Growing Up (theme), and also under Misfits & Outcasts (theme), as well as under Modern Realism (genre) and Issues of Sex (topic).

ABUSE

America, E. R. Frank (Atheneum/Richard Jackson, 2002)

Chinese Handcuffs, Chris Crutcher (Greenwillow, 1989)

Dreamland, Sarah Dessen (Viking, 2000)

Forged by Fire, Sharon Draper (Atheneum, 1997)

Freaky Green Eyes, Joyce Carol Oates (HarperCollins, 2003)

When She Was Good, Norma Fox Mazer (Scholastic, 1977)

You Don't Know Me, David Klass (Farrar, Straus & Giroux, 2001)

ADDICTION

A Hero Ain't Nothin' But a Sandwich, Alice Childress (Putnam, 1973)

Imitate the Tiger, Jan Cheripko (Boyds Mills, 1998)

AFRICAN OR AFRICAN AMERICAN EXPERIENCE AND AUTHORS

47, Walter Mosley (Little, Brown, 2005)

The Beast, Walter Dean Myers (Scholastic, 2003)

Bloods: An Oral History of the Vietnam War by Black Veterans, Wallace Terry (Ballantine, 1984)

Blue Tights, Rita Garcia-Williams (Puffin, 1996)

Bud, Not Buddy, Christopher Paul Curtis (Delacorte, 1999)

Bronx Masquerade, Nikki Grimes (Dial, 2002)

Dark Sons, Nikki Grimes (Jump at the Sun, 2005)

Fallen Angels, Walter Dean Myers (Scholastic, 1988)

The First Part Last, Angela Johnson (Simon & Schuster, 2003)

Forged by Fire, Sharon Draper (Atheneum, 1997)

A Girl Named Disaster, Nancy Farmer (Orchard, 1996)

Harlem Stomp: A Cultural History of the Harlem Renaissance, Laban Carrick Hill (Little, Brown, 2003)

Heaven, Angela Johnson (Simon & Schuster, 1998)

Her Stories: African American Folktales, Fairy Tales, and True Tales, Virginia Hamilton (Scholastic, 1995)

Hush, Jacqueline Woodson (Putnam, 2002)

I, Too, Sing America: Three Centuries of African American Poetry, Catherine Clinton ed. (Houghton Mifflin, 1998)

The Land, Mildred Taylor (Phyllis Fogelman Books, 2001)

Let the Circle Be Unbroken, Mildred Taylor (Dial, 1981)

Like Sisters on the Home Front, Rita Williams-Garcia (Lodestar, 1995)

M. C. Higgins, the Great, Virginia Hamilton (Macmillan, 1974)

Many Thousand Gone: African Americans from Slavery to Freedom, Virginia Hamilton (Knopf, 1993)

Miracle's Boys, Jacqueline Woodson (Putnam, 2000)

Monster, Walter Dean Myers (HarperCollins, 1999)

The Road to Memphis, Mildred Taylor (Dial, 1990)

Roll of Thunder, Hear My Cry, Mildred Taylor (Dial, 1976)

Sojourner Truth: Ain't I a Woman?, Patricia C. McKissack and Frederick L. McKissack (Scholastic, 1992)

Spellbound, Janet McDonald (Farrar, Straus & Giroux, 2001)

The Story of Negro League Baseball, William Brashler (Ticknor & Fields, 1994)

Toning the Sweep, Angela Johnson (Orchard, 1993)

Twists and Turns, Janet McDonald (Farrar, Straus & Giroux, 2003)

The Watsons Go to Birmingham, 1963, Christopher Paul Curtis (Delacorte, 1995)

A Wreath for Emmet Till, Marilyn Nelson (Houghton Mifflin, 2005)

ANIMAL STORIES

Dogsong, Gary Paulsen (Viking, 1987)

Every Living Thing, Cynthia Rylant (Bradbury, 1985)

My Life in Dog Years, Gary Paulsen (Delacorte, 1997)

Puppies, Dogs, and Blue Northers, Gary Paulsen (Harcourt, 1996)

Sounder, William Armstrong (HarperCollins, 1969)

Straydog, Kathe Koja (Farrar, Straus & Giroux, 2002)

Where the Red Fern Grows, Wilson Rawls (Doubleday, 1961)

Woodsong, Gary Paulsen (Simon & Schuster, 1990)

ARAB AMERICAN OR MIDDLE EASTERN EXPERIENCE

Drops of This Story, Suheir Hammad (Writers and Readers Publishing, 1996)

Habibi, Naomi Shihab Nye (Simon Pulse, 1999)

Nineteen Varieties of Gazelle: Poems of the Middle East, Naomi Shihab Nye (Greenwillow, 2002)

Under the Persimmon Tree, Suzanne Fisher Staples (Farrar, Straus & Giroux, 2005)

West of the Jordan, Laila Halaby (Beacon, 2003)

The Words Under the Words: Selected Poems, Naomi Shihab Nye (Eighth Mountain Press, 1995)

ASIAN AMERICAN EXPERIENCE/
ASIAN AMERICAN AUTHORS

American Dragons, Lawrence Yep (HarperCollins, 1993)

Farewell to Manzanar, Jeanne Wakatsuki (Houghton Mifflin, 1993)

The Joy Luck Club, Amy Tan (Putnam, 1989)

Kira-Kira, Cynthia Kadohata (Atheneum, 2004)

The Moved-Outers, Florence Crannell Means (Walker, 1945)

A Single Shard, Linda Sue Park (Clarion, 2001)

A Step from Heaven, An Na (Front Street, 2001)

When My Name Was Keoko: A Novel of Korea in World War II, Linda Sue Park (Clarion, 2002)

BIOGRAPHY

Eleanor Roosevelt: A Life of Discovery, Russell Freedman (Clarion, 1993)

Franklin Delano Roosevelt, Russell Freedman (Clarion, 1990)

The Greatest: Muhammad Ali, Walter Dean Myers (Scholastic, 2001)

I Am Somebody! A Biography of Jesse Jackson, James Haskins (Enslow, 1992)

Indian Summer: The Forgotten Story of Louis Sockalexis, the First Native American in Major League Baseball, Brian McDonald (Rodale, 2003)

Lincoln: A Photobiography, Russell Freedman (Clarion, 1987)

Sojourner Truth: Ain't I a Woman?, Patricia C. McKissack and Frederick L. McKissack (Scholastic, 1992)

DYSFUNCTIONAL OR NONTRADITIONAL FAMILY

Armageddon Summer, Bruce Coville and Jane Yolen (Harcourt, 1998)

Blind Faith, Ellen Wittlinger (Simon & Schuster, 2006)

Forged by Fire, Sharon Draper (Atheneum, 1997)

Freaky Green Eyes, Joyce Carol Oates (HarperCollins, 2003)

Gingerbread, Rachel Cohn (Simon & Schuster, 2002)

Homecoming, Cynthia Voigt (Atheneum, 1981)

Lord of the Deep, Graham Salisbury (Delacorte, 2001)

Margaux with an X, Ron Koertge (Candlewick, 2004)

Martyn Pig, Kevin Brooks (Scholastic, 2002)

Miracle's Boys, Jacqueline Woodson (Putnam, 2000)

The Moonlight Man, Paula Fox (Bradbury, 1985)

Rules of the Road, Joan Bauer (Putnam, 1998)

The Same Stuff as Stars, Katherine Paterson (Clarion, 2002)

A Solitary Blue, Cynthia Voigt (Atheneum, 1983)

Stotan!, Chris Crutcher (Greenwillow, 1986)

Up Country, Alden Carter (Putnam, 1989)

When She Was Good, Norma Fox Mazer (Scholastic, 1977)

You Don't Know Me, David Klass (Farrar, Straus & Giroux, 2001)

The Young Man and the Sea, Rodman Philbrick (Scholastic, 2004)

ENVIRONMENTAL

Beardance, Will Hobbs (Atheneum, 1993)

Bearstone, Will Hobbs (Atheneum, 1989)

California Blue, David Klass (Scholastic, 1994)

FANTASY/FAIRY TALE

Abarat, Clive Barker (Harper Trophy, 2003)

Abarat: Days of Magic, Nights of War, Clive Barker (Joanna Cotler Books, 2004)

The Amber Spyglass, Philip Pullman (Knopf, 1999)

Artemis Fowl, Eoin Colfer (Hyperion, 2001)

Artemis Fowl: The Arctic Incident, Eoin Colfer (Miramax, 2003)

Artemis Fowl: The Eternity Code, Eoin Colfer (Miramax, 2003)

Artemis Fowl: The Opal Deception, Eoin Colfer (Miramax, 2005)

Being Dead, Vivian Vande Velde (Harcourt, 2001)

The Black Cauldron, Lloyd Alexander (Holt, 1965)

City of the Beasts, Isabel Allende (HarperCollins, 2002) (trans.)

Dragonflight, Anne McCaffrey (Atheneum, 1976)

Dragon Rider, Cornelia Funke (Scholastic, 2004)

Eldest, Christopher Paolini (Knopf, 2005)

Ella Enchanted, Gail Carson Levine (HarperCollins, 1997)

Eragon, Christopher Paolini (Knopf, 2003)

Farthest Shore, Ursula Le Guin (Atheneum, 1972)

Forest of the Pygmies, Isabel Allende (HarperCollins, 2005) (trans.)

The Golden Compass, Philip Pullman (Knopf, 1996)

The Goose Girl, Shannon Hale (Bloomsbury, 2003)

Harry Potter and the Chamber of Secrets, J. K. Rowling (Arthur Levine Books, 1999)

Harry Potter and the Goblet of Fire, J. K. Rowling (Arthur Levine Books, 2000)

Harry Potter and the Half-Blood Prince, J. K. Rowling (Scholastic, 2005)

Harry Potter and the Order of the Phoenix, J. K. Rowling (Arthur Levine, 2003)

Harry Potter and the Prisoner of Azkaban, J. K. Rowling (Arthur Levine Books, 1999)

Harry Potter and the Sorcerer's Stone, J. K. Rowling (Arthur Levine Books, 1998)

Heir Apparent, Vivian Vande Velde (Harcourt, 2002)

The Hobbit, J. R. R. Tolkien (Houghton Mifflin, 1951)

I Am Mordred, Nancy Springer (Philomel, 1998)

Inkheart, Cornelia Funke (Chicken House/Scholastic, 2003)

Inkspell, Cornelia Funke (Chicken House/Scholastic, 2005)

Kingdom of the Dragon, Isabel Allende (HarperCollins 2004) (trans.)

The Lion, the Witch and the Wardrobe, C. S. Lewis (Macmillan, 1950)

Lord of the Rings, J. R. R. Tolkien (Houghton Mifflin, 1954)

The Magic Circle, Donna Jo Napoli (Dutton, 1993)

The Merlin Conspiracy, Diana Wynne Jones (Greenwillow, 2003)

Parzival: The Quest of the Grail Knight, Katherine Paterson (Lodestar, 1998)

A Sending of Dragons, Jane Yolen (Delacorte, 1987)

Stravaganza, City of Masks, Mary Hoffman (Bloomsbury, 2002)

The Subtle Knife, Philip Pullman (Knopf, 1997)

Sword of the Rightful King: A Novel of King Arthur, Jane Yolen (Harcourt, 2003)

The Thief Lord, Cornelia Funke (Chicken House/ Scholastic, 2002)

The Tombs of Atuan, Ursula Le Guin (Atheneum, 1972)

Witch's Wishes, Vivian Vande Velde (Holiday House, 2003)

A Wizard of Earthsea, Ursula Le Guin (Houghton Mifflin, 1968)

FUTURISTIC

Feed, M. T. Anderson (Candlewick, 2002)

The Giver, Lois Lowry (Houghton Mifflin, 1993)

House of the Scorpion, Nancy Farmer (Atheneum, 2002)

Jennifer Government, Max Barry (Doubleday, 2003)

The Last Book in the Universe, Rodman Philbrick (Blue Sky Press/Scholastic, 2000)

Tomorrowland: 10 Stories about the Future, Michael Cart, ed. (Scholastic, 1999)

GRAPHIC NOVEL

The 101 Best Graphic Novels, Stephen Weiner (NBM, 2001)

Age of Bronze, Eric Shanower (Image Comics, 2001) (seven volumes)

Blankets, Craig Thompson (Top Shelf, 2003)

Bone: 1, 2 and 3, Jeff Smith (Scholastic Graphix, 2005, 2005, 2006)

Club 9, Kobayashi Makoto (Dark Horse Comics, 1994)

Courageous Princess, Rod Espinosa (Antarctic Press, 2003)

Ghost World, Daniel Clowe (Fantagraphic, 2001)

Gotham Central, Greg Rucka and Ed Brubaker, Michael Lark ill. (DC Comics, 2004)

Maus, Art Spiegelman (Pantheon, 1986)

Maus II, Art Spiegelman (Pantheon, 1992)

Nausicaa of the Valley of the Wind, Hayao Miyazaki (VIZ Mechia, 2004)

The Sandman, Neil Gaiman (DC Comics, 1993)

Supernatural Law, Batton Lash (Exhibit A Press, 2000)

V is for Vendetta, Alan Moore (Vertigo, 2005)

Watchmen, Alan Moore (DC Comics, 1995)

HISTORICAL FICTION

Cast Two Shadows, Ann Rinaldi (Harcourt, 1998)

Catherine Called Birdy, Karen Cushman (Clarion, 1994)

Eyes of the Emperor, Graham Salisbury (Wendy Lamb Books, 2005)

Fever, 1793, Laurie Halse Anderson (Simon & Schuster, 2000)

Grasslands, Deb Seely (Holiday House, 2003)

Hiroshima, A Novella, Laurence Yep (Scholastic, 1995)

Island of the Blue Dolphins, Scott O'Dell (Houghton Mifflin, 1960)

The Kite Rider, Geraldine McCaughrean (HarperCollins, 2002)

The Land, Mildred Taylor (Phyllis Fogelman Books, 2001)

The Last Mission, Harry Mazer (Delacorte, 1979)

The Legend of Bass Reeves, Gary Paulsen (Wendy Lamb Books, 2006)

Lyddie, Katherine Paterson (Dutton, 1992)

Mary, Bloody Mary, Carolyn Meyer (Gulliver, 2001)

Matilda Bone, Karen Cushman (Clarion, 2000)

Maus, Art Speigelman (Pantheon, 1986) (allegorical)

The Midwife's Apprentice, Karen Cushman (Clarion, 1995)

Milkweed, Jerry Spinelli (Random House, 2003)

Mississippi Trial, 1955, Chris Crowe (Phyllis Fogelman Books, 2002)

The Moved-Outers, Florence Crannell Means (Walker, 1945)

My Brother Sam Is Dead, James Lincoln Collier and Christopher Collier (Scholastic, 1991)

A Northern Light, Jennifer Donnelly (Harcourt, 2003)

Out of the Dust, Karen Hesse (Scholastic, 1996)

The River Between Us, Richard Peck (Dial, 2003)

Sarny: A Life Remembered, Gary Paulsen (Laurel Leaf, 1999)

Shakespeare Scribe, Gary Blackwood (Dutton, 2000)

Shakespeare Stealer, Gary Blackwood (Dutton, 1998)

Sing Down the Moon, Scott O'Dell (Houghton Mifflin, 1970)

A Single Shard, Linda Sue Park (Clarion, 2001)

The True Confessions of Charlotte Doyle, Avi (Orchard, 1990)

Under the Blood-Red Sun, Graham Salisbury (Delacorte, 1994)

Walking Up a Rainbow, Theodore Taylor (Harcourt, 1994)

When My Name Was Keoko: A Novel of Korea in World War II, Linda Sue Park (Clarion, 2002)

The Winter People, Joseph Bruchac (Dial, 2002)

Witness, Karen Hesse (Scholastic, 2002)

Wolf by the Ears, Ann Rinaldi (Scholastic, 1991)

HOLOCAUST

Never to Forget: The Jews of the Holocaust, Milton Meltzer (HarperCollins, 1976)

Number the Stars, Lois Lowry (Houghton Mifflin, 1989)

One by One: Facing the Holocaust, Judith Miller (Simon & Schuster, 1990)

Schindler's List, Thomas Keneally (Simon & Schuster, 1982)

HORROR

Jade Green: A Ghost Story, Phyllis Reynolds Naylor (Atheneum, 2000)

More Scary Stories to Tell in the Dark, Alvin Schwartz (Lippincott, 1984)

Scary Stories III: More Tales to Chill Your Bones, Alvin Schwartz (HarperCollins, 1991)

Scary Stories to Tell in the Dark, Alvin Schwartz (Lippincott, 1981)

Short Circuits: Thirteen Shocking Stories by Outstanding Writers for Young Adults, Don Gallo, ed. (Delacorte, 1974)

Skeleton Man, Joseph Bruchac (HarperCollins, 2001)

Vampires, A Collection of Original Stories, Jane Yolen (HarperCollins, 1991)

HUMOR

The Amazing Life of Birds: The Twenty Day Puberty Journal of Duane Homer Leech, Gary Paulsen (Wendy Lamb Books, 2006)

Angus, Thongs and Full-Frontal Snogging, Louise Rennison (HarperCollins, 2000)

Backwater, Joan Bauer (Putnam, 1999)

Best Foot Forward, Joan Bauer (Putnam, 2005)

The Earth, My Butt and Other Big Round Things, Carolyn Mackler (Candlewick, 2003)

Flush, Carl Hiaasen (Random House/Knopf, 2005)

The Gospel According to Larry, Janet Tashjian (Holt, 2001)

Holes, Louis Sachar (Farrar, Straus & Giroux, 1998)

Hoot, Carl Hiaasen (Knopf, 2002)

A Long Way from Chicago, Richard Peck (Penguin, 1998)

Ninjas, Piranhas, and Galileo, Greg Leitich Smith (Little, Brown, 2003)

No More Dead Dogs, Gordon Korman, (Hyperion, 2002)

On the Bright Side, I'm Now the Girlfriend of a Sex God: Further Confessions of Georgia Nicolson, Louise Rennison (HarperCollins, 2001)

Rats Saw God, Rob Thomas (Simon Pulse, 1996)

Rules of the Road, Joan Bauer (Putnam, 1998)

The Secret Diary of Adrian Mole, Aged 13 3/4, Sue Townsend (HarperTempest, 2003)

Shakespeare Bats Cleanup, Ron Koertge (Candlewick, 2003)

Sleeping Freshmen Never Lie, David Lubar (Dutton Juvenile, 2005)

Slot Machine, Chris Lynch (HarperCollins, 1995)

Son of the Mob, Gordon Korman (Hyperion, 2002)

Surviving the Applewhites, Stephanie Tolan (HarperCollins, 2002)

Tofu and T. Rex, Greg Leitich Smith (Little, Brown, 2005)

The True Meaning of Cleavage, Mariah Fredericks (Simon & Schuster, 2003)

INNOVATIVE FORMAT/RADICAL NARRATIVES

Girl Goddess #9, Francesca Lia Block (HarperCollins, 1996)

Love that Dog, Sharon Creech (HarperCollins, 2001)

Missing Angel Juan, Francesca Lia Block (HarperCollins, 1993)

Monster, Walter Dean Myers (HarperCollins, 1999)

The Music of Dolphins, Karen Hesse (Scholastic, 1996)

Wasteland, Francesca Lia Block (Joanna Cotler Books, 2003)

Weetzie Bat, Francesca Lia Block (HarperCollins, 1989)

A Wreath for Emmet Till, Marilyn Nelson (Houghton Mifflin, 2005)

INTOLERANCE

Bury My Heart at Wounded Knee: An Indian History of the American West, Dee Brown (Holt, 1971)

The Drowning of Stephan Jones, Bette Greene (Bantam, 1991)

The Last Safe Place on Earth, Richard Peck (Delacorte, 1995)

Miriam's Well, Lois Ruby (Scholastic, 1993)

Nothing but the Truth, Avi (Orchard, 1991)

Skin Deep, Lois Ruby (Scholastic, 1994)

Slap Your Sides, M. E. Kerr (HarperCollins, 2002)

Whale Talk, Chris Crutcher (Greenwillow, 2001)

Witness, Karen Hesse (Scholastic, 2002)

Wounded Knee, Neil Waldman (Atheneum, 2001)

A Wreath for Emmet Till, Marilyn Nelson (Houghton Mifflin, 2005)

ISSUES OF SEX (SEXUAL IDENTITY, EXPERIENCE, ASSAULT)

Annie on My Mind, Nancy Garden (Farrar, Straus & Giroux, 1982)

Are You There, God? It's Me, Margaret, Judy Blume (Bradbury, 1970)

Arizona Kid, Ron Koertge (Little, Brown, 1988)

Boy Meets Boy, David Levithan (Random House, 2003)

Deliver Us from Evie, M. E. Kerr (HarperCollins, 1994)

The Drowning of Stephan Jones, Bette Greene (Bantam, 1991)

Hard Love, Ellen Wittlinger (Simon & Schuster, 1999)

Hello, I Lied, M. E. Kerr (HarperCollins, 1997)

Love and Sex: Ten Stories of Truth, Michael Cart, ed. (Simon & Schuster, 2001)

Night Kites, M. E. Kerr (HarperCollins, 1986)

Rainbow Boys, Alex Sanchez (Simon & Schuster, 2001)

Rainbow High, Alex Sanchez (Simon & Schuster, 2003)

Rainbow Road, Alex Sanchez (Simon & Schuster, 2005)

So Hard to Say, Alex Sanchez (Simon & Schuster, 2004)

Speak, Laurie Halse Anderson (Farrar, Straus & Giroux, 1999)

LATINO/LATINA EXPERIENCE AND LATIN AMERICAN SPANISH TRANSLATIONS

Always Running: La Vida Loca: Gang Days in L.A., Luis Rodriguez (Curbstone, 1993)

Bless Me, Ultima, Rudolfo Anaya (TQS Pub, 1976)

Breaking Through, Francisco Jiménez (Houghton Mifflin, 2002)

Caramelo, Sandra Cisneros (Knopf, 2002)

Circuit: Stories from the Life of a Migrant Child, Francisco Jiménez (University of New Mexico Press, 1997)

City of the Beasts, Isabel Allende (HarperCollins, 2002)

Cool Salsa: Bilingual Poems on Growing Up Latino in the United States, Lori Carlson, ed. (Holt, 1994)

Esperanza Rising, Pam Muñoz Ryan (Scholastic, 2000)

Forest of the Pygmies, Isabel Allende (HarperCollins, 2005)

The House on Mango Street, Sandra Cisneros (Random House, 1984)

Jesse, Gary Soto (Harcourt, 1994)

Kingdom of the Dragon, Isabel Allende (HarperCollins 2004) (trans.)

The Latina's Bible: The Nueva Latina's Guide to Love, Spirituality, Family, and La Vida,

Sandra Guzman (Three Rivers Press, 2002)

My Own True Name, Pat Mora (Arte Publico, 2000)

Parrot in the Oven: Mi Vida, (Joanna Cotler Books, 1996)

The Words Under the Words: Selected Poems, Naomi Shihab Nye (Eighth Mountain Press, 1995)

LIVING AGAINST THE GRAIN

Big Mouth and Ugly Girl, Joyce Carol Oates (HarperCollins, 2002)

Blubber, Judy Blume (Bradbury, 1974)

Born Blue, Han Nolan (Harcourt, 2001)

Buddha Boy, Kathe Koja (Farrar, Straus & Giroux, 2003)

Catcher in the Rye, J. D. Salinger (Little, Brown, 1951)

Feed, M. T. Anderson (Candlewick, 2002)

Gingerbread, Rachel Cohn (Simon & Schuster, 2002)

The Gospel According to Larry, Janet Tashjian (Holt, 2001)

I Never Loved Your Mind, Paul Zindel (HarperCollins, 1970)

Miriam's Well, Lois Ruby (Scholastic, 1993)

The Outsiders, S. E. Hinton (Viking, 1967)

Scorpions, Walter Dean Myers (HarperCollins, 1988)

Send Me Down a Miracle, Han Nolan (Harcourt, 1996)

Sweetblood, Pete Hautman (Simon & Schuster, 2003)

LOVE, FOR BETTER OR FOR WORSE

Dreamland, Sarah Dessen (Viking, 2000)

Forever, Judy Blume (Bradbury, 1975)

If I Love You, Am I Trapped Forever?, M. E. Kerr (HarperCollins, 1973)

Mr. and Mrs. Bo Jo Jones, Ann Head (Putnam, 1967)

My Darling, My Hamburger, Paul Zindel (HarperCollins, 1970)

Romiette and Julio, Sharon Draper (Atheneum, 1999)

Making a Difference/Taking a Stand

Best Foot Forward, Joan Bauer (Putnam, 2005)

California Blue, David Klass (Scholastic, 1994)

Nothing but the Truth, Avi (Orchard, 1991)

Oh, Freedom! Kids Talk about the Civil Rights Movement with the People Who Made It Happen, Casey King and Linda Barrett Osborne (Knopf, 1997)

Slap Your Sides, M. E. Kerr (HarperCollins, 2002)

Sonny's War, Valerie Hobbs (Farrar, Straus & Giroux, 2002)

Speak, Laurie Halse Anderson (Farrar, Straus & Giroux, 1999)

Stefan's Story, Valerie Hobbs (Frances Foster, 2003)

Vote for Larry, Janet Tashjian (Holt, 2004)

Memoir/Autobiography

Always Running: La Vida Loca: Gang Days in L.A., Luis Rodriguez (Curbstone, 1993)

Bad Boy, Walter Dean Myers (Amistad, 2001)

The Bell Jar, Sylvia Plath (Penguin, 1963)

Circuit: Stories from the Life of a Migrant Child, Francisco Jiménez (University of New Mexico Press, 1997)

Drops of This Story, Suheir Hammad (Writers and Readers Publishing, 1996)

Guts: The True Stories Behind Hatchet and the Brian Books, Gary Paulsen (Delacorte, 2001)

Hole in My Life, Jack Gantos (Farrar, Straus & Giroux, 2002)

How Angel Peterson Got His Name, Gary Paulsen (Wendy Lamb Books, 2003)

I Know Why the Caged Bird Sings, Maya Angelou (Random House, 1976)

King of the Mild Frontier: An Ill-Advised Autobiography, Chris Crutcher (Greenwillow, 2003)

Knots in My Yo-Yo String, Jerry Spinelli (Knopf, 1998)

Oddballs, William Sleator (Dutton, 1993)

The Pigman and Me, Paul Zindel (HarperCollins, 1992)

Woodsong, Gary Paulsen (Simon & Schuster, 1990)

MENTAL ILLNESS

The Bell Jar, Sylvia Plath (Penguin, 1963)

The Bumblebee Flies Anyway, Robert Cormier (Pantheon, 1983)

A Corner of the Universe, Ann Martin (Scholastic, 2002)

Damage, A. M. Jenkins (HarperCollins, 2001)

Dancing on the Edge, Han Nolan (Harcourt, 1997)

I Never Promised You a Rose Garden, Hannah Green (Holt, 1964)

Inside Out, Terry Trueman (Harper Tempest, 2003)

Invisible, Pete Hautman (Simon & Schuster, 2005)

Izzy, Willy-Nilly, Cynthia Voigt (Atheneum, 1986)

Memories of Summer, Ruth White (Farrar, Straus & Giroux, 2000)

Notes for Another Life, Sue Ellen Bridgers (Knopf, 1981)

Warrior Angel, Robert Lipsyte (HarperCollins, 2003)

MENTALLY OR PHYSICALLY CHALLENGED YOUTH

Cruise Control, Terry Trueman (HarperTempest, 2004)

Inside Out, Terry Trueman (HarperTempest, 2003)

Joey Pigza Loses Control, Jack Gantos (Farrar, Straus & Giroux, 2000)

Joey Pigza Swallowed the Key, Jack Gantos (Farrar, Straus & Giroux, 1998)

Stefan's Story, Valerie Hobbs (Farrar, Straus & Giroux, 2003)

Stuck in Neutral, Terry Trueman (HarperCollins, 2000)

Tangerine, Edward Bloor (Harcourt, 1997)

Whale Talk, Chris Crutcher (Greenwillow, 2001)

What Would Joey Do?, Jack Gantos (Farrar, Straus & Giroux, 2002)

MISFITS & OUTCASTS

Dinky Hocker Shoots Smack, M. E. Kerr (HarperCollins, 1972)

Fat Kid Rules the World, K. L. Going (Putnam, 2003)

Freak the Mighty, Rodman Philbrick (Scholastic, 1993)

Holes, Louis Sachar (Farrar, Straus & Giroux, 1998)

Hoot, Carl Hiaasen (Knopf, 2002)

Kissing the Rain, Kevin Brooks (Chicken House/Scholastic, 2004)

Mariposa Blues, Ron Koertge (Joy Street, 1991)

Max the Mighty, Rodman Philbrick (Scholastic, 1998)

The Misfits, James Howe (Atheneum, 2001)

Nick and Norah's Infinite Playlist, David Levithan and Rachel Cohn (Random House/Knopf, 2006)

On the Fringe, Don Gallo, ed. (Dial, 2001)

One Fat Summer, Robert Lipsyte (HarperCollins, 1977)

Out of Order, A. M. Jenkins (HarperCollins, 2003)

Pardon Me, You're Stepping on My Eyeball, Paul Zindel (HarperCollins, 1976)

Prom, Laurie Halse Anderson (Viking, 2005)

Rules of the Road, Joan Bauer (Putnam, 1998)

Rumble Fish, S. E. Hinton (Delacorte, 1976)

Small Steps, Louis Sachar (Delacorte, 2006)

Speak, Laurie Halse Anderson (Farrar, Straus & Giroux, 1999)

Stargirl, Jerry Spinelli (Knopf, 2000)

Stoner & Spaz, Ron Koertge (Candlewick, 2002)

Straydog, Kathe Koja (Farrar, Straus & Giroux, 2002)

Taming the Star Runner, S. E. Hinton (Delacorte, 1988)

Tex, S. E. Hinton (Delacorte, 1979)

That Was Then, This Is Now, S. E. Hinton (Viking, 1971)

Things Not Seen, Andrew Clement (Philomel, 2002)

Touching Spirit Bear, Ben Mikaelson (HarperCollins, 2001)

True Confessions of a Heartless Girl, Martha Brooks (Farrar, Straus & Giroux, 2003)

Whale Talk, Chris Crutcher (Greenwillow, 2001)

When Zachary Beaver Came to Town, Kimberly Willis Holt (Holt, 1999)

MODERN REALISM

Chinese Handcuffs, Chris Crutcher (Greenwillow, 1989)

Crazy Horse Electric Game, Chris Crutcher (Greenwillow, 1987)

A Day No Pigs Would Die, Robert Newton Peck (Knopf, 1973)

Dunk, David Lubar (Clarion, 2002)

Godless, Pete Hautman (Simon & Schuster, 2004)

Ironman, Chris Crutcher (Greenwillow, 1995)

Make Lemonade, Virginia Euwer Wolff (Holt, 1993)

My Heartbeat, Garret Freymann-Weyr (Houghton Mifflin, 2002)

My Name is Asher Lev, Chaim Potok (Knopf, 1972)

Olive's Ocean, Kevin Henkes (Greenwillow, 2003)

The Pigman, Paul Zindel (HarperCollins, 1968)

Running Loose, Chris Crutcher (Greenwillow, 1983)

Speak, Laurie Halse Anderson (Farrar, Straus & Giroux, 1999)

Stotan!, Chris Crutcher (Greenwillow, 1986)

There's a Girl in My Hammerlock, Jerry Spinelli (Simon & Schuster, 1991)

MULTICULTURAL

Destination Unexpected, Don Gallo, ed. (Candlewick, 2003)

First Crossing: Stories About Teen Immigrants, Don Gallo (Candlewick, 2004)

Join In: Multiethnic Short Stories, Don Gallo, ed. (Delacorte, 1993)

Shabanu, Daughter of the Wind, Suzanne Fisher Staples (Knopf, 1989)

This Same Sky: A Collection of Poems from Around the World, Naomi Shihab Nye (Simon & Schuster, 1992)

MYSTERY/SUPERNATURAL

The Body of Christopher Creed, Carol Plum-Ucci (Harcourt, 2000)

The Dark and Deadly Pool, Joan Lowery Nixon (Delacorte, 1987)

Fade, Robert Cormier (Delacorte, 1988)

I Am the Cheese, Robert Cormier (Knopf, 1977)

I Know What You Did Last Summer, Lois Duncan (Little, Brown, 1973)

The Lovely Bones, Alice Sebold (Little, Brown, 2002)

Mr. Was, Pete Hautman (Simon & Schuster, 1996)

Never Trust a Dead Man, Vivian Vande Velde (Harcourt, 1999)

New Moon, Stephenie Meyer (Megan Tingley, 2006)

The Other Side of Dark, Joan Lowery Nixon (Delacorte, 1986)

The Owl Service, Alan Garner (Walck, 1967)

The Rag and Bone Shop, Robert Cormier (Delacorte, 2001)

Séance, Joan Lowery Nixon (Harcourt, 1980)

Summer of Fear, Lois Duncan (Little, Brown, 1976)

Twilight, Stephenie Meyer (Megan Tingley, 2005)

Whispers from the Dead, Joan Lowery Nixon (Delacorte, 1989)

Who Killed Mr. Chippendale?: A Mystery in Poems, Mel Glenn (Lodestar, 1996)

NATIVE AMERICAN

Bone Dance, Martha Brooks (Bantam Doubleday, 1997)

Bury My Heart at Wounded Knee: An Indian History of the American West, Dee Brown (Holt, 1971)

Code Talker, Joseph Bruchac (Scholastic, 2005)

Fool's Crow, James Welch (Viking, 1986)

From Sand Creek: Rising in This Heart Which Is Our America, Simon Ortiz (Thunder's Mouth Press, 1981)

Geronimo, Joseph Bruchac (Scholastic, 2005)

The Heart of a Chief, Joseph Bruchac (Puffin, 2001)

Indian Chiefs, Russell Freedman (Holiday House, 1986)

Indian Shoes, Cynthia Leitich Smith (HarperCollins, 2002)

Indian Summer: The Forgotten Story of Louis Sockalexis, the First Native American in Major League Baseball, Brian McDonald (Rodale, 2003)

The Lone Ranger and Tonto Fistfight in Heaven, Sherman Alexie (Atlantic Monthly Press, 1993)

Love Medicine, Louise Erdrich (Holt, 1984)

Men on the Moon: Collected Short Stories, Simon Ortiz (University of Arizona Press, 1999)

Moccasin Thunder: American Indian Stories for Today, Lori Carlson ed. (Harper Collins, 2005)

Morning Girl, Michael Dorris (Hyperion, 1992)

My Name Is Seepeetza, Shirley Sterling (Sagebrush reprint, 2001)

Navajo Long Walk: Tragic Story of a Proud People's Forced March From Homeland, Joseph Bruchac and Shonto Begay (National Geographic, 2002) (picture book)

The Owl's Song, Janet Campbell Hale (Doubleday, 1974)

Rain Is Not My Indian Name, Cynthia Leitich Smith (HarperCollins, 2001)

Reservation Blues, Sherman Alexie (Warner, 1996)

Sing Down the Moon, Scott O'Dell (Houghton Mifflin, 1970)

Skeleton Man, Joseph Bruchac (HarperCollins, 2001)

Ten Little Indians, Sherman Alexie (Grove, 2004)

Touching Spirit Bear, Ben Mikaelson (HarperCollins, 2001)

Toughest Indian in the World, Sherman Alexie (Grove 2001)

When the Legends Die, Hal Borland (HarperCollins, 1963)

Who Will Tell My Brother? Marlene Carvell (Hyperion, 2002)

The Winter People, Joseph Bruchac (Dial, 2002)

Wounded Knee, Neil Waldman (Atheneum, 2001)

NONFICTION

Andy Warhol: Prince of Pop, Jan Greenberg and Sandra Jordan (Random House/Delacorte, 2004)

Bury My Heart at Wounded Knee: An Indian History of the American West, Dee Brown (Holt, 1971)

From Sand Creek: Rising in This Heart Which Is Our America, Simon Ortiz (Thunder's Mouth Press, 1981)

Getting Away with Murder: The True Story of the Emmett Till Case, Chris Crowe (Penguin Putnam, 2003)

Harlem Stomp: A Cultural History of the Harlem Renaissance, Laban Carrick Hill (Little, Brown, 2003)

Indian Chiefs, Russell Freedman (Holiday House, 1986)

Many Thousand Gone: African Americans from Slavery to Freedom, Virginia Hamilton (Knopf, 1993)

Navajo Long Walk: Tragic Story of a Proud People's Forced March From Homeland, Joseph Bruchac and Shonto Begay (National Geographic, 2002) (picture book)

Oh, Freedom! Kids Talk about the Civil Rights Movement with the People Who Made It Happen, Casey King and Linda Barrett Osborne (Knopf, 1997)

One by One: Facing the Holocaust, Judith Miller (Simon & Schuster, 1990)

The Race to Save the Lord God Bird, Phillip Hoose (Farrar Straus & Giroux, 2004)

Wounded Knee, Neil Waldman (Atheneum, 2001)

NONFICTION ABOUT TEENS

Branded: The Buying and Selling of Teenagers, Alissa Quart (Perseus Publishing, 2003)

Hiding to Survive: Stories of Jewish Children Rescued from the Holocaust, Maxine B. Rosenberg (Orchard, 1995)

The Latina's Bible: The Nueva Latina's Guide to Love, Spirituality, Family, and La Vida, Sandra Guzman (Three Rivers Press, 2002)

Ophelia Speaks: Adolescent Girls Write about Their Search for Self, Sara Shandler (HarperCollins, 1999)

Teenagers Who Made History, Russell Freedman (Holiday House, 1961)

OUTDOOR ADVENTURE

Beardance, Will Hobbs, (Atheneum, 1993)

Bearstone, Will Hobbs (Atheneum, 1989)

Between a Rock and a Hard Place, Alden Carter (Scholastic, 1995)

Brian's Hunt, Gary Paulsen (Random House, 2003)

Brian's Return, Gary Paulsen (Delacorte, 1999)

Deathwatch, Robb White (Doubleday, 1972)

Down the Yukon, Will Hobbs (HarperCollins, 2001)

Downriver, Will Hobbs (Atheneum, 1991)

Far North, Will Hobbs (HarperCollins, 1996)

Ghost Canoe, Will Hobbs (HarperCollins, 1996)

Hatchet, Gary Paulsen (Bradbury, 1987)

Jason's Gold, Will Hobbs (HarperCollins, 1999)

Julie of the Wolves, Jean George (HarperCollins, 1982)

Leaving Protection, Will Hobbs (HarperCollins, 2004)

Lord of the Deep, Graham Salisbury (Delacorte, 2001)

Sniper, Theodore Taylor (Harcourt, 1989)

Wildman Island, Will Hobbs (HarperCollins, 2002)

Woodsong, Gary Paulsen (Simon & Schuster, 1990)

PLAYS

Center Stage: One-Act Plays for Teenage Readers and Actors, Don Gallo, ed. (HarperCollins, 1990)

Pizza with Shrimp on Top, Aaron Levy (Dramatic Publishing, 2006)

POETRY COLLECTIONS

A Maze Me: Poems for Girls, Naomi Shihab Nye (Greenwillow, 2005)

Cool Salsa: Bilingual Poems on Growing Up Latino in the United States, Lori Carlson, ed. (Holt, 1994)

Dark Sons, Nikki Grimes (Jump at the Sun, 2005)

God Went to Beauty School, Cynthia Rylant (HarperCollins, 2003)

Heart to Heart: New Poems Inspired by Twentieth-Century American Art, Jan Greenberg, ed. (Abrams, 2001)

I, Too, Sing America: Three Centuries of African American Poetry, Catherine Clinton, ed. (Houghton Mifflin, 1998)

Joyful Noise: Poems for Two Voices, Paul Fleischman (HarperCollins, 1998)

Love that Dog, Sharon Creech (HarperCollins, 2001)

My Own True Name, Pat Mora (Arte Publico, 2000)

Nineteen Varieties of Gazelle: Poems of the Middle East, Naomi Shihab Nye (Greenwillow, 2002)

This Same Sky: A Collection of Poems from Around the World, Naomi Shihab Nye (Simon & Schuster, 1992)

Walking on the Boundaries of Change, Sara Holbrook (Boyds Mills, 1998)

What Have You Lost?, Naomi Shihab Nye, ed., photos by Michael Nye (Harper Tempest, 2001)

REGIONAL AMERICA

Eyes of the Emperor, Graham Salisbury (Wendy Lamb Books, 2005) (Hawaii-historical fiction)

A Fine White Dust, Cynthia Rylant (Bradbury, 1986) (Appalachia)

Grasslands, Deb Seely (Holiday House, 2003) (Great Plains)

A Long Way from Chicago, Richard Peck (Penguin, 1998) (small town Midwest)

M. C. Higgins, the Great, Virginia Hamilton (Macmillan, 1974) (Appalachia)

Memories of Summer, Ruth White (Farrar, Straus, & Giroux, 2000) (Appalachia)

RELUCTANT READERS

Adrenaline High, Christine Forsyth (Lorimer, 2003)

At-Risk, Jacqueline Guest (Lorimer, 2004)

The Baitchopper, Silver Donald Cameron (Lorimer, 1982)

Blood Is Thicker, Paul Langan and D. M. Blackwell (Townsend, 2004)

Body Art, Tamara Williams (Lorimer, 2005)

Brothers in Arms, Paul Langan and Ben Alirez (Townsend, 2004)

Bull Rider, Marilyn Halvorson (Orca, 2003)

The Bully, Paul Langan (Townsend, 2002)

Camp Wild, Pam Withers (Orca, 2005)

Ceiling Stars, Sandra Diersch (Lorimer, 2004)

Clearcut Danger, Lesley Choyce (Lorimer, 1995)

Dark End of a Dream, Lesley Choyce (Lorimer, 1994)

Dead-End Job, Vicki Grant (Orca, 2005)

Every Move, Peter McPhee (Lorimer, 2004)

Good Idea Gone Bad, Lesley Choyce (Lorimer, 1998)

Grind, Eric Walters (Orca, 2004)

The Gun, Paul Langan (Townsend, 2002)

In the Paint, Jeff Rud (Orca, 2005)

Juice, Eric Walters (Orca, 2005)

Klepto, Lori Weber (Lorimer, 2004)

Lightning Rider, Jacqueline Guest (Lorimer, 2000)

Lost and Found, Anne Schraff (Townsend, 2002)

A Matter of Trust, Anne Schraff (Townsend, 2002)

My Time as Caz Hazard, Tanya Lloyd Kyi (Orca, 2004)

No More Pranks, Monique Polak (Orca, 2004)

On the Game, Monique Polak (Lorimer, 2005)

Out of Time, Peter McPhee (Lorimer, 2003)

Queen of the Toilet Bowl, Frieda Wishinsky (Orca, 2005)

Racing Fear, Jacqueline Guest (Lorimer, 2004)

Someone to Love Me, Anne Schraff (Townsend, 2002)

Something Girl, Beth Goobie (Orca, 2005)

Split, Lori Weber (Lorimer, 2005)

Summer of Secrets, Paul Langan (Townsend, 2004)

Tattoo Heaven, Lori Weber (Lorimer, 2006)

Until We Meet Again, Anne Schraff (Townsend, 2002)

Secrets in the Shadows, Anne Schraff (Townsend, 2002)

SCIENCE FICTION

47, Walter Mosley (Little, Brown, 2005)

Children of Dune, Frank Herbert (Orion, 1976)

The Dark Side of Nowhere, Neal Shusterman (Starscape, 1997)

Dune, Frank Herbert (Chilton, 1965)

Dune Messiah, Frank Herbert (Putnam, 1969)

Eldest, Christopher Paolini (Knopf, 2005)

Ender's Game, Orson Scott Card (Tor, 1985)

Eragon, Christopher Paolini (Knopf, 2003)

Feed, M. T. Anderson (Candlewick, 2002)

House of the Scorpion, Nancy Farmer (Atheneum, 2002)

House of Stairs, William Sleator (Dutton, 1974)

Interstellar Pig, William Sleator (Dutton, 1984)

Left Hand of Darkness, Ursula Le Guin (Ace, 1969)

Mickey & Me: A Baseball Card Adventure, Dan Gutman (HarperCollins, 2003)

Mr. Was, Pete Hautman (Simon & Schuster, 1996)

Parasite Pig, William Sleator (Dutton, 1984)

Shoeless Joe and Me: A Baseball Card Adventure, Dan Gutman (Harper Trophy, 2003)

Stranger in a Strange Land, Robert Heinlein (Putnam, 1963)

Stravaganza, City of Masks, Mary Hoffman (Bloomsbury, 2002)

The Time Hackers, Gary Paulsen (Wendy Lamb Books, 2005)

Tomorrowland: 10 Stories about the Future, Michael Cart, ed. (Scholastic, 1999)

Turnabout, Margaret Peterson Haddix (Simon & Schuster, 2000)

SHORT STORY COLLECTIONS

American Dragons, Lawrence Yep (HarperCollins, 1993)

Athletic Shorts, Chris Crutcher (Greenwillow, 1991)

Baseball in April, Gary Soto (Harcourt, 1990)

Destination Unexpected, Don Gallo, ed. (Candlewick, 2003)

Dreams & Visions: Fourteen Flights of Fantasy, M. Jerry Weiss and Helen S. Weiss, ed. (Starscape, 2006)

First Crossing: Stories About Teen Immigrants, Don Gallo, ed. (Candlewick, 2004)

First French Kiss and Other Traumas, Adam Bagdasarian (Farrar, Straus & Giroux, 2002)

Island Boyz: Short Stories by Graham Salisbury, Graham Salisbury (Random House, 2002)

Join In: Multiethnic Short Stories, Don Gallo, ed. (Delacorte, 1993)

Lost and Found, Jerry and Helen Weiss (Tor, 2000)

Love Medicine, Louise Erdrich (Holt, 1984)

Love and Sex: Ten Stories of Truth, Michael Cart ed. (Simon & Schuster, 2001)

Men on the Moon: Collected Short Stories, Simon Ortiz (University of Arizona Press, 1999)

Moccasin Thunder: American Indian Stories for Today, Lori Carlson, ed. (HarperCollins, 2005)

Necessary Noise: Stories About Our Families as They Really Are, Michael Cart, ed. (Joanna Cotler, 2003)

No Easy Answers: Stories about Teens Making Tough Choices, Don Gallo, ed. (Delacorte, 1997)

On the Fringe, Don Gallo, ed. (Dial, 2001)

Rush Hour: Sin, Michael Cart, ed. (Delacorte, 2004)

Rush Hour: Bad Boys, Michael Cart, ed. (Delacorte, 2004)

Rush Hour: Face, Michael Cart, ed. (Delacorte, 2005)

Ten Little Indians, Sherman Alexie (Grove, 2004)

Time Capsule, Don Gallo, ed. (Delacorte, 1999)

Tomorrowland: 10 Stories about the Future, Michael Cart, ed. (Scholastic, 1999)

Toughest Indian in the World, Sherman Alexie (Grove, 2001)

Ultimate Sports: Short Stories by Outstanding Writers for Young Adults, Don Gallo, ed. (Delacorte, 1995)

Vampires: A Collection of Original Stories, Jane Yolen (HarperCollins, 1991)

Within Reach, Don Gallo, ed. (Delacorte, 1993)

SPORTS

Beneath the Armor of an Athlete: Real Strength on the Wrestling Mat, Lisa Whitsett (Wish, 2002)

The Brave, Robert Lipsyte (HarperCollins, 1993)

Bull Rider, Marilyn Halvorson (Orca, 2003)

The Contender, Robert Lipsyte (HarperCollins, 1967)

The Greatest: Muhammad Ali, Walter Dean Myers (Scholastic, 2001)

Hard Ball, Will Weaver (HarperCollins, 1998)

High Heat, Carl Deuker (Houghton Mifflin, 2003)

Home of the Braves, David Klass (Farrar, Straus & Giroux, 2002)

Imitate the Tiger, Jan Cheripko (Boyds Mills, 1998)

Indian Summer: The Forgotten Story of Louis Sockalexis, the First Native American in Major League Baseball, Brian McDonald (Rodale, 2003)

Jump Ball: A Basketball Season in Poems, Mel Glenn (Lodestar/Dutton, 1997)

Mickey & Me: A Baseball Card Adventure, Dan Gutman (HarperCollins, 2003)

The Moves Make the Man, Bruce Brooks (HarperCollins, 1984)

Out of Order, A. M. Jenkins (HarperCollins, 2003)

Pinned, Alfred Martino (Harcourt, 2005)

Rat, Jan Cheripko (Boyds Mills, 2002)

Shadow Boxer, Chris Lynch (HarperCollins, 1993)

Shoeless Joe and Me: A Baseball Card Adventure, Dan Gutman (Harper Trophy, 2003)

Something for Joey, Richard E. Peck (Bantam, 1978)

The Story of Negro League Baseball, William Brashler (Ticknor & Fields, 1994)

Stotan!, Chris Crutcher (Greenwillow, 1986)

Striking Out, Will Weaver (HarperCollins, 1993)

Tangerine, Edward Bloor (Harcourt, 1997)

Tears of a Tiger, Sharon Draper (Atheneum, 1994)

Ultimate Sports: Short Stories by Outstanding Writers for Young Adults, Don Gallo, ed. (Delacorte, 1995)

Vision Quest, Terry Davis (Viking, 1979)

Warrior Angel, Robert Lipsyte (HarperCollins, 2003)

Whale Talk, Chris Crutcher (Greenwillow, 2001)

When the Legends Die, Hal Borland (HarperCollins, 1963)

Wrestling Sturbridge, Rich Wallace (Knopf, 1996)

STORIES TOLD IN VERSE

Back to Class, Mel Glenn (Clarion, 1988)

Bronx Masquerade, Nikki Grimes (Dial, 2002)

Frenchtown Summer, Robert Cormier (Delacorte, 1999)

Heartbeat, Sharon Creech (Joanna Cotler, 2004)

Jump Ball: A Basketball Season in Poems, Mel Glenn (Lodestar/Dutton, 1997)

Out of the Dust, Karen Hesse (Scholastic, 1996)

Split Image, Mel Glenn (HarperCollins, 2000)

Taking of Room 114: A Hostage Drama in Poems, Mel Glenn (Lodestar/Dutton, 1997)

Who Killed Mr. Chippendale? A Mystery in Poems, Mel Glenn (Lodestar, 1996)

TEEN PARENTING

The First Part Last, Angela Johnson (Simon & Schuster, 2003)

Heaven, Angela Johnson (Simon & Schuster, 1998)

Mr. and Mrs. Bo Jo Jones, Ann Head (Putnam, 1967)

Spellbound, Janet McDonald (Farrar, Straus & Giroux, 2001)

True Believer, Virginia Euwer Wolff (Atheneum, 2001)

TROUBLE AT SCHOOL

Back to Class, Mel Glenn (Clarion, 1988)

Beyond the Chocolate War, Robert Cormier (Random House, 1985)

Buddha Boy, Kathe Koja (Farrar, Straus & Giroux, 2003)

The Chocolate War, Robert Cormier (Pantheon, 1974)

Class Dismissed, Mel Glenn (Clarion, 1982)

Confess-O-Rama, Ron Koertge (Orchard, 1996)

Killing Mr. Griffin, Lois Duncan (Little, Brown, 1978)

Othello: A Novel, Julius Lester (Scholastic, 1995)

Prom, Laurie Halse Anderson (Viking, 2005)

Running Loose, Chris Crutcher (Greenwillow, 1983)

Sleeping Freshmen Never Lie, David Lubar (Dutton Juvenile, 2005)

Speak, Laurie Halse Anderson (Farrar, Straus & Giroux, 1999)

Split Image, Mel Glenn (HarperCollins, 2000)

Whale Talk, Chris Crutcher (Greenwillow, 2001)

UNLIKELY FRIENDS

The Cay, Theodore Taylor (Doubleday, 1969)

Defiance, Valerie Hobbs (Farrar, Straus & Giroux, 2005)

Looking for Alaska, John Green (Penguin Group/Dutton, 2005)

Margaux with an X, Ron Koertge (Candlewick, 2004)

Stoner & Spaz, Ron Koertge (Candlewick, 2002)

WAR

Amaryllis, Craig Crist-Evans (Candlewick, 2003)

Bloods: An Oral History of the Vietnam War by Black Veterans, Wallace Terry (Ballantine, 1984)

Dateline: Troy, Paul Fleischman (Candlewick, 2006)

Everything We Had: An Oral History of the Vietnam War by Thirty-three American Soldiers, Al Santoli (Ballantine, 1981)

Fallen Angels, Walter Dean Myers (Scholastic, 1988)

Farewell to Manzanar, Jeanne Wakatsuki (Houghton Mifflin, 1993)

In the Combat Zone: An Oral History of American Women in Vietnam, Kathryn Marshall (Little, Brown, 1987)

Johnny Got His Gun, Dalton Trumbo (Lippincott, 1939)

The Last Mission, Harry Mazer (Delacorte, 1979)

My Brother Sam Is Dead, James Lincoln Collier and Christopher Collier (Scholastic, 1991)

Soldier Boys, Dean Hughes (Atheneum, 2001)

Soldier's Heart, Gary Paulsen (Delacorte, 1998)

Sonny's War, Valerie Hobbs (Farrar, Straus & Giroux, 2002)

Tree by Leaf, Cynthia Voigt (Atheneum, 1988)

When My Name Was Keoko: A Novel of Korea in World War II, Linda Sue Park (Clarion, 2002)

Zazoo, Richard Moser (Houghton Mifflin, 2001)

WHEN THINGS DON'T GO ACCORDING TO PLAN

Driver's Ed, Caroline B. Cooney (Delacorte, 1994)

Speak, Laurie Halse Anderson (Farrar, Straus & Giroux, 1999)

Tears of a Tiger, Sharon Draper (Atheneum, 1994)

Whirligig, Paul Fleischman (Holt, 1998)

A Boy Growing Up

Between a Rock and a Hard Place, Alden Carter (Scholastic, 1995)

Dark Sons, Nikki Grimes (Jump at the Sun, 2005)

The First Part Last, Angela Johnson (Simon & Schuster, 2003)

How Angel Peterson Got His Name, Gary Paulsen (Wendy Lamb Books, 2003)

The Outsiders, S. E. Hinton (Viking, 1967)

The Perks of Being a Wallflower, Stephen Chbosky (MTV, 1999)

Rat, Jan Cheripko (Boyds Mills, 2002)

Rats Saw God, Rob Thomas (Simon Pulse, 1996)

Running Loose, Chris Crutcher (Greenwillow, 1983)

Scorpions, Walter Dean Myers (HarperCollins, 1988)

The Secret Diary of Adrian Mole, Aged 13 $^3/_4$, Sue Townsend (HarperTempest, 2003)

A Separate Peace, John Knowles (Macmillan, 1961)

Shadow Boxer, Chris Lynch (HarperCollins, 1993)

Slap Your Sides, M. E. Kerr (HarperCollins, 2002)

Slot Machine, Chris Lynch (HarperCollins, 1995)

Soldier Boys, Dean Hughes (Atheneum, 2001)

Something for Joey, Richard E. Peck (Bantam, 1978)

Stand Tall, Joan Bauer (Putnam, 2002)

A Step from Heaven, An Na (Front Street, 2001)

Stotan!, Chris Crutcher (Greenwillow, 1986)

Tears of a Tiger, Sharon Draper (Atheneum, 1994)

Touching Spirit Bear, Ben Mikaelson (HarperCollins, 2001)

Up Country, Alden Carter (Putnam, 1989)

Very Far Away from Anywhere Else, Ursula Le Guin (Atheneum, 1976)

Vision Quest, Terry Davis (Viking, 1979)

Whale Talk, Chris Crutcher (Greenwillow, 2001)

When Zachary Beaver Came to Town, Kimberly Willis Holt (Holt, 1999)

Whirligig, Paul Fleischman (Holt, 1998)

Wrestling Sturbridge, Rich Wallace (Knopf, 1996)

You Don't Know Me, David Klass (Farrar, Straus & Giroux, 2001)

Young Man and the Sea, Rodman Philbrick (Scholastic, 2004)

A GIRL GROWING UP

A Maze Me: Poems for Girls, Naomi Shihab Nye (Greenwillow, 2005)

Angus, Thongs and Full-Frontal Snogging, Louise Rennison (HarperCollins, 2000)

Beneath the Armor of an Athlete: Real Strength on the Wrestling Mat, Lisa Whitsett (Wish, 2002)

Bloomability, Sharon Creech (HarperCollins, 1998)

Blue Tights, Rita Garcia-Williams (Puffin, 1996)

The Canning Season, Polly Horvath (Farrar, Straus & Giroux, 2003)

Catalyst, Laurie Halse Anderson (Viking, 2000)

Chicks Up Front, Sara Holbrook (Cleveland State University Press, 1998)

Girls in Pants: The Third Summer of the Sisterhood, Ann Brashares (Delacorte, 2005)

Habibi, Naomi Shihab Nye (Simon Pulse, 1999)

Hope Was Here, Joan Bauer (Putnam, 2000)

I Never Said I Wasn't Difficult, Sara Holbrook (Boyds Mills, 1992)

Jacob Have I Loved, Katherine Paterson (Crowell, 1980)

Keeper of the Night, Kimberly Willis Holt (Holt, 2003)

Letting Go of Bobby James: Or How I Found My Self of Steam, Valerie Hobbs (Farrar, Straus & Giroux, 2004)

Like Sisters on the Home Front, Rita Williams-Garcia (Lodestar, 1995)

Make Lemonade, Virginia Euwer Wolff (Holt, 1993)

A Northern Light, Jennifer Donnelly (Harcourt, 2003)

Olive's Ocean, Kevin Henkes (Greenwillow, 2003)

On the Bright Side, I'm Now the Girlfriend of a Sex God: Further Confessions of Georgia Nicolson, Louise Rennison (HarperCollins, 2001)

Ophelia Speaks: Adolescent Girls Write about Their Search for Self, Sara Shandler (HarperCollins, 1999)

Out of the Dust, Karen Hesse (Scholastic, 1996)

Pop Princess, Rachel Cohn (Simon & Schuster, 2004)

Prom, Laurie Halse Anderson (Viking, 2005)

Rules of the Road, Joan Bauer (Putnam, 1998)

The Same Stuff as Stars, Katherine Paterson (Clarion, 2002)

The Second Summer of the Sisterhood, Ann Brashares (Delacorte, 2003)

Send Me Down a Miracle, Han Nolan (Harcourt, 1996)

The Sisterhood of the Traveling Pants, Ann Brashares (Delacorte, 2001)

Someone Like You, Sarah Dessen (Viking, 1998)

Sonny's War, Valerie Hobbs (Farrar, Straus & Giroux, 2002)

Speak, Laurie Halse Anderson (Farrar, Straus & Giroux, 1999)

Spellbound, Janet McDonald (Farrar, Straus & Giroux, 2001)

Split Image, Mel Glenn (HarperCollins, 2000)

Straydog, Kathe Koja (Farrar, Straus & Giroux, 2002)

There's a Girl in My Hammerlock, Jerry Spinelli (Simon & Schuster, 1991)

Toning the Sweep, Angela Johnson (Orchard, 1993)

Tree by Leaf, Cynthia Voigt (Atheneum, 1988)

True Believer, Virginia Euwer Wolff (Atheneum, 2001)

True Confessions of a Heartless Girl, Martha Brooks (Farrar, Straus & Giroux, 2003)

The True Meaning of Cleavage, Mariah Fredericks (Simon & Schuster, 2003)

Turnabout, Margaret Peterson Haddix (Simon & Schuster, 2000)

Twists and Turns, Janet McDonald (Farrar, Straus & Giroux, 2003)

Walk Two Moons, Sharon Creech (HarperCollins, 1994)

When My Name Was Keoko: A Novel of Korea in World War II, Linda Sue Park (Clarion, 2002)

When She Was Good, Norma Fox Mazer (Scholastic, 1977)

Zazoo, Richard Moser (Houghton Mifflin, 2001)

Literary Elements

It's much easier to meet your reading/literature standards with books that are rich in certain literary elements. I recommend the following books to help students analyze these literary element.

CHARACTER

The Canning Season, Polly Horvath (Farrar, Straus & Giroux, 2003)

Catalyst, Laurie Halse Anderson (Viking, 2000)

The Chocolate War, Robert Cormier (Pantheon, 1974)

A Northern Light, Jennifer Donnelly (Harcourt, 2003)

The Sisterhood of the Traveling Pants, Ann Brashares (Delacorte, 2001)

FLASHBACK

Mr. Was, Pete Hautman (Simon & Schuster, 1996)

Soldier's Heart, Gary Paulsen (Delacorte, 1998)

FORESHADOWING

The Music of Dolphins, Karen Hesse (Scholastic, 1996)

The Shakespeare Stealer, Gary Blackwood (Puffin, 2000)

Walk Two Moons, Sharon Creech (HarperCollins, 1994)

PLOT

The Contender, Robert Lipsyte (HarperCollins, 1967)

Driver's Ed, Caroline B. Cooney (Delacorte, 1994)

The Drowning of Stephan Jones, Bette Greene (Bantam, 1991)

The Heart of a Chief, Joseph Bruchac (Puffin, 2001)

Holes, Louis Sachar (Farrar, Straus & Giroux, 1998)

Stand Tall, Joan Bauer (Putnam, 2002)

Whale Talk, Chris Crutcher (Greenwillow, 2001)

POINT OF VIEW

Kissing the Rain, Kevin Brooks (Chicken House/Scholastic, 2004)

Letting Go of Bobby James: Or How I Found My Self of Steam, Valerie Hobbs (Farrar, Straus & Giroux, 2004)

Monster, Walter Dean Myers (HarperCollins, 1999)

Stuck in Neutral, Terry Trueman (HarperCollins, 2000)

SETTING

Down the Yukon, Will Hobbs (HarperCollins, 2001)

A Fine White Dust, Cynthia Rylant (Bradbury, 1986)

Grasslands, Deb Seely (Holiday House, 2003)

The House on Mango Street, Sandra Cisneros (Random House, 1984)

My Own True Name, Pat Mora (Arte Publico, 2000)

Out of the Dust, Karen Hesse (Scholastic, 1996)

SUSPENSE

The Body of Christopher Creed, Carol Plum-Ucci (Harcourt, 2000)

I Know What You Did Last Summer, Lois Duncan (Little, Brown, 1973)

THEME

The Beast, Walter Dean Myers (Scholastic, 2003)

Clearcut Danger, Lesley Choyce (Lorimer, 1995)

Defiance, Valerie Hobbs (Farrar, Straus & Giroux, 2005)

Fallen Angels, Walter Dean Myers (Scholastic, 1988)

Rat, Jan Cheripko (Boyds Mills, 2002)

Sonny's War, Valerie Hobbs (Farrar, Straus & Giroux, 2002)

Toning the Sweep, Angela Johnson (Orchard, 1993)

Touching Spirit Bear, Ben Mikaelson (HarperCollins, 2001)

When the Legends Die, Hal Borland (HarperCollins, 1963)

In addition to the suggestions in this chapter, the books listed in Chapter 4: In the Authors' Words are proven winners. The myriad publications, websites, organizations, and awards designed to inform readers of the quality and nature of young adult books today (some of which we discuss in Chapter 3) are also good places to consult when choosing books for students. The following rubric also might be a helpful way to evaluate and compare potential choices.

Young Adult Book Evaluation Form

BOOK TITLE	The Outsiders
PUBLISHER Major name in young adult literature?	Penguin Puffin (yes)
REVIEWS Multiple, favorable reviews in major publications and/or online? What age range is suggested?	Recognized as classic within YA genre. Grades 7–9
AWARDS Multiple awards? Specific awards for genre of cultural portrayals?	Chicago Tribune Book, 1967; Media and Methods Maxi Award, 1975; ALA Best Young Adult Books, 1975; Massachusetts Children's Book Award, 1979 (and more)
AUTHOR Award-winning author? For what reading level and age does this author generally write?	S. E. Hinton. Recognized as one of the best YA authors. Ages 12–16
CONTENT Who are the characters? What are their issues?	Characters: Ponyboy, Sodapop, Darrell, Dallas, Two-Bit, and Johnny. Issues: gangs, class divisions, violence, family, friendship
POSSIBLE USE Circle those that apply. Readability test quotient: _____	Whole class Independent reading with parent approval Read-aloud Genre Literature circle Theme Independent reading

Young Adult Book Evaluation Form

BOOK TITLE	
PUBLISHER Major name in young adult literature?	
REVIEWS Multiple, favorable reviews in major publications and/or online? What age range is suggested?	
AWARDS Multiple awards? Specific awards for genre of cultural portrayals?	
AUTHOR Award-winning author? For what reading level and age does this author generally write?	
CONTENT Who are the characters? What are their issues?	

POSSIBLE USE

Circle those that apply.

Readability test quotient: _____

Whole class

Read-aloud

Literature circle

Independent reading

Independent reading with parent approval

Genre

Theme

Closing Thoughts

A wondrous experience is just one book away for every teen reader. Armed with the information in this chapter, you should be able to set your students up for success with a number of books that fit them well and provide others they can choose from as they see fit. A little time spent investigating content, reading level, and the response a book has received from young readers and from the adult experts on adolescent literature will not only pay off in a successful class experience but may also make a lifelong difference for a newly inspired reader, whether it's that first enjoyable book ever or an author who becomes a cherished favorite.

What about the people behind the books, the authors? Knowing more about them can shed a completely new light on their work. When a young person makes a connection with an author's work, he or she will enjoy knowing more about that author's life, will become something of an expert on that author, and will be hungry for other books by that favorite writer. In the next chapter, In the Authors' Words, we let the authors speak for themselves. For each the 70 authors listed, you will find a short biography and an annotated bibliography of some of his or her best books. I've also included interviews with many of them. This information may become important in keeping a newly inspired reader going when he or she gets to the end of a great book and says, "Hey! That was fun; what else can I read just like that one?"

CHAPTER 4

IN THE AUTHORS' WORDS

INTERVIEWS, SHORT BIOGRAPHIES, AND RECOMMENDED WORKS FROM THE TOP AUTHORS OF YOUNG ADULT LITERATURE

For each of the following authors, I've included some biographical information and plot summaries of some of his or her books. Interviews are included for 32 of the authors. Since most of these interviews appeared in either the *Journal of Adolescent and Adult Literacy* or *The ALAN Review* immediately following the publication of a new book, the questions in the interview will often focus on that particular book.

Much more complete and lengthy works with longer biographies and complete annotated listings of these authors' works are available as multiple volumes (most often found in libraries) or as compendiums that concentrate on a small number of authors. What I have done here is attempt to give enough information on many authors to help you choose books for your students.

Although the following information about authors and their books could be shared with individual students whenever the interest or need arises, I suggest three approaches for sharing this information with your classes as a whole.

BOOK WEEK

Early in each semester schedule a number of days in a row (I found that three was about right) to take students through a list of books and authors. The teacher can provide the information or even ask students to become experts and each choose an author or two. During the Book Week days, the expert or teacher describes each author's background, especially the interesting parts (Gary Paulsen raced in the Iditarod and was stomped by a moose!), and gives a little description of some of that author's most famous books. Students who have read the author can share their insights, as well as tell about additional books by that author that they recommend.

 MY DAILY RECOMMENDATIONS

I have been modeling this method with my university students for the last seven years, and it works well, too. As part of my class opening, I make two or three book recommendations. I project an image of the books onto the video screen, and pass the books around. I tell a little bit about the author, and describe each book's major premise (What if you thought the picture of a kidnapped child on a milk carton looked a lot like you?), giving just enough information about the plot, setting, and characters to pique the students' interest but not enough to give away too much of the book's story.

3 **"AUTHOR'S VISIT"**

Armed with the biography, book summaries, and the interviews from this book, students can come to class as a famous author, talk to the class, and have one of their friends interview them. Creative costuming might mean "Joan Bauer" wearing a waitress uniform, or perhaps "Robert Lipsyte" wearing boxing gloves and protective headgear.

LAURIE HALSE ANDERSON

Laurie Halse Anderson grew up in upstate New York, where her father was a Methodist minister. For part of Laurie's childhood, her father was a chaplain for Syracuse University, and Laurie has pleasant memories of the campus as a young girl. As a teenager, she worked on a dairy farm where she did a variety of farm work, including milking cows.

Laurie attended Onondaga Community College in Syracuse, New York, and then transferred to Georgetown University in Washington, D.C., where she earned a degree in linguistics. Laurie continues to live in upstate New York in a beautiful house built from the ground up by her husband, Scot.

Laurie's novels for young adults go beyond telling a good story and illustrate her affinity for the artful use of language and her joy in works of literary substance. She often deals, in a thoughtful and careful way, with traumatic events many teenagers may face.

BOOKS

♦ *Speak*: In the summer before ninth grade, Melinda finds herself at a high school beer party. When a popular older boy rapes hers, she calls 911 but cannot bring herself to tell the police or anyone else what has happened. As her first year of high school unwinds, she is not only suffering from the unresolved issue of the attack but also the ostracism of her schoolmates, who see her only as the girl who "ratted out" their illegal celebration. Grades 8–12

♦ *Catalyst*: Kate Malone finds herself in her senior year of high school without a backup plan if she is rejected by MIT—her dream university. As her friends are accepted to various Ivy League schools, Kate's penchant for obsessing over life's obstacles drives her to the verge of a physical breakdown. Meanwhile, her father, a minister, brings Teri Litch, the most outcast of Kate's classmates, into their home along with all of Teri's family's social ills. Kate grows to understand that failing to get into your dream college is not the worst thing that can happen to someone. Grades 8–12

♦ *Prom*: Ashley Hannigan is the last person anyone would expect to go to her high school prom, let alone help put it on. When a wayward math teacher embezzles the prom funds and Ashley's best friend and next-door neighbor, Natalie Schmulensky, nobly attempts to pick up the pieces and make the cancelled prom a reality, Ashley finds herself helping with and eventually in charge of the prom despite a principal who is out to get her, an apathetic student body, and a long list of unpredictable obstacles. Grades 9–12

A Conversation With Laurie Halse Anderson

Adapted from Blasingame, James. (2005). Interview with Laurie Halse Anderson. *Journal of Adolescent and Adult Literacy, 49*(1), 72–73.

JB: In your book *Prom* (Viking, 2005) the protagonist, Ashley Hannigan, is hardly the person to care about the prom, but in the end she takes on 90 percent of the responsibility for making sure this prom-that-wasn't-going-to-happen does happen and becomes something of a folk hero in her school. How/why did you ever shoulder this sort of counter-culture-march-to-her-own-drummer person like Ashley with the burden of making sure the quintessential symbol of school social acceptability is a success? Ashley + Prom = the null set before the story—how/why could that possibly change?

LHA: Well, that's a tough question. "Null set"? Man!

I wanted Ashley to reach outside her narrowly defined world (in the preparation for the prom) and I wanted her to have a triumph (the shining moment when everyone is dancing to the same beat)

Teenagers often allow themselves to be limited by how the culture sees them. Come to think of it, some adults do, too. True freedom comes from the realization that it doesn't matter what other people think of you. When you start making decisions based on your internal compass, that's when you come to life.

The things that I resist the most often become significant pieces of my own growth and development. Eleanor Roosevelt said, "You must do the thing you think you cannot do," and those are words to live by. I handed Ashley a thing she didn't want and couldn't do, and she did it.

JB: You have captured the dialogue of teenagers masterfully (and managed to do so without needing to resort to much in the way of obscenity), including slang expressions like "bling bling" and also some real jewels of school administrator platitudes like "Listening is an opportunity, people." Did you hang out in high schools to capture these? Where did they come from?

LHA: If I (or any other YA author) were to write truly realistic dialogue, our books would overflow with curse words and they would probably not be published, but if they were, they would never make their way into bookstores and libraries and the hands of readers because a part of the American public would be outraged that authors use such filthy, inappropriate gutter language. Not all teenagers spice their daily conversations with obscenity, but most of the ones I've met do.

Teens understand this situation. They know that, just as they get in trouble for dropping the "F-bomb" in front of teachers, authors get nailed for it, too. So we have an unspoken pact about pretend language in books. It's another one of the confusing hypocrisies that makes being an American teenager so damn—I mean darn—hard. However, it presents an interesting craft challenge to the author. We must show through action and narrative details the situations of daily high school life that leads teens to curse a lot. It's fun to struggle with that.

I stole most of the administrators' platitudes while visiting high schools. When announcements are made over loudspeakers, even visiting authors have to shut up and listen. Some visiting authors take notes.

JB: Ashley describes herself as "normal." What do you think a "normal" high school student is in values and behavior?

LHA: Ashley uses the word *normal* as a defense. In her mind, those other kids, the kids you see on TV who are going to college and are given cars on their 16th birthday, there is something wrong with those kids. She is comfortable being "normal," fitting in with the world around her.

I think the average teenager just wants to get by without attracting too much attention. They live on an ice skating rink and they are trying very hard not to fall flat on their faces.

JB: Ashley *seems* to be in love with her boyfriend, T. J., all the way through the novel until the end, at which point she cuts him loose and shows no regret. Why did she do this/ what realization had she come to about him or that relationship?

LHA: Ashley is following the model of her parents' relationship: fall in love at the end of high school and commit to that first love. But she has nagging doubts about T. J. The world he offers her falls short of her dreams, though she is still figuring out what those dreams are

There is true love and respect in her parents' marriage. Over the course of the book, Ashley realizes that despite all his good qualities (and his yummy abs) E. G. cannot look beyond his own desires to see what she needs and wants. He is not good enough for her.

JB: You have successfully created a tension between two conflicting views of the prom: (1) It's all pretend and ignores the reality of life and it commands a disproportionate amount of a teenagers' or that teenager's family's discretionary spending money, especially for this one-time, short-lived social event. (2) For once in their lives, the kids will get to pretend they are glamorous socialites, and it is a once in a lifetime opportunity that they will remember the rest of their lives, lives that will have few opportunities for glamour and luxury. Even Ashley seems able to hold both contradictory ideas in her head at the same time. How do you view this American cultural phenomenon, "the prom"?

LHA: The book reflects my ambivalence about this bizarre ritual. On the one hand, proms are a wonderful celebration. High school is hard, being a teenager is hard, and they deserve a chance to dress up and party together, to push beyond the envelope of their daily routines and experiment with dressing up and feeling special.

On the other hand, the money spent on proms is truly obscene and stupid. I wonder if there are any high schools out there that have thought of deliberately scaling back the glitz. I doubt it. And I wish we could find a way to convince teenagers that this is not the night to get drunk or high or laid.

Maybe the attention that teens lavish on the prom tells us that they want more in the way of coming-of-age rituals. They want a public acknowledgment that they have moved from childhood into adulthood. Hmmm . . . .

M. T. Anderson

M. T. (Tobin) Anderson teaches in the M.F.A. program at Vermont College and believes that secondary students could, and should, work with challenging literary texts. M. T. grew up loving classical music such as the work of Handel and thought George Frederick Handel's life story would be interesting enough to young people that an illustrated picture book would be a good idea. M. T. worked briefly at McDonald's as a teenager, which helped to inspire his first novel, *Burger Wuss*. Later he went to Harvard and Cambridge universities, where he studied literature before getting an M.F.A. in creative writing from Syracuse University. M. T. lives in Boston, Massachusetts.

Books

♦ *Feed*: High school students Titus and his friends are looking for a good time, an effort that's enhanced by their "feeds," a media hybrid of TV and the Internet that's hardwired into their brains. The feeds are a sort of Internet, MTV, advertising, and instant messaging system that flash "mega" (futuristic slang for "a lot") information through their heads at lightning speed. The effect on culture is so fast that Titus's female friends arrive at a party with their hair in one style and leave the party having adopted a completely different coiffure, thanks to the information coming in through their feeds. When Titus meets Violet, the virtue of feeds comes under challenge. Violet is determined to thwart the anonymous corporate entity controlling the feeds and its efforts to brainwash and influence the behavior (especially buying behavior) of everyone on the planet. Consumerism is almost a religion in this world. M. T. Anderson creates futuristic slang that is ingenious and entertaining. Grades 9–12

♦ *Handel, Who Knew What He Liked*: This book has comical but instructive illustrations and a text that makes the life of the composer of the *Messiah* quite interesting. Grades 5–7

♦ *Burger Wuss*: When Anthony catches the love of his life, Diana, kissing a total loser who works at O'Dermott's (could this be a parody of a well-known, corporate giant burger-joint franchise?), he will go to great measures to win her back. Grades 8–10

♦ *Thirsty*: Along with all the other transitional problems of adolescence, Chris finds that he is turning into a vampire. In this comical account of a young man's attempt to deal with yet another developmental problem of being a teenager, Chris must choose between the vampire world and the human one. Grades 7–12

A Conversation With M. T. Anderson

Adapted from Blasingame, James. (2003). Interview with M. T. (Tobin) Anderson. *Journal of Adolescent and Adult Literacy, 47*(1), 98–99.

JB: The premise of *Feed*, a future world where almost everyone has an implanted microchip "feed" that constantly bombards them with information—mostly promoting and facilitating a consumer culture gone wild—obviously came from present-day trends in television, the Internet, and the consumer culture that's foisted upon young people without their knowledge. Were there any specific events, moments, or experiences in the present that drove this home for you and inspired the book?

MTA: I wrote the first two sections of the book in the week preceding the terrorist attacks in 2001. Needless to say, I stopped writing for a while afterwards. On the Friday after the attacks, I was standing in a used CD store, just an hour or two after the memorial services that had been taking place across the nation. And a young man walked in and said, "Dude! I think the truffle is totally undervalued." A while later, I overheard a young woman talking into a cell phone, saying, "God, but he *never* pukes when he chugalugs."

It was as if the attacks had never happened. Now of course, it's completely unfair to judge these two people solely by these overheard fragments—and of course, many young people were deeply, deeply affected by it, and it's my hope that they (and all of us!) will have a greater sense of the political exigencies of being a superpower in a precarious world—but still, these two statements stuck in my head as a graphic illustration of what so many of us do when confronted with disaster. We turn away. We refuse to be confronted.

So when I returned to the manuscript, I opened part three with a scene that includes those quotations.

JB: Violet and her father are the only critical thinkers in a ravished world peopled by unquestioning citizens totally under the control of a faceless corporate entity. Is their destruction your warning that we need to change our ways?

MTA: Yes, indeed. There's a real urgency in the need to change. Overpopulation, destruction of the country's forests, exploitation of other populations in the name of good business sense—these things seem like the tired maunderings of dreamy-eyed intellectuals but they're statistical realities, and they're going to have a profound impact on the way we live.

I close the book with the words "Everything must go . . ." That has particular meaning within the story, but also in a broader sense, that willingly or unwillingly, we're going to have to radically change the way we live. Our lives as Americans are built on superstructures that are not self-sustaining. Our nation has a vicious prejudice against anything that doesn't yield quick profit. There's little sense of long-term planning, and there's open scorn when ethical questions arise in opposition to short-term business goals—they're seen as airy-fairy gobbledygook, fine for the kids and grandmas, but of no concern to men who understand how the world really works.

Pragmatism is one of America's greatest inheritances, and also one of our most dangerous tools for self-deception. A good example of this is the federal government's approach to global warming—years of denial, and then, finally, when it was fully admitted, our government openly turned its back on international solutions because they seemed to threaten business interests. And yet, demonstrably, the climate is changing. This could be said of any number of key environmental and political issues.

In any case, this is why I turn to kids for answers. They haven't yet been fully inducted into the values and pieties of the adult political and financial world. They still feel outrage. We'll be handing over to them a world that is deeply destabilized and sapped. It is from them that the solutions must come.

JB: Although the future world you create is very different from the present-day world, you seem to believe that there are some constants. What are those?

MTA: Love, sadness, the need to belong, anger, joy, Coca-Cola.

JB: How did you create the slang that Titus and the others speak, and how did you arrive at the language used in the advertisements and ploys that come over the feed?

MTA: I read a lot of magazines like *Maxim, Stuff,* and *Teen.* I watched a lot of cable. Whenever I felt tired of the whole project, I went and read one of these magazines. Instantly, my anger was renewed, and I went back in, fists swinging. Studying magazines like that is actually a great school activity—I recommend it highly for classroom use. A friend of mine who teaches sixth grade took quotations from magazines for, by, and about teenagers in to her class. The kids stared at the page for a while, and got really quiet, and then one asked, "So when we become teenagers, are we going to suddenly become really stupid?" If you show kids things like this, out of their usual context, they instantly see what's up. They see all the ways in which a whole cultural *context* is being constructed for them that promotes certain kinds of sales. It's a context that soothes the consumer, produces desire, and conceals the marketing drive behind the glitter of the cool and the self-actuating.

For example, I recently looked at a website devoted to the celebration of "Real Girls" which was actually sponsored by the American Beef Council. Beef was not mentioned—being a real girl was the subject of the site—but, by chance, there were overlays of hamburgers and many vague prompts to eat great snacks. It's a great question for classrooms—how are things sold *without reference to* what the thing is or what it can do for you?

Kids are ready for these realizations, and many of them already see around the context that's being forced on them. That's one of the greatest things a teacher can do, I think—decontextualizing and recontextualizing—inviting kids to step outside their world long enough to see what we're all living in, and start to ask questions.

There are certain linguistic positions that we as Americans tend to fill with a slang term. Like the "buddy" position, used as a filler to reaffirm the connection between interlocutors—there's one in every age in America, as we move through time: sir/ sirrah, b'hoy (very trendy in the late 1840s), friend, pal, buddy, man, guy, dude. Same thing for a string of positive intensifiers: capital, bully, swell, groovy, cool, awesome, bitchin', phat, tight, etc. I started to think about these idiomatic placeholders, and I just inserted fabricated ones—"unit" and so on.

The language was huge fun to write. It irritates some readers, which is completely understandable. Sorry about that. But I do feel, in spite of everything, that this is the world we're making.

JB: Do you consider yourself to be positive or negative about today's youth?

MTA: This is a great question, and a difficult one. I have to struggle to answer it briefly. The short answer is that it depends on the day. This is, as teachers know all too well, a society with a deep suspicion of and dislike for intelligence. Our culture focuses on the young—both because that's always been an American topos, and because, more recently, marketers have realized that in the teen demographic there's a succulent coincidence of disposable cash and herd psychology. Everything's young, everything's short-term.

There's a certain late-imperial emphasis on instant gratification as a result. Because of all of this, kids have a highly adversarial relationship to education. It's sad, really, since education is, at an abstract level, about giving them a better chance, and giving them a chance to really effect change. All of that potential for growth is blocked by the stereotypes so prevalent in our mass media—of white-haired teachers, dry and out-of-touch, with nothing to offer but boredom and chalk dust, confronting a room full of the hip, the bubbling, the fun, and the sprayed, all of whom want to burst out of their seats and go dance, because that, after all, is where it's at.

In my low moments, I worry that we're producing a nation and a generation that is inarticulate and clumsy in their thought, self-absorbed, incapable of subtlety, constructed by products, unable to learn from the past since the past is forgotten, blind to global variation, violently greedy and yet unaware of how much they ask for already. I worry about what we're becoming, with so little sense of what we were.

But on my good days, I meet just one kid at a reading or in someone's classroom who says something that makes us all pause, and I think, "Wow. All right. Generation yields to generation. We're going to be okay."

JB: Are you an Internet junkie?

MTA: No, not really. I love the breadth of expression—the fact that if you type in any random phrase into a search engine you'll get a list of sites where people are telling you all about their vision of truth. I also love the possibilities inherent in the technology—that soon, we'll be able to quite efficiently and reliably cut out the system of distribution for many forms of art and entertainment—movies, music, and text are already available on the Web, and the technology to distribute them is only going to improve.

AVI

Avi uses only this three-letter name, a name his twin sister, Emily, first bestowed upon him when they were small children. Born in 1937, he grew up in New York but now makes his home in Denver, Colorado. Surprisingly, writing did not come naturally to Avi; in fact, he suffered from dysgraphia, a learning disability that causes writers to unintentionally reverse elements, misspell words, and/or write words that are not exactly what they mean to express. Although Avi struggled with writing, in his senior year of high school he vowed to become a writer.

Avi worked as a librarian in New York and London before becoming a professor and librarian at Trenton State College in 1970. Avi turned to full-time writing in 1986; he began as a playwright, but upon the birth of his oldest son, Shaun, he began writing for young people—and has never stopped. His first book, *Things That Sometimes Happen*, was published in 1970. Avi explains his view of writing for young people in this excerpt from his 2003 Newbery Medal acceptance speech in Toronto, June 22, 2003:

"That's all we who write hope to do: create stories that will enable our young readers to find the stirrings of their souls . . . . One way or another we provide stories for kids that will entertain, move, engage, and teach, stories that say again and again that yes, life may be hard, or funny, or perplexing, always risky, but in the end—worth the living."

BOOKS

♦ *Blue Heron*: Twelve-year-old Maggie spends part of the summer with her father and stepmother at a waterside cabin, where she learns that her father is very ill and that life can quickly turn bad. Her joy in the beauty of a great blue heron is threatened by a young boy who would kill it for sport. Grades 5–7

♦ *Crispin: The Cross of Lead*: This Newbery Medal winner is a fictionalized account of actual events leading up to the English Peasants' Revolt of 1381. Upon the death of his mother, a previously nameless medieval serf discovers his true name, Crispin, and finds himself inexplicably hunted by the local aristocracy. The truth of his heritage and the role he will play in the historic turn of events are revealed on his journey across England. Grades 6–9

♦ *The True Confessions of Charlotte Doyle*: When 13-year-old Charlotte Doyle takes passage on the brig *Seahawk*, she has no idea the crew will mutiny, or that she will join them, captain the ship, and eventually be charged with murder. Grades 6–8

♦ *The Fighting Ground*: Thirteen-year-old Jonathon is captured by Hessians in his first experience with war during the American Revolution. Grades 6–8

♦ *City of Light, City of Dark*: This graphic novel offers a mythological explanation of the solar cycles. Sarah and Carlos must prevent the evil Mr. Underton from procuring a magical golden token, the secret to the changing of seasons, or New York will freeze solid. Grades 6–8

A Conversation With Avi

Adapted from Blasingame, James. (2003). Interview with Avi, 2003 Newbery Medal winner for *Crispin: The Cross of Lead*. *The ALAN Review, 3*(1), 38–39.

JB: Good historical fiction reveals details of life in a given time period without beating the reader over the head with them. Without even noticing it, the reader comes away from *Crispin* with a new understanding of what life in 1377 must have been like for a peasant. How hard was it to weave in history without diminishing the story?

AVI: The problem inherent in all historical fiction is the fusion of fact and incident. One tries to root the action in historical reality. Thus Crispin is proclaimed "a wolfhead," which means, under the law of the time, that he is placed beyond the pale of law—and anyone may kill him. It is this that propels the boy into flight.

    Consider the problem of time. This story takes place before the existence of clocks—thus time is measured by the church, its canonical hours, its feast days. To use them in the story is to help the reader understand the totality of the church in people's lives.

JB: From the beginning, Crispin's wonderfully poetic language contributes to the setting. How did you so successfully create a verbal tone to suggest the time period?

AVI: The English language of the day was Middle English—not usable as such. In any case I don't know it. But in the course of my research, I read the poetry of the period, mostly Chaucer and William Langland. I then used their poetic forms and wrote about a third of the book in that style of verse. Once I got the rhythm, I restructured the lines. Thus:

> Time was the great millstone
> Which ground us to dust
> Like kernelled wheat.
> The Holy Church told us where we were
> In the alterations of the day,
> The year,
> And in our daily toil.
> Birth and death
> Alone
> Gave distinction
> To our lives . . .

JB: Starr LaTronica, chair of the 2003 Newbery Award Selection Committee, said, "Readers experience Crispin's surroundings through Avi's sensory descriptions; they see, hear, smell, taste and feel his world." You include a wealth of gritty details about how life operated back then, both in the villages and in the cities. Which details did you especially want readers to know? Were there any details of life at that time that especially shocked, surprised, or otherwise affected you?

AVI: The historian Barbara Tuchman wrote a history of this period called *A Distant Mirror*. Her thesis was that the European 14th century, in all its violence and cruelty, is a mirror to our own 20th century. Being aware of the horrors of the past hundred years primes you all too well to what life was like then.

JB: The details of the plot seem to have remarkable historical accuracy. John Ball is clearly based on a rebellious priest in the County of Kent by the same name who preached rebellion after mass, and the language of the peasants' charge echoes the language of the charter, which Walter Tighler presented to King Richard in 1381. How much research did this project require and was it done beforehand or as you went along?

AVI: I read or used more than 200 books about the period. John Ball of course is real, and his speech is a paraphrase of one he gave during the peasants' rebellion of 1381—which was extraordinarily violent—both the uprising and the suppression. It was during this rebellion that the idea that "All men are created equal" was first expressed in English.

JB: How did the Peasants' Revolt actually end, and was it a conscious choice not to write that into the novel?

AVI: The Peasants' Revolt was brutally suppressed, but it helped pave the way for the end of English feudal society.

JB: You decided in high school that you wanted to be a writer. Do you have any advice for aspiring young writers?

AVI: The art of fiction writing is the art of transforming ideas (which we all have) into written words that build a narrative design. To become a novelist, the most crucial thing one must do is read, read, and read some more. Gradually, you begin to *think* like a writer. Ideas are not found—they are shaped.

JOAN BAUER

Joan Bauer grew up in River Forest, Illinois, where she frequented the public library. The echoes of her own life experiences in River Forest often show up in her fiction. Even as a little girl, she enjoyed humor and making people laugh and thought that she might one day make a career of it. Her grandmother, Nana, was a professional humorist who, Joan acknowledges, had a tremendous influence on her. Her mother was a high school English teacher whom Joan has described as having "a great comic sense." Joan's parents divorced when she was eight. The pain of losing her father and the memory of his alcoholism stayed with her, and she has "pull[ed] from that memory regularly as a writer."

As a young woman, Joan worked in publishing sales and advertising before meeting Evan, her husband, in 1981; he supported her in her decision to switch careers and attempt professional writing. After writing newspaper and magazine articles, followed by screenwriting, Joan was in a serious car accident that left her incapacitated for some time. During her recovery she wrote her first novel for young adults, *Squashed*. Through her successful career as an author of young adult fiction Joan persists in the belief that humor not only makes life enjoyable but also "empower[s] us to overcome dark times."

BOOKS

+ *Hope Was Here*: Sixteen-year-old Hope and her Aunt Addie move from New York to a small town in Wisconsin to run the Welcome Stairways Café. When the good-hearted owner/cook decides to run for mayor, Hope learns much about life and also about dirty politics. Grades 6–10

+ *Rules of the Road*: Sixteen-year-old Jenna Boller is a master shoe salesperson for Gladstone's Shoes, a company that emphasizes quality. When Mrs. Gladstone herself fears a hostile takeover by her no-good son, she takes Jenna on the road with her as her chauffeur for a whirlwind tour of their 176 stores, in an attempt to thwart her son's effort. On the road, Jenna comes to terms with having an alcoholic father and with being an outcast at school. Grades 6–9

+ *Squashed*: Sixteen-year-old Ellie Morgan is determined that Max, her giant pumpkin, will win the county fair, despite the efforts of Cyril Pool (her evil nemesis), some pesky crows, pumpkin-smashing vandals, and a potential frost. Meanwhile she has a crush on Wes, the new boy in school. Grades 5–8

+ *Thwonk*: High school senior A. J. McCreary is in love with Peter Terris but will need some help to gain his affection. When Cupid appears and grants her one wish, Allison chooses love over her art career and finds romance may not be all she thought it would be. Grades 6–9

FRANCESCA LIA BLOCK

The best description for the work of Francesca Lia Block may be her own: "Magic realist punk fairy tales that deal with the beauty, darkness, and healing power of love." Block, who grew up in the Los Angeles area, sets her stories there as well, and extrapolates upon the already magical properties of L.A. by peopling her books with fairies, vampires, and other magical characters. These fantasy characters are part of a surrealistic mix that also includes love and sex, family dysfunction, homosexuality and sexual identity, illegal drugs, AIDS, and other not-so-otherworldly realities of life. Mythological elements appearing in her work may have origins in her father's bedtime stories, which included "bits of the Odyssey." Francesca's parents were both artists, and her father was a filmmaker as well as a painter, a fact that contributes to the strong visual nature of Block's work. Block attended the University of California at Berkeley, where she developed an interest in the magical realism of Gabriel Garcia Marquez and Isabel Allende.

Francesca distinguishes her work from the average young adult novel. She says, "I think the stereotypical young adult book is the 'problem novel' where there's a moral message. . . . I don't set out to make an example for somebody. I just want to tell a story, and it's informed with beliefs that I naturally have. Those always seem to be the healing power of creative expression, and the healing power of love." She still lives in Los Angeles with her family and their Springer spaniel, Vincent Van Go Go Boots.

BOOKS

♦ *Baby Be-Bop*: In this prequel to *Weetzie Bat*, Dirk grows up knowing he is gay and suffering the rejection and abuse of many of those around him except for his guardian, Grandma Fifi. Grades 9–12

♦ *Cherokee Bat and the Goat Guys*: Weetzie Bat's daughter, Cherokee Bat, and adopted daughter, Witch Baby, form a band called Cherokee Bat and the Goat Guys, with Angel Juan and Raphael. Experimentation with sex, drugs, and rock and roll ensues while the adults in the Weetzie Bat household are off making a film. Grades 9–12

♦ *Dangerous Angels*: A complete set of the Weetzie Bat books, including *Weetzie Bat, Witch Baby, Cherokee Bat and the Goat Guys, Missing Angel Juan,* and *Baby Be-Bop*. Grades 9–12

♦ *Girl Goddess #9*: In this short story collection Block imagines the lives of modern young women with all the issues that go with them. These stories include a little magic, a little mythological influence, and the juxtaposition of gritty reality with fantasy. Grades 9–12

JUDY BLUME

Judy Blume is one of the authors most responsible for helping to establish young adult literature as a genre of its own. She grew up in Elizabeth, New Jersey, and graduated from New York University with a B.S. in education in 1961. When asked about the source of her story ideas, Judy acknowledged that her "ideas come from everywhere—memories of my own life, incidents in my children's lives, what I see and hear and read—and most of all, from my imagination."

Judy Blume does not shy away from the daily, intimate, private issues that are part of growing up (for example, menstruation or masturbation), and this commitment to realism has won countless devoted readers who find themselves, their friends, and their real-life issues in her books. Conversely, Judy has aroused the ire of some adults who've attempted to ban her books, misunderstanding the role of literature in the lives of children and wishing to guard them from reality. Judy's reaction to this is quite respectful, particularly in regard to the letters she sometimes receives from parents: "Sometimes, of course, I hear directly from parents who don't like what I've written. I try to write back and explain if the parent has written a thoughtful letter."

Judy and her husband, George, spend time up and down the East Coast as she writes novels for both adults and young adults.

BOOKS

◆ *Are You There, God? It's Me, Margaret:* Margaret moves to a new neighborhood as a sixth grader, a difficult age for making new friends, starting in a new school, and coping with the transitions of adolescence. God becomes Margaret's best confidant. Grades 6–8

◆ *Blubber:* At first, Jill accepts the way her fifth-grade classmates torment Linda, an overweight girl who unfortunately delivers an oral report on whales and is nicknamed "Blubber" by the class witch, Wendy. Later, Jill finds herself a victim and decides to fight back. Grades 5–7

◆ *Forever:* When Katherine and Michael have sex as teenagers, Katherine knows that Michael is the one destined to be her lifelong mate. But when the two are separated one summer, Katherine begins to have feelings for another boy. The consequences of sexual activity at an early age are explored in a thoughtful and frank manner. Grades 9–12

◆ *Tiger Eyes:* Fifteen-year-old Davey Wexler and her family move from Atlantic City, New Jersey, to Los Alamos, New Mexico, when her father is killed in a robbery. Davey must come to grips with living in her aunt's house and adapting to a whole new way of life in New Mexico. Grades 8–10

ANN BRASHARES

As of 2004, Ann Brashares still had a pair of jeans from her sophomore year in high school, although they did not have the magical qualities of the jeans in her books about the sisterhood of the traveling pants. Ann is a native of Chevy Chase, Maryland, and has a degree in philosophy from Columbia University. When she was a child, she kept a scrapbook of imaginary letters she'd written as if she were traveling all over the world, which may be the antecedent to her books about Lena, Bridget, Tibby, and Carmen and their exploits all over the globe.

Today Ann and her husband, Jacob Collins, have three children and live in Brooklyn, New York.

BOOKS

♦ *The Sisterhood of the Traveling Pants*: Lena, Bridget, Carmen, and Tibby have been best friends almost from before they were born, when their mothers were in a maternity aerobics class together and began a friendship their daughters carried on through high school. When Carmen finds a pair of thrift store jeans that somehow fit all four girls, the sisterhood of the traveling pants is born, and each girl takes her turn wearing the jeans before sending them on to the next girl. As the jeans travel over the course of the summer, so does the story, from girl to girl, as they experience romance, potential divorce, death, and friendship. Grades 7–10

♦ *The Second Summer of the Sisterhood*: It is one year later, and the girls are still trading the pants over the course of the summer (although the pants have writing on them now). Again, as the pants travel, so does the story, this time, however, with each girl experiencing something different from the previous book, including romance, again, but also some new experiences, such as single parents who date, blended families, and investigating the life of a lost parent. Grades 7–10

♦ *Girls in Pants: The Third Summer of the Sisterhood*: The pants continue to travel among the four best friends as they prepare to head off to college. New problems include a pregnant mom (Carmen's) and a family tragedy (Tibby's). Grades 7–10

A CONVERSATION WITH ANN BRASHARES

Adapted from Blasingame, James. (2004). Interview with Ann Brashares. *Journal of Adolescent and Adult Literacy, 47*(4), 350.

JB: You successfully use a plot-building device of switching back and forth from character to character. Other authors who attempt this often need several pages to reestablish for the reader who each character is and what that character's piece of the story is before moving forward. It can be a little trying, if not confusing, for the reader. In both *The Sisterhood of the Traveling Pants* and its sequel, *The Second Summer of the Sisterhood*, however, switching from character to character, place to place, and conflict to conflict is instantaneous and effortless for the reader. How did you make that so seamless?

AB: I am glad it was effortless. I worried a lot about that. Particularly because I first wrote the girls' stories as four separate novellas, and then wove them together. But truthfully, I didn't go to great effort to make a seamless narrative (not consciously, anyway). I sort of took the opposite approach. I put a lot of faith in the reader. I didn't begin each new scene by rehashing where we left off with the character. I just jumped right in, figuring the readers' brains are nimble enough to fill in blanks and keep numerous plots in motion. A lot of exposition really weighs a story down and that's where you lose your reader's attention and her trust. I believe that if you keep the pace up and the emotions strong, your reader will stick with you.

I did, however, make a conscious effort to give each of the characters a distinct voice. I tried to stay close to each of the girl's thoughts and feelings, with the hope that the various scenes wouldn't begin to blur.

JB: Your characters in both books must sometimes deal with a disparity between the family that they wish they had and the family they actually have. In the first novel, this was especially true of Carmen, and in *The Second Summer of the Sisterhood* Bridget has gone in search of a lost relationship with her grandmother. How does a person overcome a past she does not want?

AB: In my books, the way she usually has to deal with it is by facing it straight on. As long as she hides from it, denies it, or tries to change what can't be changed, she causes greater torment for herself and the people she loves. The truth, of course, is more liberating than any lie.

JB: Before asking this question, let me say that I enjoyed the first book, and so I was excited to hear about and read the second one (which surpassed my expectations), but even so, do you consider it a "girl's book"? Are you writing mostly to young women?

AB: I don't mean to exclude any readers (although I believe certain readers are too young for some of the subject matter). I love when boys and men read my books. I feel especially gratified if they enjoy them. But I am realistic enough to know that a book with the word *sisterhood* in the title and a pair of pants on the cover won't be widely embraced by boys. I do hope in the future to write other things that will be embraced by boys, but for the moment, I am very happy to have a special writing relationship with girls.

KEVIN BROOKS

Kevin Brooks is among the most multitalented of people on the planet. He is an artist (painting, in particular), musician (he actually performed in a rock and roll band), and of course, author. He has also worked at the London Zoo, as well as at a crematorium. Interestingly enough, one of his own favorite genres is the detective novel, and he feels especially influenced by Raymond Chandler. Once Kevin broke into publishing with his book *Martyn Pig*, he took the young adult literature world by storm, publishing book after book and winning the Flying Start Award from Publishers Weekly. Kevin and his wife, also a talented artist, live in Manningtree, Essex, in the U.K.

BOOKS

♦ *Martyn Pig*: When teenaged Martyn Pig accidentally kills his abusive father, rather than face murder charges or (even worse) be sentenced to live with his aunt, he attempts to dispose of the body. Grades 9–12

♦ *Kissing the Rain*: Moo Nelson, an overweight outcast at school and in life, is an unlikely and reluctant hero when he comes between a crime boss and the local police, neither of whom are above hurting Moo's family if he doesn't testify in court the way they demand. Grades 9–12

♦ *Candy*: Purely by accident, a 15-year-old suburbanite falls in love with a teenaged London prostitute. Can he save her from her heroin addiction? Can he save both of them from her pimp? Grades 10–12

A CONVERSATION WITH KEVIN BROOKS

Adapted from Blasingame, James. (2004). Writing to the Teenager Inside: A Talk with Kevin Brooks. *The ALAN Review, 31*(3), 72–77.

JB: In *Kissing the Rain* you introduce the reader to your protagonist and narrator, Mike Nelson, nicknamed Moo by his classmates, in reference to his weight problem. "Kissing the rain" is Moo's expression for embracing the insulting remarks about his obesity that rain down on him from his classmates. How did you come up with that expression? Is it from your own life?

KB: I think it's one of those things that just pops into my head, actually. I wanted to somehow draw together the taunting and the rain; the point of it being that if you're in that situation where you're being bullied, which ties into the larger dilemma that Moo faces with the police and the gangster, you haven't got too many options, really. One of the options is that you stand up and face it, but that means you become kind of like the people who are making your life hell. Another way is to just sort of put up with it and run away.

The kissing the rain part is almost like embracing the attitude, which is thrust at you, which is hurting you, rather than fighting or running away from it. That's what I was attempting to capture.

JB: Are most kids rainmakers or rain-takers?

KB: Given a chance, most of them would be rainmakers, I think. There's that sort of pecking order thing, so at least they'll be the top bully in their group. I think Moo does it to an extent with his only friend, Brady.

As I created Moo's personality, I didn't want the reader to just feel sorry for him, but rather I wanted the reader to bounce on the edge of feeling sorry for him—acknowledging the problems in his life, but also from the negative side, seeing why he was in the situation he was in. He's not the most attractive, the nicest person in the world. I wanted the reader to see him from different sides, and I attempted to keep the balance between two perspectives on Moo.

JB: Moo's narration is almost stream of consciousness—a rapid-fire delivery mixing long sentences with sentences of only two words, followed by words or phrases in capitals to emphasize a point. It's easy to follow but it's kind of like watching an MTV music video or a television advertisement in that lots of images and ideas come very quickly. In this writing style of yours, you accurately convey a grand number of ideas in a very small space. Do you notice the myriad of details in real life?

KB: I've always felt that the details are of great importance to a writer, and I have always tended to notice everything around me. I think it's the small things that actually characterize life. You put them all together and that's what comprises the whole. I have always noticed, for example, the way that someone moves their eyes, the way they stand. The small things are everywhere, and they make up the world. In good writing the author can more accurately convey the essence of something through a multitude of details rather than long, direct descriptions.

JB: You demonstrate a skill for portraying the cruelty, madness, strangeness, and humor of school and how teenage kids, especially outcasts, experience it. For example, in the typical school cafeteria, like Mike Nelson's school cafeteria, the unpopular kid faces the daily problem that no one will let him eat lunch at their table. How do you know kids this age so well? Were you ever a teacher?

KB: I was never a teacher, but what I do remember very well from when I was a teenager are the emotions. I know exactly how I felt in certain situations, and I still feel some of the same emotions in similar situations now. I am much better at dealing with them now, but if I go into a room full of strange people now, I'll feel virtually the same as I did when I was a kid. Now, of course, I've done it so many times that I've learned how to deal with it, but beneath that, the same instinctive, emotional reaction takes place.

Those kinds of things that seem small now didn't seem small at all back then. Every single day, every single minute, there is stuff for a teenager to deal with it. As we get older, it's probably still there, but we have learned to deal with it.

Until I was 11, I went to a small village school, but then I won a scholarship to a big, wealthy private school. Suddenly I found myself away from the kids I grew up with and with kids who were much wealthier. I often took sanctuary in books. Twenty years later, I was commuting to work in London, sitting on the train among lots of people, reading a book, and I realized that not much had changed. Adults drive cars instead of bikes, and carry briefcases instead of satchels and talk about markets, but it's all pretty much the same, just the outer layer changes. The real stuff is still the same.

JB: Speaking of sanctuary, real or figurative, Mike Nelson finds sanctuary at a bridge where he passes time watching the traffic go by and escaping from the world. When you were his age, did you have a bridge or place of sanctuary where you went, and do you think that's a common thing for adolescents?

KB: Yes. Although I had two brothers, I quite enjoyed—I enjoy being on my own. The house I grew up in had a sort of an attached garage with a flat roof and a little parapet. You could get down on the roof from the landing window, and I used to spend a lot of time on the garage roof. I would spend a lot of time just sitting up there, really, on my own, and I never got tired of looking down.

Maybe not everyone is this way—some people find sanctuary in the company of other people rather than being alone, but I think everybody has a place where they go to feel sanctuary. Even now, I have a place; my sanctuary now is sitting in my little room in front of my computer, writing.

JB: The bridge works well for Mike Nelson because it works as a plot device in the conflict because he sees the murder take place there, and it works in the characterization of Moo, as well.

KB: I think about stories a lot before I write them. Before the writing of this book, I actually saw a boy on a bridge. He seemed to be wrapped in a sort of loneliness but peacefulness, as well. That fit with the ideas about which I was getting ready to write.

JB: One of the things that makes Mike Nelson appealing is that he has this intelligent, dry, but dark sense of humor. As the narrator, the opportunity is often there for him to make fun of himself, and he takes it. It seems to be a tool that he uses to defend himself. Is this dryness common to the British sense of humor? Is Moo's sense of humor actually your sense of humor?

KB: It's mine. I'm not a bleak person, but I am sort of dry in my sense of humor. Sometimes when I'm writing some of the humor comes through but some may need to be explained to Americans because it can be in the British style. I suppose there are different national senses of humor; it's risky to generalize, but I think there can be differences. I think humor works very well in dark situations. A story is hard to read if it is all dark, but the humor makes it readable.

It can't all be dry, either, and different styles of humor work in different ways. Some of the best comedy I have seen, like the American television show *The Simpsons*, isn't just funny but has some point to make. I even like sort of middle-of-the-road things like *Cheers* and *Friends*. They're funny in a different way, and actually English humor isn't always dry; we have Benny Hill type of humor, as well.

JB: Early in *Kissing the Rain*, Moo's dad has on a Homer Simpson shirt, so I couldn't help but from that point on think of him as Homer Simpson. Was that intentional on your part?

KB: Just a little inside-out joke. The image goes into the back of your mind and a character is built without having to say, "He looks like so and so," in an overt description.

JB: Moo's dark and quirky sense of humor, the twists and turns of the plot and your distinctive writing style combine to give the book a sort of Chris Crutcher, Ken Kesey, Hunter Thompson flavor with perhaps some overtones of Robert Cormier. Your writing is more sophisticated than just telling a story. Have you had to work to attain this style, or does it come naturally? Does it take a lot of revision to get that kind of complexity?

KB: That's a nice list of names. I especially like Ken Kesey. The writing does come kind of naturally now, but it didn't when I first started writing. When I was writing stuff for adults, I was unpretentiously trying to write the great masterpiece, the great novel to show how good I was. But you can lose track of the story that way. When I started writing for and about teenagers, the story became the main thing. You've got to write a good story first. I found that all the nice little bits of prose and poetry that I like in a piece could still go in, but they are almost like the garnish to the main course, which is the story.

I've always loved really good writing, especially good writing that includes a good story; that's the ideal—when great writing doesn't get too much in the way of the story. That's what I have aimed to do in my writing. I sometimes have to be a bit hard on myself and edit out stuff [I have written] I like, passages that are really good writing but maybe get in the way of the story. I've had to learn how to do editing like that with the help of my publisher. I still enjoy the art of words and style.

JB: Your word choice is masterful, and sometimes you even invent words like "hipponotic" and "a nonfat smile." The language of your writing is enjoyable even just for its own sake.

KB: I enjoy writing in that fashion, and I never really change the nuts and bolts of how I write. I may change the direction slightly depending on the audience, but my basic structure and style remain the same. I don't change much. It should be writing that could be enjoyed by people of different ages.

MICHAEL CART

Michael Cart is an influential figure in the growth and development of young adult literature as a genre. He is past president of the Young Adult Library Services Association (YALSA), former director of the Beverly Hills Public Library, and past president of the Assembly on Literature for Adolescents of the National Council of Teachers of English. In addition to writing articles for numerous newspapers and professional journals (e.g., *Los Angeles Times*, *The New York Times*, *San Francisco Chronicle*, *Booklist*), he has served on selection committees for young adult literature awards for such groups and awards as the American Library Association, the *Los Angeles Times* Book Prize for Young Adult Literature, and the National Book Award. He chaired YALSA's committee that created the Printz Award, one of the most distinguished awards available for young adult literature. Michael is both an author and editor of novels and short story collections for young adults. He is the host of the syndicated television program *In Print* and teaches courses in young adult literature at UCLA.

BOOKS

(Michael Cart edited the following books.)

♦ *The Best American Nonrequired Reading 2002*: A collection of hip pieces from such publications as *Rolling Stone* and *The Onion*. For readers 16–24 years of age.

♦ *Love and Sex*: Stories about love and the aches and pains it brings for adolescents by Joan Bauer, Michael Lowenthal, Garth Nix, Sonya Sones, Laurie Halse Anderson, Emma Donoghue, Louise Hawes, Chris Lynch, Shelley Stoehr, and Angela Johnson. Grades 8–12

♦ *Necessary Noise: Stories About Families as They Really Are*: Ten short stories about families from among the best authors of young adult fiction: Joan Bauer, Michael Cart, Walter Dean Myers, Rita Williams-Garcia, Sonya Sones, Norma Howe, Lois Lowry, Nikki Grimes, Joyce Carol Thomas, and Emma Donoghue. Grades 8–12

♦ *Rush Hour: Sin*: *Rush Hour* is described as "A Journal of Contemporary Voices" published twice a year. Volume one, *Sin*, includes poems, stories, and nonfiction pieces by Joan Bauer, Sonya Sones, Marc Aronson, Hazel Rochman, Emma Donoghue, Terry Davis, and Elizabeth Lorde-Rollins. Grades 8–12

♦ *Rush Hour: Bad Boys*: Volume two of *Rush Hour* includes pieces about young men who've been characterized as "bad," accurately or inaccurately—stories include those from Chris Gall, E. R. Frank, Eugenie Doyle, Edward Averett, Jan Greenberg and Sandra Jordan, Michael Simmons, Ron Koertge, Julia Jarcho, John O'Brien, Nick Larocca, David Lubar, Marie G. Lee, Jeff Newman, Robert Lipsyte, and Jacqueline Woodson. Grades 8–12

A Conversation With Michael Cart

Interview conducted by e-mail on November 12, 2004.

JB: What advantages do short stories have over other genres for YA readers?

MC: In a word, they're short! Surveys conducted by the Young Adult Library Services Association have shown that many young adults claim they would gladly read more if they only had the time. Since many of them have schedules these days that rival those of heads of multinational corporations, I don't dispute their claim. But even if they can't find the time to read a book-length work, I do think they can find time to read a short story. I tell them to carry an anthology or short story collection with them and read while they're on the bus or waiting to meet friends or in the middle of any other period of "down" time. And the short story, which doesn't require the sustained periods of concentration that the novel does, can be an attractive alternative and a viable way to get YAs reading.

JB: You seem to select short stories/authors for your collections very carefully. What qualities do you believe make them worth publishing?

MC: First of all, the stories need to be well written in a lively, engaging style, and they need to tell a good story. The traditional *New Yorker* story that is essentially an actionless mood piece or moment-of-truth story simply doesn't cut it with young adult readers. The story also has to have a dynamic central character with whom the reader can identity and empathize. And I would hope the story has enough thematic substance to stimulate lively discussion among its readers.

JB: You have chosen some engaging themes. How did you arrive at these thematic choices?

MC: I'm tempted to say "through prayer and fasting," but the truth is that I've tried to think of themes that are provocative, not in a prurient sense but in the sense that they provoke thought and discussion. I also strive to find themes that are relevant to contemporary young adult life and interests (love and sex, for example!) and that also address issues that teens are anxious to learn more about.

JB: Why have you chosen to devote your life to literature, especially literature for young adults?

MC: At the risk of sounding corny, I'd say my devotion derives from a fundamental belief that literature is civilizing. Literature teaches empathy, tolerance, and respect for the dignity and worth of every individual, especially those individuals who are, in whatever way, regarded as "different" and, thus, are marginalized, vilified, scorned, stereotyped, and—in general—made to undervalue or even loathe themselves. At no time in life are people more vulnerable to this pattern of external abuse by their peers than in their teen years. And, therefore, at no other time in their lives do they more urgently need to see their own faces in the pages of good books and to learn, thereby, that they are not alone. I value life, I value the future, and—oh, boy—do I ever value civilization. That's why I've devoted my life to bringing young adults and good books together.

SANDRA CISNEROS

Sandra Cisneros grew up in Chicago and went to Loyola University for her undergraduate degree before attending the fabled Writers' Workshop at the University of Iowa. She burst on the young adult literature scene in 1983 with *The House on Mango Street*, fiction based on Cisneros's own life, short pieces about Esperanza, a teenaged Latina growing up in Chicago. Like her main character, Sandra also experienced life in various houses in the Chicano neighborhoods of Chicago and traveled to visit family in Mexico. In 2002, Sandra returned to a very similar autobiographical scenario in *Caramelo*, the story of Lala Reyes, whose family claims both Mexico and the U.S. as home, and who experiences both loyalty to and alienation from the two distinct cultures. Cisneros's literary talent has been recognized as more than simply the ability to tell an interesting and accurate story. Her books have been praised for their artful and poetic prose. Sandra captures not only the conflicting emotions and the sometimes painful, sometimes pleasant experiences of adolescence but also the issues of being equally comfortable and uncomfortable in two different cultures.

BOOKS

♦   *The House on Mango Street*: In a series of snapshots in prose and poetry, Esperanza tells the story of growing up in the Latino section of Chicago. Esperanza recognizes the faults and foibles of those around her and experiences the joys and frustrations, not only of adolescence but also of being Latina. Grades 6–12

♦   *Woman Hollering Creek: And Other Stories*: A collection of short stories about life as a Mexican American on the Texas-Mexico border. Grades 8–12

♦   *Loose Woman: Poems*: Poems about love and emotion told from the point of view of the female narrator. Grades 8–12

♦   *Caramelo*: Lala Reyes is the youngest of seven children living in Chicago near her uncles, aunts, and cousins. The extended family makes an annual trip to Mexico City to visit relatives, specifically Awful Grandmother and Little Grandfather. Living in the middle between two cultures provides Lala with ongoing conflict and curiosity. Grades 11 and up

♦   *My Wicked, Wicked Ways*: Poems about life and love told from the point of view of a young woman. Grades 8–12

DAVID CLEMENT-DAVIES

David Clement-Davis is a native of London and attended Westminster School. He studied history and English literature at Edinburgh University, specializing in the Renaissance. A lifetime aspiration to work in the theater sublimated into writing, and David has made his mark as a travel writer and a novelist. He has traveled all over the world and experienced many exotic things. David takes his laptop along and writes wherever he is. He lives in London, but continues to explore the world.

BOOKS

* *Fire Bringer*: This animal fantasy effectively tells a story of the supernatural with animals as the characters, including a deer born with the image of an oak leaf in his antlers, and a prophecy about overcoming evil. Grades 7–10

* *The Sight*: Transylvanian wolves have supernatural powers, including the powers of good and evil. One lone wolf, Fell, has special powers, powers feared by the dark side. Grades 8–12

* *Fell*: In this sequel to *The Sight*, Fell continues his fight against the dark side. Grades 8–12

* *The Telling Pool*: In this blend of the Arthurian legend and Richard the Lionheart's Crusade, young Rhodri Falcon must navigate his destiny through a maze of magic, hatred, and war. Grades 8–12

* *The Alchemist of Barbal*: In a fantasy realm where the golden masked Mardak would rule all and know all, young Silas Root sets out to defeat the dark lord, armed with only a talisman and a will to succeed. Grades 7–12

A CONVERSATION WITH DAVID CLEMENT DAVIES

Adapted from Blasingame, James (2006). Interview with David Clement-Davies. *Journal of Adolescent and Adult Literacy, 50*(1), 76–78.

JB: *The Telling Pool* is a definite cut above the great majority of fantasy fiction about knights and wizards in that your setting has accurate details rooted in the known history of England, the speculative prehistory of England, the literary ancestry of the Arthurian legend and the popular culture concept of King Arthur, Merlin, and Excalibur. How do you know about all these things?

DCD: Wow! Well, I hope I do know about all those things, but I suppose it started with a youthful love of stories that developed into a love of history. Books like *The Crystal Cave*, *The Sword in the Stone* and *The Once and Future King* gave me an unforgettable introduction to King Arthur, and those were classics that combined a sense of real history with a passion for a literary tradition. I could never decide whether to study history or literature at university, so I did both and took a joint degree. One of my finals papers was on the Crusades, hence the backdrop for my tale. It's a fascinating period and one that has important resonances for our own times, and the dangerous climate of fear and ignorance that might prevail if we go back to old stereotypes. I read *The Morte D'Arthur* of course and other Arthurian cycles, but actually the Arthurian story is deeply embedded in the whole tradition of English literature. I suppose I am a literary writer, more than many storytellers perhaps, and I think that a study of history is really an act of imagination, too. It's about recovering a texture, a feel, as much as dates or significant events. My favorite fantasy books always reached for that authenticity, and when they synthesized the possibility of a living magic with realistic settings, I always found it the most wonderful.

JB: You have done a masterful job of weaving ancient religion, modern religion, and magic together in this book; in fact; there is a seamless flow across the three. What do you think the England of Arturus, the historic King Arthur, was really like? Did people believe in magic? And what about the time of the Crusades—did the English people accept the Roman Catholic Church as the one true and just church of God?

DCD: Thank you so much. If Arturus was the "real King Arthur" I simply don't know. But I am as much interested in the literary creation of Arthur as I am in a real man. It is the very creation of those cycles, and how they reflected the beliefs of a society, and the sublimation of pagan traditions into Christian ones that I find so interesting and powerful. So in trying to retell them I am trying to get at what lies behind those myths, and makes them work as archetypal stories.

People have of course believed in magic for thousands of years and some still do, while the Catholic Church fought long and hard to suppress supposedly evil elements of paganism. For a writer, the very fact of making up a story can be a kind of magic, and of course for a fantasy writer the idea of "making things happen" with the wave of a wand is irresistible. But I am more interested in genuinely spiritual ideas that exist within Earth magic. Natural healing, for instance, that was often the preserve of women in local countryside communities employing a tradition of herb lore, or in the idea of the masculine and the feminine in nature. I practice tai chi, which is all about the flow of life and the interaction of yin and yang. I am not religious myself in any formal sense, but I suppose I am powerfully drawn by the religious, or certainly the spiritual, because it is a theme in all my books.

The Catholic Church certainly considered itself the one true and just church when the first Crusade was called to take back Jerusalem, but the whole movement of the Crusades, which lasted over a long period, was as much about social forces, land hunger, private ambitions, and so on, as it was a religious phenomenon. When we study them from a secular perspective it is often easy to forget, though, that the motivations of many of its actors were deeply religious. They believed actively in miracles and divine reality on a daily basis, and I think we can only understand the Crusades if we understand that. Equally, we can only understand some suicide bombers and terrorists if we realize that they actually believe that what they are doing is just and that they will go straight to heaven. But within the Catholic Church of course there have always been many doctrinal disputes and conflicts and many differing heresies, since it earliest beginnings.

JB: King Richard the Lionheart and his participation in the Crusades are an important part of the book. Did you manipulate any of the facts about him or did you stick to history? Did you intend any parallels to current events in the year 2006?

DCD: Well, my greatest manipulation of the facts about Richard were that Homeria the enchantress played a direct role in his imprisonment, which is of course pure invention. That makes *The Telling Pool* more fantasy than history. But otherwise I tried to build the fiction around real and known facts, and some things that Richard actually said, too. I realize that this can be a problem for readers because I do think in the end that the truth of history is more important than its fictionalization. I hope readers will take it as a good tale first, but with hopefully important truths at its core, too.

I did intend parallels with the present, very specifically, most especially in trying to question all the belief structures that the characters carry around with them in the book, from pagan to Christian to Jewish and Islamic, and I imply both positive and negative things about them all. Rhodri's journey through that is to find his own way and to see what he has the courage to care for and to stand up for, too.

When the Crusaders went to fight in the Holy Lands many of them settled and became assimilated into Eastern cultures, and many were attacked at the time for doing it. History reminds us of the great sophistication of Islamic and Arabic culture and the debt the West owes to it. Indeed, in many ways the Crusaders, in their sacking the city of Byzantium, for instance, were the real barbarians. But that is in no way a vindication of the fanaticism that has come out of Islam in recent years. The danger is trying to fight that kind of lunacy on its own terms.

Elements in the book also try to give a realistic depiction of what war is like and how terrible it can be. I really think there is a reality gap going on, because when we all watched Desert Storm or the attack on Baghdad on our TV screens it was like some ghastly video game. It takes an act of realism and imagination to remember that at the other end of bombs and extraordinarily powerful and sophisticated weapons, bodies are being torn apart, limbs severed, and lives ended.

CAROLINE COONEY

Caroline Cooney grew up in Old Greenwich, Connecticut. She has loved writing stories since she was a girl, remembering her sixth-grade teacher, Mr. Albert, and how he encouraged creative writing. As a teen, Caroline performed as a piano player, and served as a choir director, and a church organist. She enjoyed reading series novels as a young woman, such as the Hardy Boys and Cherry Ames, Student Nurse.

Caroline explains that writing involves a degree of "teamwork," and that she and her editor talk about her writing often. Caroline loves writing and books and spends much of her time in libraries and bookstores. The ideas for some of her books, such as *Emergency Room* and *Flight #116 Is Down!*, come from her own experience and the experiences of her children, Harold, Sayre, and Louisa.

BOOKS

♦ *The Face on the Milk Carton*: Janie is struck by the familiarity of a lost little girl's picture on milk carton and realizes it may be her. As she investigates her own past, the truth is revealed. Grades 7–9

♦ *Family Reunion*: With great apprehension, 15-year-old Shelley travels to Iowa for her family reunion. She discovers that even "perfect" families are not perfect. Grades 7–9

♦ *Whatever Happened to Janie*: In this sequel to *The Face on the Milk Carton*, Janie and her two families must find a way to move forward. Grades 8–10

♦ *What Janie Found*: Janie discovers a secret about her abductor in this fourth book in the Milk Carton series and acts to confront the issues of her past. Grades 8–10

♦ *The Voice on the Radio*: Janie's boyfriend uses her story of abduction on his college radio program without her permission. Grades 8–10

♦ *Driver's Ed*: A harmless prank turns out to be fatal when driver's education students steal a stop sign. Grades 8–10

♦ *Flashfire*: Wildfire roars through affluent Pinch Canyon before residents can escape or firefighters can save them. Grades 8–10

♦ *The Terrorist*: Sixteen-year-old Laura tries to find the terrorist whose bomb killed her brother. Grades 8–10

♦ *Flight #116 Is Down!*: Heidi's life is changed when Flight #116 crashes on her family's land. Grades 7–9

♦ *Emergency Room*: Teenage volunteers experience the chaos of a hospital emergency room. Grades 7–9

ROBERT CORMIER

The late Robert Cormier was a native of Leominster, Massachusetts, and chose to live his adult life there, as well. He was one of nine children and attended Roman Catholic schools, which would later inspire some of his plot premises. In the eighth grade, for example, he saw his own home in flames from the classroom window, but he later explained that the nuns would not let him leave until he had said the required prayers.

Robert attended Fitch State College in Fitchburg, Massachusetts, where a story submitted for class so impressed his teacher, Professor Florence Conlon, that she submitted it for publication in a national magazine, for which it was accepted and earned $75.

Robert remained in Fitchburg after college to work in journalism, eventually working for 23 years as a reporter and then editor for the *Fitchburg Sentinel*. He was involved in some form of publishing, including fiction writing for major magazines, for 30 years.

Cormier broke onto the young adult literature scene in 1974 with *The Chocolate War*, a wildly popular and often banned book about life in an all-boys Catholic high school. *Chocolate War*, often challenged for language deemed inappropriate for teenagers by parents or other adults, is ranked fourth on the American Library Association's 100 Most Frequently Challenged Books of 1990–2000 (ALA). Cormier might be characterized as having an interest in both the less noble aspects of human nature, such as intimidation and cruelty, and the greater aspects, such as courage and fortitude. Cormier's stories are typically dark portrayals of human nature.

BOOKS

- *The Chocolate War*: Trinity Catholic School freshman Jerry Renault finds himself caught between a tyrannical priest, Brother Leon, and a secret gang leader, Archie Costello. When Jerry refuses to knuckle under to either, he becomes one of the first anti-heroes in young adult literature. Grades 8–10

- *The Bumblebee Flies Anyway*: A mystery of psychological suspense in which teenage Barney attempts to find the truth about his identity and his role in an experimental clinic. Grades 7–9

- *Beyond the Chocolate War*: In this sequel to *The Chocolate War*, Archie Costello, leader of the secret society called the Vigils, finds his authority challenged. Archie's total lack of conscience is frightening, as is the lack of human decency in a private Catholic school. Grades 8–10

- *We All Fall Down*: Teenage vandals commit obscene crimes against a nice girl and her family. A dark view of human nature. Grades 8–10

- *Tunes for Bears to Dance To*: Eleven-year-old Henry's employer, Mr. Hairston acts out his racist, abusive nature. He enlists Henry's help to perpetrate a senseless crime on a Holocaust survivor. Grades 7–9

- *In the Middle of the Night*: Sixteen-year-old Denny Colbert must cope with the fact that townspeople blame his father for an accident that killed 22 children more than two decades earlier. Grades 7–10

- *Heroes*: After World War II, Francis Cassavant returns to his hometown so horribly disfigured from combat that he's unrecognizable, a fact that contributes to his intention of seeking revenge on Larry Lasalle, a former youth counselor who committed a horrible crime against Nicole Renard, Francis's teenage love. Grades 8–10

- *Rag and Bone Shop*: Twelve-year-old Jason doesn't believe he committed the murder of a seven-year-old neighbor girl until a skilled interrogator applies sufficient psychological pressure to crack Jason's will. When the real murderer is caught, the story isn't over. Grades 7–9

BRUCE COVILLE

Bruce Coville has lived in central New York state for most of his life. He grew up in dairy country near his grandparents' farm. As a boy he enjoyed reading comic books and series novels, like the Hardy Boys. He traces his writing career's origin to a story he wrote in the sixth grade, although he identifies the age at which he decided on a writing career as age 17. After a variety of jobs to make ends meet as he continued to write, Bruce became an elementary school teacher. He also married Kathy, who would partner with him on many books as an illustrator. The majority of Bruce's books are for upper elementary students, but some, like *Armageddon Summer*, have high-school-age protagonists and deal with complex issues of growing up. He has published more than 200 books and believes that fun reading helps create avid future readers.

BOOKS

♦ *Armageddon Summer* (cowritten with Jane Yolen): Told in alternating chapters from the point of view of each of the two teenage protagonists, Jed and Marina, whose parents have found the answer to life's chaos and unhappiness in a cult. The cult members are essentially imprisoned on a mountaintop in Massachusetts awaiting the coming of the new millennium, which religious hucksters are predicting will bring the chaos foretold in Revelations. Jed's sense of humor and wry wit as he explains events are delightful. Grades 7–10

♦ *My Teacher Is an Alien*: Susan Simmons pursues the likelihood that her substitute teacher is an alien when she sees him peel off his face. When she uncovers his horrible plans for the kids, who will believe her? Grades 4–6

♦ *Goblins in the Castle*: Young William solves the mysteries of the castle in which he grew up. A good transition book for readers who will enjoy fantasy books for older readers as they mature. Grades 4–6

♦ *The Dragonslayers*: Princess Wilhelmina would rather attempt to slay a dragon than be forced into an arranged marriage. Grades 4–6

SHARON CREECH

Sharon Creech is a native of a suburb of Cleveland, Ohio, but her childhood summers were spent with relatives near Quincy, Kentucky, near the Ohio River, a place where she would later set much of her fiction. Sharon's relatives' experiences and her own childhood would supply many of the characters and events in her novels as an adult, including her father, Arvel, who was the basis for the character Uncle Arvie in *Pleasing the Ghost*. A trip from Ohio to Idaho that Sharon took as a young girl would inspire her Newbery Medal–winning novel, *Walk Two Moons*. Sharon has a B.A. from Hiram College in Ohio, and an M.A. from George Mason University in Virginia.

Sharon credits much of her character as a writer to the influences of teaching and parenting. Being around students taught her what kids will respond to in a story and also how important it is that kids have good books in their lives. It was her experience with her own son's individuality as a learner that taught her the value of celebrating and respecting the unique characteristics of all kids.

BOOKS

♦ *Walk Two Moons* (Newbery Award winner): Thirteen-year-old Sal goes on a road trip with her hip grandparents to be reunited with her mother. A secret about Sal's mother is kept from the reader until the end although clues are dropped along the way. Grades 6–8

♦ *The Wanderer*: Thirteen-year-old Sophie joins her uncles and cousin on a sailing ship to cross the Atlantic Ocean and visit her grandfather. Grades 6–8

♦ *Chasing Redbird*: Thirteen-year-old Zinny Taylor renovates a long-lost trail that crosses her family's property and uncovers some fascinating events from the past. Grades 6–8

♦ *Love That Dog*: Middle-school-aged Jack doubts he is going to like poetry when school begins. His teacher has some strange practices, however, and he soon finds himself mimicking the poetry of some very famous poets, like Robert Frost, William Carlos Williams, and Walter Dean Myers. Poetry turns out to be a vehicle for Jack to express some deep feelings he has been suppressing about a tragic event. When he invites Walter Dean Myers to make a school visit, and Myers accepts, Jack finds meaning in his own poetry. Grades 6–8

♦ *Absolutely Normal Chaos*: Thirteen-year-old Mary Lou Finney is assigned to keep a journal over the summer. Her take on things is often funny, and so are some of the quirky characters who people her world. Grades 6–8

♦ *Ruby Holler*: Twin orphans Dallas and Florida have known a succession of orphanages and foster homes and doubt that Ruby Holler, the home of an older couple whose own children have grown, will be any different; in fact, they plan to run away just as soon as they get there. But as they get to know Tiller and Sairy, their ideas about adults start to change. Grades 6–8

CHRIS CROWE

Chris Crowe has traced his interest in reading to the summer following sixth grade, when he immersed himself in *The Complete Works of Sir Arthur Conan Doyle*, which led to a relationship with the works of Edgar Rice Burroughs, H. G. Wells, and Jules Vernes. Chris was so inspired by his reading that he attempted to write his own short stories and even a novel on the family's antique typewriter.

When Chris was a teenager, the family moved from California to Arizona, and Chris's life became largely defined by sports at McClintock High School in Tempe, Arizona, where he played football and basketball and competed in track and field. Like all four boys in the Crowe family, Chris earned a football scholarship to a university—in his case, Brigham Young University, in Provo, Utah. It didn't seem like a career as a writer and a career as an athlete were compatible, but that was only temporary.

After marrying Elizabeth and beginning his ten years as a high school English teacher back at McClintock High School, Chris returned to his love of writing and began banging out both fiction and nonfiction. Chris acknowledges that he loves the spirit of adolescence, which may explain why he continues to enjoy reading and writing about adolescents. Chris is now a professor of English at Brigham Young University. He is a past president of the Assembly on Literature for Adolescents.

BOOKS

♦ *From the Outside Looking In: Short Stories for LDS Teenagers*: These 15 stories may have teenagers of the Church of Jesus Christ of Latter Day Saints as characters, but the feelings and experiences they go through will prove meaningful to all teenagers. Grades 7–12

♦ *Mississippi Trial, 1955*: This book is a fictional account of the murder of Emmett Till, a 14-year-old youngster from Chicago. While visiting relatives in Mississippi in 1955, Emmett is accused of making a rude remark to a white woman and is brutally murdered. Later the murderers are acquitted in a sham of a trial. Grades 7–12

♦ *Getting Away With Murder: The True Story of the Emmett Till Case*: This nonfiction work recounts the events of the 1955 murder of Emmett Till, and the resulting murder trial. These events have been cited as the possible ignition of the fire that became the civil rights movement in the United States. Grades 7–9

A Conversation With Chris Crowe

Adapted from Blasingame, James. (2003) A Crime That's So Unjust! Chris Crowe Tells About the Death of Emmett Till. *The ALAN Review, 30*(3), 22–24.

JB: Chris, congratulations on having your very first young adult novel, *Mississippi Trial, 1955,* win so many awards. Readers are also finding that your nonfiction work, *Getting Away With Murder: The True Story of the Emmett Till Case,* is a wonderful complement to the fictionalized account. The research and the two books were quite a project. Were you thinking of a specific readership as you began?

CC: I'm always thinking about young adult readers, so when I learned about the Emmett Till case, I knew that I wanted to tell the story for teenagers. Emmett was only 14 when he was murdered, so I thought his story would be especially important for YA readers. There are many stories about teenagers in the civil rights movement, and Emmett's death and the trial of his killers was a catalyst for the Montgomery Bus Boycott that took place just months later. The story of Emmett Till was a story I had been ignorant of, and it's a story everyone should know. I thought it would make sense to share it with YAs. I started the novel first, without any plans for a nonfiction book. It wasn't until I finished the novel and looked over the stacks of notes and research material that I realized I had enough information for a nonfiction book about the case. And because this was such an important event in U.S. history, I wanted to present teenage readers with the straight story, illustrated with photographs from the case. I wanted YA readers to know the facts of the murder of Emmett Till without any doubt about what was fact and what was fiction.

JB: In the acknowledgments to *Getting Away With Murder: The True Story of the Emmett Till Case,* you thank Mildred D. Taylor, author of the Logan Family series—*Roll of Thunder, Hear My Cry; Let the Circle be Unbroken; The Road to Memphis;* and *The Land*—"an awe-inspiring writer, who first sent me in search of Emmett." Was this a figurative or literal sending? Can you tell us about that?

CC: It was more figurative than literal. When I was working on a book about Mildred D. Taylor, I came across a comment she made about the impact the murder of Emmett Till had on her when she was a high school student. That reference sent me in search of the story because I wondered if it might have had some influence on her writing as well. As I said, previous to this, I'd never heard anything about Emmett Till, so when I found the photo of his corpse in *Jet Magazine,* I was shocked. I was shocked because it was such a horrible crime, but I was also shocked because the murder had been a huge event in 1955 but somehow it never made it into most history books. In all my years as a student and a teacher, I'd never read about it. My ignorance of this major historical event shamed me.

142

JB: Speculating about the truth is perhaps one of the biggest requirements of writing a fictional account of an actual event. In *Mississippi Trial, 1955*, you had to imagine or speculate about the truth of what happened during those seven days in 1955, a truth that may have also died, in part, with Emmett Till. How did you accomplish that?

CC: I wanted to make sure that any speculation I did was based on fact, so I did lots of research. As I learned about the people involved in the crime, I tried to imagine what they were like, what would make someone believe that they could justify murder. To create the fictional character of R. C. Rydell, I tried to imagine what sort of childhood a boy would have to have in order to grow up capable of doing awful, cruel things. I imagined what his home life must have been like and what might have warped him. In terms of the events, I read as many accounts of the murder and trial as I could find. Because it was such a sensational crime in 1955, there were lots of newspaper and magazine articles written about it. The trial transcripts have been "lost," so those weren't available, but I did make good use of microfilm records and even some video interviews of people involved in the case. I even spent a week in Greenwood, Mississippi, the same week in August that Emmett had been there, so I could have an accurate sense of the setting—the weather, the towns, the way people spoke.

JB: There is more going on with your characters in *Mississippi Trial* than just the story that people could have read in the news. What did you mean for your characters to show about the human experience?

CC: I suppose I was thinking most about Hiram Hillburn, my narrator. In many ways, mainly the cowardly ways, Hiram is a lot like I was when I was a teenager. Hiram's oblivious to the racism around him, oblivious to the goodness of his own father, oblivious to the unsavory qualities of many of the people he admires. Hiram was a racist without being aware of it. He also was a part of an intergenerational family conflict. Hiram hates his father. Hiram's father hates his father. As I said, some of this comes from my own teen years. When I was in high school, I didn't get along very well with my own father, and it was my fault. After I got married, and especially after I had kids of my own, I realized what a dope I had been, and I regretted that I hadn't made a better effort at understanding Dad when I was a teenager. Anyway, my dad died while I was working on *Mississippi Trial, 1955*, and that caused me to reflect a lot on what my relationship had been with him and what I wish it had been.

One of the nice things about fiction is that it gives you a chance to work out some angst, and that's what I did through Hiram. I knew that this novel couldn't be about the Emmett Till case—it had to be a story that stood on its own, a story affected by the case rather than about the case. For Hiram, I wanted it to be a story of reconciliation; I wanted him to come to see his father in a new light, and I wanted him to learn about racism and how evil it is. Having him get caught up in the Emmett Till case provided the catalyst for both those lessons to take place.

So, I wanted Hiram to learn that our perceptions of others aren't always accurate. I wanted him to learn that the people he loves can still do bad things. I wanted him to face something really scary and find the courage to do what was right, even if he didn't want to. I guess those are the same things I wish I would have learned when I was 16.

JB: Both books required an enormous amount of research (more than 50 sources in the bibliography of *Getting Away With Murder*), and the facts you uncovered were hardly benign. As you were searching for Emmett's story, what was going on with you on a personal level? What experiences along the way most affected you?

CC: The research was both fascinating and agonizing. I learned facts about the case, of course, but I also learned an awful lot about the Jim Crow South and many of the terrible things that happened following the 1954 *Brown* vs. *Board of Education* ruling by the Supreme Court. I'd never realized how that decision had inflamed the South. So the educational part of the research was fascinating. But it was agonizing because much of what I was reading and writing about was so awful. Emmett wasn't the only African American murdered in Mississippi in 1955, and reading about the hate and violence that was erupting then made me feel awful.

The details of the Emmett Till case, of course, are singularly horrifying. Here's a boy, barely 14 years old, the only child of a widow, who ends up kidnapped, tortured, and murdered for being rude to a white woman. The blatant racism during the trial was incomprehensible to me, and the cocky pride his murderers had for "doing their duty" was simply stunning. It was hard for me to believe that there really are people like that. Anyway, being immersed in this story for the years I spent researching and writing about this case kept me in a perpetual dark cloud of sadness. I have to admit that when I finally finished both books, I felt a ton of relief, not just because the projects were done, but because I could finally emerge from all the dark stuff I'd been dealing with for so very long.

JB: You could have chosen a much safer, less challenging topic for your first attempt at a novel. Why did you choose the story of Emmett Till for your opening endeavor?

CC: I suppose I may have thought that historical fiction might be easier because it provided a ready-made story for a framework. Man, was I wrong about that! I found that it was incredibly difficult blending history with fiction because my fictional plot and characters kept bumping up against real history, so I had to keep rechecking facts to make sure I was faithful to the historical events. I chose the story of Emmett Till because I felt it had to be told, that kids should know about the murder of this 14-year-old boy and its place in American history. Looking back, I realize that I was pretty naive about what this work would entail. It was painful being immersed in the facts of this case for so long, but I'm glad I did what I did and that it's turned out all right.

JB: Lastly, I wonder if you have any advice for aspiring writers—of historical fiction, or any kind of writing at all?

CC: A writer is someone who writes. If you want to be a writer, you've got to sit down and write; you've got to make time for writing. I also recommend that writers find trusted mentors, someone who can read their work and tell them what's working and what's not. Aspiring writers also need to read widely. Of course, they should read the sorts of books they hope to write, but they also need to read all kinds of other books too. It's all grist for the writing mill; you can never know how what you read will influence you as a person and as a writer.

CHRIS CRUTCHER

hris Crutcher grew up in Cascade, Idaho, a small logging community 80 miles north of Boise. His father ran a gas and oil business with Chris's grandfather, sometimes running a tanker truck across Idaho. Chris has portrayed himself when a boy as small, hardheaded, and determined.

Chris Crutcher writes often about athletics, misfits, and dysfunctional families, three things with which he is very familiar. He was a four-sport athlete in high school and competed as a swimmer for Central Washington University. He spent many years in education, including time as the principal of an alternative school. He continues to work as a family therapist in Spokane.

Chris's work has been banned often due to his refusal to ignore certain important issues of adolescent life. His frank (but not disturbingly graphic) depictions of sexual and physical abuse, homosexuality, and other favorite targets of censorship have won him spots on the American Library Association's 100 Most Banned Books list for 1990–2000 for *Athletic Shorts* and *Running Loose*.

BOOKS

- *Athletic Shorts: Six Short Stories*: Six stories involving athletics in which young people must deal with issues such as abusive parents, death, and disease. Grades 8–12

- *Chinese Handcuffs*: Sixteen-year-old triathlete Dillon attempts to cope with his older brother's suicide and the sexual abuse his girlfriend experienced from her father and stepfather. Grades 8–12

- *King of the Mild Frontier*: Chris Crutcher recalls and explains life in Cascade, Idaho, in the 1950s and 60s. The title refers to the pop culture icon of the time, Davy Crockett, as portrayed in a Walt Disney movie and television program. Young Chris is never short of spirit or grit in an attempt to overcome an older brother's pranks or an alleged lack of athletic prowess. This autobiography mixes humor and tragedy evenly. Grades 8–12

- *Staying Fat for Sarah Byrnes*: Eric and Sarah have been friends since childhood, helping each other through difficulties with peers brought on by Eric's obesity and Sarah's unattractive burns. When Eric starts losing pounds as a high school swimmer, he chooses to thwart the weight loss for Sarah's benefit. When Sarah's childhood secret begins to come out, their friendship is crucial. Grades 8–12

- *Stotan!*: Walker, Nortie, Jeff, and Lion make up a four-man swim team in their last year at Robert Frost High School in Spokane, Washington. A Zen master–like swim coach invites them to become "Stotans" for a brief period during Christmas break. A Stotan is a person who combines the characteristics of a Spartan and a Stoic, especially when it comes to athletic training. The lessons learned and the bonds of friendship see them through some pretty difficult events. Grades 8–12

A Conversation With Chris Crutcher

Adapted from Blasingame, James. (2003). Interview with Chris Crutcher. *Journal of Adolescent and Adult Literacy, 46*(8), 696–697.

JB: Your brother John seems to have been like most other big brothers in that he tempted you into acting in ways that were not in your best interest but often in his. How does he feel about being revealed these many years later?

CC: Needless to say we don't see those events through the exact same-colored lens. I recently spoke at his retirement party (he was wrapping up about 35 years as an accountant) and I read the "Wanna do something neat?" section to raucous laughter. I *think* he was laughing, too. About a quarter of the guests were attorneys, and I haven't heard from any of them on his behalf, so it seems my meager royalties are safe for now.

JB: Are there advantages to growing up in a small town, and if so, what are some of them?

CC: Well, you have a huge extended family, so in general it feels safer. When I was growing up there wasn't a locked door in my entire neighborhood. The three backyards of ours and our neighbors on either side made one large hide-and-seek/kick-the-can playground. People who would have disappeared in larger cities were taken care of: given odd jobs or handouts or places to live. In larger cities they would have been homeless. It's hard to let a person freeze or go hungry when you know his or her name. And if you had rough or uncompromising (or deceased) parents, you could find people to take up some of that slack. There is a tribal quality.

JB: Are there *dis*advantages to growing up in a small town, and if so, what are some of them?

CC: I think every small-town inhabitant complains that everyone knows his or her business. Once embarrassed, always embarrassed. And there is a certain lack of worldliness, for want of a better term. For me it translates into a less "allowing" atmosphere that is much less forgiving of behavior that falls outside the norm. Nobody cut classes when I was in school. If some downtown merchant saw a kid on the street between the hours of 8:30 and 3, he made two phone calls: one to the kid's parents and one to the school. So I guess I'd say the edges are pretty close together in a small town. I think I found my identity more easily there, but I had to get away to celebrate it.

JB: You make the distinction between being "correct" and being "right" in chapter 12 of *King of the Mild Frontier* over the issue of ultra-correct table manners. What's the difference and why is one preferable over the other?

CC: In that instance, "correct" meant by the numbers, but "right" had to do with whether or not it was a good idea to demand all that protocol simply to get human fuel from the plate to the stomach. There was a certain low-level trauma to a meal when my dad got on one of his manners kicks. I guess in a larger arena it meant the difference between following protocol at the expense of relationship.

JB: *King of the Mild Frontier* is often hilarious. It's also humor that could be called self-deprecating; you seem to make fun of yourself rather than other people most of the time. Do you prefer that kind of humor?

CC: I do prefer that kind of humor because I know what a sharp edge making fun of other people can take on. I live for humor. Without it I would not be a therapist, and I would not be a writer. There are few things that, when applied correctly, are more healing. There is a certain meanness to making fun of others, unless you are intimately acquainted with them and have earned "fun-making permission." The more you know about a subject or a person, the deeper the humor can run, and I know myself better than anyone or anything else, so I can practice my best forms of humor on myself. Also the best humor is ironic, and my entire life is nothing if not that. I also use it to highlight what little wisdom I possess.

JB: You recount your efforts as a very young man to deal with the idea of death. It was difficult, and you handled it without help, but you seem to have come to terms with the idea. In your experience as a counselor, do you find that dealing with death is a common issue for everyone? Is it common for kids?

CC: The common issue is loss, and death is the trump card of loss. In the preface to one of the short stories in *Athletic Shorts*, I said this: "There is a case to be made that from the time of birth, when we lose a warm, enclosed, safe place to be, our lives are made up of a series of losses and that our grace can be measured by how we face those losses, and how we replace what is lost." What I'm talking about there is the process of grief, which is one of the most important things we do as humans; taking the risk of losing one thing so we can go on to the next. I believe our culture doesn't understand that very well, and often tries to force us to hold on to old perceptions and beliefs that have little or no further use, and that keep us stuck and afraid. If we do learn to face death, accommodate and accept it, there are few lesser changes that can tip us over, though there are certainly "fates worse than death." So yeah, I think it's common for kids, at their developmental level, and it is common for us at ours.

JB: Like the characters in your books, the people from your real life are not romanticized in *King*; they can have bad breath, acne, and total egomania. Do you enjoy capturing true-to-life human qualities, and if so, how do you go about doing it?

CC: Man, I have a ringside seat for watching true-to-life qualities, starting with my own

Books That Don't Bore 'Em

successes and failures and ending with the infinite stories (if you can "end" with something infinite) I've heard as a counselor and a questionable educator. I am fascinated by human response. My own responses to the world have allowed me to soar and brought me crashing to the ground. I go about capturing all that by simply paying attention, and applying my sense of humor to all I see.

JB: There seems to be a huge gap between the "coonskin cap–wearing, pimply-faced, 123-pound offensive lineman" and the tall, handsome, former college athlete with several best-selling books and a career helping dysfunctional families who we see at young adult literature conferences. Will you fill in the gap and continue your autobiography through the college and early teaching, coaching and counseling years at some point?

CC: I think I might. I had way more fun writing this book than I deserved. The gap isn't as huge as it might seem, however. I've been afraid all my life. When I think of my preadolescence, I think of that 11- or 12-year-old boy staring at the picture of the dead kid in [*Saturday Evening*] *Post* magazine (readers will have to read the book to appreciate the circumstance), paralyzed at the thought of what might have happened to him and at the thought of being gone; and ashamed that I couldn't get a handle on it. I have always been terrified of being a disappointment, of never being enough— as a human, as an athlete, as a lover, as a friend, as an example. I regularly give myself reasons to keep right on being terrified. But what I'm describing here is simply the business of being human. I'm afraid of the same things everyone else is afraid of; my circumstance is in no way special. As one of my greatest mentors once reminded me, Planet Earth is a tough town. If I've given myself one thing over the years that's helped, it's the capacity to not be so afraid to be afraid. The coonskin cap–wearing, pimply-faced, 123-pound offensive lineman lives within me.

CHRISTOPHER PAUL CURTIS

Christopher Paul Curtis grew up in Flint, Michigan, the setting for all three of his popular young adult novels. Christopher is one of the most loved and generous writers of today's young adult literature. Point in proof: at the 2000 ALAN Breakfast held at the National Council of Teachers of English Convention in Milwaukee, Wisconsin, Christopher finished his speech by asking how many of the 300 or so people attending his talk were new or aspiring teachers who could not yet afford memberships in the Assembly on Literature for Adolescents. When 50 or so responded, he promptly bought them all memberships out of his own profit.

Christopher grew up in a loving family with his mother, father, and four siblings. His father was a doctor who wound up working at the Fisher Body auto plant in Flint when his poor patients could not pay. Chris's mother, a Michigan State Spartan, wanted Chris to go immediately to college upon graduating from high school in 1971, but the lure of big dollars on the assembly line, and the prospect of buying a new car, held greater appeal, and Chris vowed to attend college a little later. He eventually graduated from the University of Michigan.

A talent for words and writing could not be subverted even by an assembly line full of car doors, and Chris wrote in a spiral notebook in between hanging doors at Fisher Body. When his wife, Kaysandra, urged him to take a year away from the auto plant and give his writing a real chance, he ended up with the manuscript for *The Watsons Go to Birmingham, 1963*, which he entered in the Delacorte First YA Novel Contest. Christopher's entry in the contest caught the attention of Random House editor Wendy Lamb, and Christopher was on his way to being one of most widely read of young adult authors.

In his second attempt at a young adult novel, Christopher wrote *Bud, Not Buddy*, which won both the Newbery Medal and the Coretta Scott King Award.

BOOKS

- *The Watsons Go to Birmingham, 1963*: Kenny, his older brother, Byron, their little sister, Joetta, and their parents head to Birmingham, Alabama, when Byron's juvenile delinquency requires the iron hand of a child-rearing pro, their tiny but powerful grandmother. Kenny experiences the awful cruelty and violence of the racially motivated church bombings in Birmingham that year firsthand, an evil he must come to grips with emotionally and psychologically. Grades 5–9

- *Bud, Not Buddy* (Newbery Award winner): When Bud (don't call him "Buddy") loses his mother, he experiences life in an orphanage, as well as the cruel injustice that orphans often face in foster homes. He has never known his father, but he has a picture of a jazz and blues trombone player he believes is his dad, and he sets out in 1930s Michigan to find the man in the picture. Grades 5–9

◆ *Bucking the Sarge*: Luther is a kind and moral 15-year-old who loves science (he wins first place in the school science fair every year) and the moral virtues found in ancient philosophy. His slumlord mother, nicknamed "the Sarge" for her love of military order and discipline, loves power and money. Her plans for Luther to make her even richer—by managing the government-scamming group homes for the elderly that she owns—are not what he has in mind for his future. Grades 6–9

A CONVERSATION WITH CHRISTOPHER PAUL CURTIS

Adapted from Blasingame, James, and Todd Goodson. (1999) A Conversation with Christopher Paul Curtis. *The Writers' Slate, 15*(1) 1–7.

JB: Let me start by asking how you became a writer. You have often told the story of your first job out of high school, making excellent money working on the assembly line at, was it Ford, Chevy?

CPC: General Motors, Fisher Body Number One.

JB: How did you make the transition from the auto assembly line to writing for young adults?

CPC: The process was kind of convoluted, actually. I never really intended to be a writer, and I think if you say you want to be a writer when you're growing up, you get encouragement, but you're also told that's not something you can make a living at, that it's very difficult to make any kind of money, and I think that the average writer in the United States, professional writer, makes $5,000 a year. When you consider you've got people like John Grisham and Stephen King making billions, and then you've got everybody else, it's not even that good. So I never really planned on being a writer; it was something that, with the encouragement of my wife, I was able to pursue. It's something that I love to do. I find it very relaxing to sit down and write. I think, if I'm having problems, the problems seem to go away while I write. And I think I work on the problems when I'm writing. Your mind works on so many different levels.

JB: Your books seem to draw quite a bit on family and family memories. Even at the end of *Bud, Not Buddy,* in the afterword you encourage kids to listen to their elders. Could you address that for a little bit about how you go about mining your own experiences, your family experiences?

CPC: I think that for first-time writers that's pretty common. It's easier, more comfortable to deal with something that you're really familiar with. And when I talk to young students about writing, I tell them it's such a wonderful thing because you can draw on so many different things to make a story. It doesn't have to have happened to you; it could be a story that you heard from someone else, but as a writer you can incorporate that into your story and make it part of your own story, so when you tell it in first person, as I do in both books, I feel that a writer has a tremendous advantage because there are so many things that you can draw from. Family and family history are two of those things. As I say in the afterword of *Bud, Not Buddy,* I blew a really great opportunity because both my grandfathers were these fascinating men, but I was a typical young person, and when they'd start to talk, I didn't want to hear them. I'd think, "Oh, God, Grampa, shut up. Please." And I'd try to get away from them. But they both had fascinating stories. It wasn't until actually after they had died, and I'd gone to family reunions, and people started talking about these things, and I'm old enough now where I can appreciate it, but I don't have my grandfathers to listen to, and that's why I try to tell the kids and tell anybody that if you've got those resources, you won't have to do what I had to do; I spent a lot of time in the library reading books, and it's a shame if you have to do that. When there was at one time the resource of my grandparents, and I didn't take advantage of it. That's why I say to kids, "Listen to what they have to say. I know it's boring, but maybe you can hold on. It's not boring, actually. Once you realize the place of history that it goes to, you have a real advantage."

JB: That's hard for kids.

CPC: It is, and even if I was this wonder kid at that age, and could sit there and say, "Oh, yeah! Tell me more, Grampa," I probably wouldn't have been able to write it down in a way which would mean anything. But if you have the stories, at least you have the memories to fall back on. I, unfortunately, don't have a lot of memories of my grandparents to fall back on.

JB: How is it that you came to write for young people?

CPC: Originally when I wrote *The Watsons,* my wife and I agreed that I would take a year off work. Originally I just wanted to write a book. I wasn't intending to write for young people. So I wrote the book, the way I write: I sit down, I don't know where the story's going, I don't know what the story's going to be about, but then I start to write. A lot of times, I start with a conversation, and then a character will come to me.

It's a very cumbersome process in the beginning, but as time goes on, it kind of focuses, and I end up getting a voice, and both times it was a 10-year-old voice. Even though it's told by a 10-year old, when I first wrote *The Watsons,* I didn't think it was a book for young people, I really didn't because the language was saltier; Byron was a juvenile delinquent, thug, and he spoke like one. He used the language that the kids use on the schoolyard, and there were a couple of scenes in there that were too intense, my editor felt they were not suitable for children. And actually the reason it was published as a children's book was I didn't know how else to get it read by anybody. It's really hard to get anybody to read anything you've written, so I sent it to those two contests [Delacorte First Middle Novel and Delacorte First Young Adult Novel] and they're both for young-adult readers. And the shocking thing to me was they didn't consider it young adult, they considered it middle reader. They go pretty much by the age of the narrator, and they have found that students won't generally read anything narrated by someone who is more than two years younger than them. So the upper limit is about 12 years old.

JB: Where did you go to college?

CPC: The University of Michigan. During the time I was in the factory, I'd go evenings, and they had a wonderful thing at General Motors where you could take time off. You wouldn't get paid, but you wouldn't lose your seniority. Your seniority would continue. They had educational leave, so I took educational leave.

JB: Did you study English?

CPC: Political science.

JB: So you didn't study creative writing?

CPC: No, I seriously wasn't—didn't start writing until—I had started in my twenties, or maybe even in my teens, I had tried to write fiction and it just wasn't right in my twenties. It wasn't right. And you know when you've written something really bad, and I knew this was really bad what I was writing. Fiction is something that is really strange because I think it takes a lot of time to develop into a fiction writer. The kind of proof of that is there are no writing prodigies, no really young people who put out brilliant, wonderful books, and I think it's something that you have to develop, that you have to live for a while, and you have to take a lot of time. So I didn't really start to write fiction until I was in my late thirties.

JB: What has life been like since your first manuscript caught the attention of Random House and your books took the country by storm, winning tons of awards?

CPC: I write full time. I write and travel around giving presentations. I could do 60 engagements a year if I wanted to. It's unusual how well I do. I have no complaints. It's a wonderful, wonderful life. I recommend it.

I think one of the reasons why *The Watsons* was so successful was that it fell into a niche. There are very few African-American male writers. There is Walter Dean Myers, and Julius Lester occasionally. It's mostly just Walter Dean Myers and me, and I've just got two books, so it's not a big market out there. And there's a need for that. Kids have asked me when I go to places what book really touched me when I was a child, and there really wasn't a book, and I think it has to do with the fact that there weren't any books for, by, or about me. Not that that's the only books that you have to read, but I think [it's powerful] if you can connect with a book on some level, something about you or something you know about.

JB: What did you write when you first started writing? You mentioned writing in journals during the 30 minute breaks at the factory.

CPC: I kept a journal, and I tell the young students when they ask me about writing that it's important, not what you write, but the fact that you're doing it, that you' re putting pen to paper, that you're going through the process of thinking about what you're going to write. That's what's really important because it helps you to develop flexibility as a writer, and I never get blocked. I think part of the reason is, number one I don't believe in that, number two, if you start to think about it, it'll happen to you.

I think that, from doing all the writing that I've done, there's a way around anything, any thought that you want or anything that you want to tell, you can get to it if you look at it the right way. *The Watsons Go to Birmingham* was originally called *The Watsons Go to Florida, 1963,* and I got them to Florida and the story just stopped. They met Grandma Sands and that was the end of the story, and I knew something was wrong and I set it aside. And Steven, my son, brought home "The Ballad of Birmingham," the poem by Dudley Randall about the bombing of the 16th Street Baptist Church. As soon as I heard that I knew that the Watsons didn't want to go to Florida, they wanted to go to Birmingham. So I went back and changed it all around. So I know that when the story stopped, it's that there's a flaw somewhere in the story, that somewhere in the story the characters have gone off in a way that they don't want to go and after awhile they just stop cooperating.

JB: You've alluded to some things about when and where and what part of your writing you do; for example, you do part of your writing at the Windsor [Canada] library. Could you speak to the when, where, and what?

CPC: OK, I do it kind of as a two-step process really. I go to the library to write and I sit in the children's section to write, and the public library hours were cut, so I had to start going to the Windsor University Library. This was totally coincidence, but I noticed I was sitting in the education section and the whole wall is filled with children's books. So I sit there and just write for two or three hours. Then the next day I get up at five. I wake up at five every morning. Then I start to edit. As I said I'm a very unstructured, undisciplined writer, really. Whenever I'm writing, if a character goes off on a tangent, I never stop the tangent, and a lot of times that will lead to another tangent, and to another tangent, and I can blow a whole day of writing just on that: things that I can't use in that story, but I never throw anything away because you never know when you might be able to fit that into another story.

154

I spend two or three hours a day writing and more time, probably, paring the story down so that it'll fit into whatever direction I'm going to take the story. I kind of look at it as the afternoon is kind of a creative time, and the morning is the grunt work where you're cutting through and slugging it out. That's my editorial time when I say, "Where is this story going?" Then I'll try to get a form for that, then I go back and starting actually from where I ended my editorial work. And the story takes structure from there.

JB: You're successful. You don't just make the $5,000 a year you mentioned as the national average. People like your stories. To whom or what do you attribute your success?

CPC: A lot of things. I think my parents kind of gave us a love of reading and a love of books. Both of them were avid readers. There were always books in the house. I remember coming home from school, I must have been in about the second or third grade, and there was a smell in the house I hadn't smelled before. My father had us all line up, and he marched us into the hallway, and there was a new bookcase, and there were *World Books*. He bought *World Books* and *Childcraft*, and they were beautiful green and gold and red bindings. And he said, "These damn books cost three hundred dollars, and if I see a crayon or a glass around one of them I'm going to kill you. [*laughter*] They did that, and they always read. I think my parents were very important.

My wife is very important. She gave me the time to do this. It would have been very easy to say, "No, get a better job," instead of saying "Take a year off [to write]." She is an [intensive care] nurse, so she works, but she also does all the bookings and handles the business end. That's wonderful, too, because I'm not a businessperson.

I think a lot of the success of the book has to do with Random House, my editor especially, Wendy Lamb. I think editing has got to be one of the worst jobs in the world. To take what someone has written and say something is wrong with it and how you're going to form this. Not only that but you have to deal with the writer. You know writers are kind of famous for being petulant and hard to deal with. I think that's an important part of the success, too.

PAULA DANZIGER

The late Paula Danziger loved kids and was loved in return. She taught middle school and high school, as well as college. While working on a master's degree in reading, Paula wrote her first big novel, *The Cat Ate My Gymsuit*. She was a student in Dr. M. Jerry Weiss's adolescent literature class at Montclair State College at the time, and when Dr. Weiss promised to find a publisher if she would turn it into a novel, she did.

Paula met life's setbacks with a sense of humor; for example, when she suffered two back-to-back car accidents in the early 1970s, she decided she might as well become a full-time writer before she was hit by a truck. After becoming a full-time writer, Paula was known for her heavy travel regimen as she went around the country speaking to kids, teachers, librarians, and parents.

BOOKS

+ *P.S. Longer Letter Later* (coauthored with Ann M. Martin): When 12-year-old best friends Tara and Elizabeth are separated, they try to maintain their close relationship by mail, which turns out to be a medium that highlights the difficulties and pains adolescents face. Paula Danziger writes as Tara and Ann M. Martin is the voice of Elizabeth. Grades 6–9

+ *The Cat Ate My Gymsuit*: Marcie Lewis suffers from acne, a weight problem, an abusive father, and a lack of self-respect. When her favorite teacher is unfairly dismissed, Marcie finds herself standing up for what she believes, despite the odds. The title refers to excuses kids use to avoid the public undressing that is a part of gym class. Grades 6–9

+ *The Divorce Express*: Phoebe's life as a high school freshman is complicated by having to cope with two different households rather than one stable one. The Divorce Express is the nickname given to a bus on which many of the passengers are kids being ferried to one parent or the other after divorce has split their households and their lives. Grades 7–9

+ *There's a Bat in Bunk Five*: In this sequel to *The Cat Ate My Gymsuit*, Marcy becomes a camp counselor on the recommendation of her favorite teacher, Mrs. Finney. Marcy has the opportunity to experience life with a degree of independence and romance. Grades 6–8

KATE DICAMILLO

Kate DiCamillo, her brother, and their mother moved from Philadelphia to a small town in Florida when she was 5 years old. Kate was a sickly girl who suffered from chronic pneumonia, and doctors suggested the warm, moist Florida air would help her. Kate had a much-loved companion during this time in Nanette, a black standard poodle.

Kate did not begin writing until the age of 29, when she found herself surrounded by children's books all day long at her job in a book warehouse. Before her success, Kate used to get up early in the morning to write before going to work at a bookstore, a habit she has continued ever since.

BOOKS

* *Because of Winn-Dixie*: India Opal Buloni and her father move to Florida, after India's mother runs out on them. Things seem to improve in her life when she adopts an ugly mutt running loose at the grocery store and names him for the store, Winn-Dixie. Grades 6–8

* *The Tale of Desperaux*: This Newbery Award winner is fairy tale–style story about Desperaux, a noble, romantic mouse (who loves art, music, and literature) who winds up in a dark and dreary dungeon when he describes his love for a human princess. Desperaux, a rat named Chiaroscuro, and a lowly serving girl named Miggery Sow adventure through the dungeon and into the castle. Grades 4–6

* *The Tiger Rising*: Twelve-year-olds Rob Horton and Sistine Bailey, victims of bullies at their small northern Florida school, figure out how to release a tiger they discover caged in the woods. Grades 4–6

SHARON DRAPER

Sharon Draper was born in Cleveland, Ohio, and makes her home in Cincinnati. She earned her undergraduate degree from Pepperdine University and her masters from the University of Miami. Sharon received her National Board for Professional Teaching Certification when the certification was new and served on the National Board for Professional Teaching Standards Board of Directors in its early years.

Sharon's success as an author might be traced back to her answer to a student's challenge when she entered and won an essay contest with "The Touch of a Teacher," which won $5,000 and publication. In 1997, after nearly 30 years in the classroom, Sharon was named National Teacher of the Year.

BOOKS

◆   *Tears of a Tiger*: Andy Jackson, a star basketball player, struggles with the memory of his best friend's death. Andy cannot escape the memory that his own drunken driving resulted in the fatal accident. Grades 6–9

◆   *Romiette and Julio*: Two 16-year-olds fall in love in a Cincinnati high school. Problems develop from the differences in their backgrounds. Romiette Capelle is the daughter of two highly successful African-American parents and the granddaughter of college professors. Julio Montague has moved to Cincinnati from Corpus Christi, Texas, in an attempt to escape his gang involvement. Grades 6–9

◆   *Forged by Fire*: In this prequel to *Tears of a Tiger*, Gerald, the protagonist, must confront an abusive stepfather who sexually assaults Gerald's stepsister. Grades 8–10

◆   *The Battle of Jericho*: How much humiliation will high school junior Jericho Prescott endure to become a member of the Warriors of Distinction at Frederick Douglass High School? He is about to find out. Grades 7–9

A CONVERSATION WITH SHARON DRAPER

Adapted from Blasingame, James. (2000) Conversations: Sharon Draper. *The Writers' Slate 15*(2), 1–4.

JB: You've won a lot of awards with your writing. Which one or ones have meant the most to you?

SD: Probably the writing award that means the most is the very first one because that was the first time that anybody recognized my writing as having any kind of quality or that it was a cut above the normal. So when I won the Coretta Scott King Genesis

Award, I was thrilled and I got to give a speech at the American Library Association) conference, and there were several hundred people in the room. It was probably one of the most exciting days of my life because I was a brand new writer and there were writers who'd been writing for years that never got any recognition. All of a sudden, my very first book is getting all kinds of wonderful recognition. But I don't write for the awards. I write for the young people, and I think, more than the awards, are the letters that I get from young people, who write me and they say things like, "I read your book. It changed my life. "I read your book. It made a difference." Please write another book. "Is there anything else that you wrote that's any good?" Those are the kinds of things that make me want to go and write more because I'm making a difference in the lives of kids I've never even met.

JB: As Teacher of the Year in 1997, you represented all educators nationwide. What messages did you feel it was important for you to convey?

SD: As Teacher of the Year, I considered myself to be a representative for all teachers. I didn't consider myself to be the best teacher in the country; I just considered myself fortunate enough to be a representative for all those teachers that couldn't get out of the classroom, that didn't have a voice, that didn't have anybody to speak for them and say they are valuable and doing a good job, that they need to be honored, they need to be cherished, they need to be praised, and that's kind of what I said to them when I got the chance to go all over the country and speak to them and speak about them and speak for them. So I had a chance to be their voice for a year, and I really enjoyed it.

JB: You obviously respect the profession of teaching very much. What makes a good teacher?

SD: A good teacher is a teacher that hasn't forgotten the magic that, in spite of the rules and the regulations and the standards and the tests and the proposals that come down from above that teachers have to follow, that there are still teachers that find the magic and find the joy and find the connection between kids and learning and know how to connect with kids, even very difficult kids. A good teacher smiles. A good teacher is happy. A good teacher doesn't teach the subject matter. For instance, I tell my student teachers, "You don't teach math. You teach children. And you teach math to children. You are a teacher of children first, and what you are teaching these children is math." And if you look at it from that point of view and keep the children first—keep the children in the main focus—then that teacher can make it for 30 or 35 years and be successful. It's very hard to define what a good teacher is. It's really easy to see what a good teacher isn't, and so you take the opposite of that. A person who is not a good teacher is complaining and whining and does less than their best. A good teacher does the exact opposite of that—always cheerful, always optimistic, always trying, always doing more because they actually care about what they're doing and they care about their children.

JB: Who are some of your favorite characters from your novels and where did they come from?

SD: Favorite characters from my novels. I have no idea where they come from. I sit down and they fall out of my fingertips. They really do. And then once they start to develop, they take on personalities of their own. I hate to get to the end of a book because I like the characters so much I don't want to leave them. I like the kind of quirky characters. I like Destiny from *Romiette and Julio* because she's so effervescent and so different. She has such a positive outlook on life. And Ben, with the blue hair or the orange hair or the green hair, whose attitude is "Live and let live and enjoy life. Don't get stressed about anything." The characters that kind of go beyond their expectations are the ones I like. I like Ziggy because Ziggy speaks with a Jamaican accent and Ziggy is funny and Ziggy eats unusual foods and nothing ever bothers Ziggy. He's always in a good mood, he's always happy and always operating on an upbeat note. So those are the characters that I remember the most. I'm working on one now. It's another kind of character like that. It's a girl—in a new book—that can't tell the truth. She just cannot tell the truth. It's just totally impossible for the truth to come out of her mouth, which ends up getting her in trouble all the time. But she's fun to develop because everything I write about her is a lie, and so it's fun. So those are the kinds of characters I enjoy.

JB: What did you read when you were the age of many of your readers, and what do you read now?

SD: I read everything when I was in school; I read voraciously, copiously, all the time. We had these summer reading clubs, where they would give you a little dot for every book you read. You were supposed to have read 10 books over the summer, and they had to put special lines on there for me because I would read 40, 50, 60 books in a summer. And the chart was just filled up with my little dots because I read so many books. So I had a very, very wide variety of readings. So, because I had such a vast background, that was all input. So that was all information that was coming into my head that I used maybe 20 years later and I don't even know where it came from. So a book I may have read on Polynesia will somehow show up somewhere down the line. So everything that I read or things that I read back then was input. I read an awful lot of the award winners, but I did not know that they were award winners.

I read just about anything. I might read historical fiction, I might read a biography, I might read just a current pulp fiction. I won't read a whole book. I'll put it down if it isn't any good. And I'm not talking about if the story is good. If it's not well written, I don't have any patience with it.. The words have to be well crafted and well put together. That will make any story good. But I don't care what the story is. If it's not well-written, I won't have patience with it and I won't read it. I just can't.

JB: Any tips for beginning writers?

SD: I tell student writers that the first thing you have to do to be a good writer is to be a good reader and to go read. Put your pencil down and go read. Read and read and read and read and read so you have all that input so that you have background, so you have something to draw on, so you have some knowledge about how words work together.

LOIS DUNCAN

Lois Duncan grew up in Sarasota, Florida. She has always been a writer. She submitted her first piece of writing at age ten and first published a piece in a girls' magazine at age 13, She continued her successful writing career as a high school student, writing stories for *Seventeen*.

As an adult, Lois moved to Albuquerque, New Mexico, with her second husband, Don Arquette, and their five children. She continued to write for various magazines, in addition to teaching in the journalism department at the University of New Mexico from which she received her B.A. in 1977. Her novels *I Know What You Did Last Summer* (1973) and *Killing Mr. Griffin* (1979) brought Lois acclaim throughout the 1970s. Both books were made into popular movies. *I Know What You Did Last Summer* spawned a sequel, but Lois did not feel that the movie reflected her book accurately: "There's a double-identity twist that makes it much more interesting and it doesn't contain all the gore that's in the slasher film."

Tragedy befell her family in 1989, when her daughter, Kaitlyn, was murdered in what Albuquerque police called a "random drive-by shooting." They refused to investigate. Evidence in 2004 points to the possibility that Kaitlyn's death was not an accident, but was related to a crime ring about which Kaitlyn had become aware and was about to report to the police, unaware that authorities were implicated in the crime ring.

Lois often writes about teenagers who are involved in mysteries, and sometimes the paranormal enters in. These protagonists sometimes have psychic powers and are often outsiders. When asked why she likes to use outsiders as main characters, Lois answered: "Outsiders make sympathetic protagonists because they have no preestablished support group and must find the strength to overcome adversity on their own."

BOOKS

- *I Know What You Did Last Summer*: Julie, Helen, Barry, and Ray have covered up the fact that they were involved in a hit-and-run accident in which a little boy was killed. A mysterious stalker seems to be extracting justice. Grades 8–10

- *They Never Came Home*: When Dan and Larry don't return from a mountain camping trip, Larry's sister suspects they are more than just lost hikers. Grades 8–10

- *Summer of Fear*: When Rachel's cousin Julia comes to live with her and her family, strange things start to occur. Rachel suspects witchcraft. Grades 8–10

- *Killing Mr. Griffin*: A plot to get even with a mean English teacher goes all wrong for five teenagers. Grades 8–10

Nancy Farmer

Nancy Farmer grew up in Phoenix and Yuma, Arizona. Her father was the manager of a rough-and-tumble tavern in downtown Phoenix (a tavern that remains in operation today and with the same name, Ted's), until he moved the family to Yuma, where they managed a hotel. As a teenager, Nancy was assigned the job of night manager for the hotel and consequently rubbed elbows with its unusual clientele, including circus performers, rodeo cowboys, and an occasional gangster. Nancy graduated from Reed College in Oregon before serving two years in the Peace Corps in India.

She returned to the U.S. to study chemistry but soon left the States again, this time to journey to South Africa, where she worked as an entomologist before meeting her husband, Harold, an English professor. After 20 years in South Africa, Nancy, Harold, and their son, Daniel, settled in the United States.

Nancy's travels all over the world provide excellent background for her novels. She enjoys researching the topic or the setting of her books, such as *Sea of Trolls,* which takes place in England and the Scandinavian Peninsula during the Dark Ages. Nancy extensively researched Norse mythology and Viking history to find historical seeds for the myths about trolls and pixies. She also did extensive research on cloning for her National Book Award–winning *The House of the Scorpion.*

Nancy and her husband live in Menlo Park, California.

Books

♦ *A Girl Named Disaster*: When 11-year-old Nhamo is orphaned in her African village, she is at the mercy of anyone and everyone. When she is about to be forced to become the fourth wife of a cruel man, she runs away, and begins an odyssey of learning and spirituality in the African wilderness. Grades 6–8

♦ *The Ear, the Eye and the Arm*: In the year 2194, three aristocratic children in Zimbabwe, Tendai, Rita, and Kuda, explore the wonders of the world outside their pampered existence, only to be kidnapped. Three mutant detectives with special talents (the Eye, the Ear, and the Arm) are called in to find the children. Grades 6–9

♦ *The House of the Scorpion*: Somewhere in the not-too-distant future, Mateo (Matt) is a very special relative of El Patron. El Patron is a rich and powerful drug lord in the country of Opium, which lies between the United States and Mexico. Matt is special because he is El Patron's clone; he leads the life of an aristocrat as if he were El Patron's favorite son. There is a horrible price to pay for this existence, however, and some day soon, when El Patron (at 140 plus years of age) is in need of a heart transplant, Matt will be forced to make the ultimate sacrifice (unless he can escape). Grades 8–12

- *Sea of Trolls:* This includes some factual history about the Viking raids on England with what is known of Norse life in the Dark Ages and a good helping of historical speculation (were the Picts the inspiration for the fantasy creatures known as pixies?), as well as fantasy, traditional fairy tales, and science fiction. Teenaged amateur wizard Jack, a Saxon boy kidnapped by Vikings, must travel to the land of the trolls to save his sister from the evil Viking Queen Frith. Grades 8–12

A CONVERSATION WITH NANCY FARMER

Adapted from Blasingame, James. (2004). Interview with Nancy Farmer. *Journal of Adolescent and Adult Literacy, 48*(1), 78–79.

JB: *Sea of Trolls* is unlike any fantasy that I have ever read in that it is not entirely fantasy; it actually has some basis in historical and anthropological fact. The time and place are very real, as are the Northmen (the Vikings), and of course the Saxons and the Picts, but the trolls have some basis in fact, too. Can you explain the historical basis for the trolls? What are some other elements of your story that, while developed with a supernatural element, are actually to some degree speculation about a very real past?

NF: Trolls are mentioned seriously in Norse histories, not at all as though they were mythical creatures. They controlled the high ground in Norway until the advent of Christianity around 800 A.D., and some old Norwegian families trace themselves back to a troll ancestor. Troll males and females are mentioned by name and have family trees and distinct personalities. This is not at all like the dragons and giants of British folklore, who are described in general terms—"terrible," "fire-breathing," or "stupid." I would like to believe they were Neanderthals, but the evidence is against it. Still, preserved Neanderthals were found in salt mines during the Middle Ages and earlier, and may have fueled the stories.

My guess is that trolls were a unique tribe like the Ainu of Japan or the Chuckchee of Siberia. They were suited to cold—all the stories have them living in ice and snow—and they are named things like Fonn, Drifa, or Mjoll (words for snow) or Hrimgerth (frost). A numbing chill may creep over a hero before he meets a troll maiden or snow begins to fall.

Picts are almost as elusive as trolls. No one is quite sure where they came from or when they vanished. No one understands their language. They appear in Roman chronicles as naked headhunters covered with tattoos. Hadrian's Wall was built to keep them out. Later, the Vikings describe them as small people who only came out at dusk. It seems likely they were the original Pixies. In spite of their unsavory reputation, Picts were magnificent artists. Their metalwork and stone carving exist all over Scotland, and Pictish art found its way into the Lindesfarne Gospel and the Book of Kells.

JB: How did you go about researching the possibilities for this storyline?

NF: I did a great deal of research for *Sea of Trolls*. Except for the giant spiders, which I couldn't resist, the animals came out of Norse mythology. Golden Bristles, the troll-boar, was one of Freya's pets, and her cart was drawn by giant cats. I was surprised to learn how complicated Norse mythology was. It was a religion spread across Northern Europe and Britain, with a lot of local variations. It had a distinct mind-set behind it that has never entirely disappeared. *Lord of the Rings* is moving because we still understand the principles of heroism, loyalty, and the sacrifice behind them.

JB: Jotunheim, the land of the trolls, is fraught with danger. There are troll bears and dragons and spiders as big as semi-trucks, not to mention the warlike trolls themselves. Was the journey of Jack and Thorgil through this dangerous land in any way based on or similar to your own life experience?

NF: Jotunheim is a land where everything is bigger. It is also a matriarchy. In Middle Earth, things are run by men. In Jotunheim we find the Mountain Queen with her harem, and troll females (who are larger) capturing males for mates. We also have a female dragon, a giant mother spider and a giant female grouse with her chicks. The most powerful figures are not the gods, but mysterious female entities called Norns. I drew on my oceanography and marine biology experiences for the descriptions of Northmen. I met several wannabe berserkers, including the captain of an oceanography vessel. His nickname was Captain Crunch because he ran into so many things, and he used to stand naked at the helm with a bottle of rum by his side.

JB: As it turns out, the trolls, while extremely fearsome, are quite honorable, and are capable of great kindness. What suggested this premise to you?

NF: In the course of my travels I have met people who were very dangerous, but who were, so to speak, on vacation. They could be charming under the right circumstances. When I was in Mozambique I hired several off-duty terrorists to handle boats and fishing nets. The 16-year-old soldiers in the Mozambique army (Frelimo) used to fire off tracer bullets, rocket launchers, and so forth for sport. Imagine a drunk 16-year-old with an AK-47 and you get the idea. I met witch doctors, too. They were friendly, but I never trusted them. In this country, I've been to parties with the Hell's Angels and haven't trusted them either. I think I've been lucky not to be around when such people *stopped* being on vacation. It's important to know when to head for the door.

JB: Coming not too long after *The House of the Scorpion*, *Sea of Trolls* represents almost a mirror opposite of the earlier book. You go into the past instead of the future, you go into the far North instead of the Southwest. You speculate on the roots of our past instead of what the future may hold. What special problems did this book pose over the earlier work and how would you compare your experiences in writing each?

NF: *The House of the Scorpion* contains a lot of biographical elements. For that reason it was emotionally difficult to write and I was glad to finish it. *Sea of Trolls* was a glorious vacation from beginning to end. However, the inspiration for it, the attack on 9/11, was serious. I wanted to deal with the theme on a mythological level children could tolerate. It's my experience that children have to come to terms with such things symbolically. *Hansel and Gretel* explains uncaring parents. *The Snow Queen* deals with emotional paralysis. Such themes are too devastating to be approached directly. Thus, with *Sea of Trolls*, I describe another unexpected and undeserved tragedy, which is solved by courage and a belief in the value of life. It's no good discussing 9/11 with children unless you offer them hope.

JB: You have been described as having boundless energy and a sense of adventure that hasn't waned one bit as you have gone through life. How do you account for that? What was the biggest adventure of your life?

NF: Why, thank you. The truth is I am a timid adult who knows how to act brave. I was a timid child, too. It bothered me no end that the rest of my family was courageous while I was scared of everything. And so I forced myself from an early age to do the things that frightened me. I picked up tarantulas, explored dark alleys, and walked along the edges of tall buildings. The result was that I got a taste for adventure. (My definition of "adventure" is something that is horrible at the time, but fun to talk about later.) I was lucky to be born into a family of extremely lively people who were interested in everything and communicated it to me. The biggest adventure of my life will probably be death, which I plan to put off for a long time.

Paul Fleischman

Paul Fleischman grew up in Santa Monica, California, and after stops in many other places, lives in California today. Writing seems to run in Paul's family. His father, Sid Fleischman, won the Newbery Medal for his book *The Whipping Boy* in 1987; only two years later Paul himself won the Newbery Medal for his book, *Joyful Noise: Poems for Two Voices*. When Paul was growing up, his father would sometimes read from his works in progress, and the family would make suggestions for the story. Nevertheless, Paul says he didn't gravitate toward writing as a child but recalls that he and his sister much preferred riding their bikes around their hometown looking for discarded or lost treasures.

But his love of language eventually won out. After Paul graduated from the University of New Mexico, he went on to found the "grammar watchdog groups" ColonWatch and the Society for the Prevention of Cruelty to English. Paul's Newbery Medal winner, *Joyful Noise: Poems for Two Voices*, was an innovative work of poems designed to be read by two alternating voices. The topic of the book is insects.

Paul has two grown sons, Seth and Dana. He and his wife, Patty, currently live in Aromas, California.

Books

♦ *Joyful Noise: Poems for Two Voices*: This Newbery Medal winner about insects broke new ground with poems designed to be read by two alternating voices. Grades 6–8

♦ *I Am the Phoenix: Poems for Two Voices*: These poems, designed to be read by alternating voices, are about birds, from the legendary to the extinct. Grades 6–8

♦ *Bull Run*: Sixteen voices tell the story of the Battle of Bull Run in verse. Grades 6–8

♦ *Whirligig*: Sixteen-year-old Brent Bishop must fulfill an unusual request from the mother of the girl he killed while he was driving drunk. Grades 7–10

♦ *Breakout*: A seventeen-year-old runaway assumes a new name, a new identity, and a new view of life as a performance artist whose topic for stand-up comedy will later become the lives of people trapped on the Santa Monica Freeway during a traffic jam. Grades 8–11

♦ *Dateline Troy*: Fleischman presents the Trojan War and suggests parallels to current events through the placement of newspaper clippings about modern, but similar, happenings. Grades 9–12

RUSSELL FREEDMAN

Nonfiction writer Russell Freedman grew up in San Francisco and went to the University of California at Berkeley. Russell believes that historical nonfiction is boring only when it is told in a boring fashion. Freedman was a reporter and editor for the Associated Press and worked in publicity for television networks, so he learned how to write with energy and verve. In addition, he includes carefully chosen photographs in his work, saying: "Photos make the past come alive; scenes show that the subjects are time-bound; expressions are timeless."

BOOKS

- *Give Me Liberty: The Story of the Declaration of Independence*: The story of events in history that lead up to the signing of this historic document that changed the world. Grades 6–8

- *Babe Didrikson Zaharias*: Mildred Didrikson, an Olympic gold medal winner, goes on to help found the Ladies Professional Golf Association. Grades 6–8

- *Eleanor Roosevelt: A Life of Discovery*: This 1994 Newbery Honor Book tells the story of how Roosevelt worked for the good of unfortunates in the U.S. Grades 6–8

- *Kids at Work: Lewis Hine and the Crusade Against Child Labor*: Freedman follows the travels and photographic record of Lewis Hine, investigating for the National Child Labor Committee in 1908. Grades 6–8

- *The Wright Brothers: How They Invented the Airplane*: Two bicycle mechanics turn inventors and conquer the air. Includes photographs by Wilbur and Orville Wright. Grades 6–8

- *Out of Darkness: The Story of Louis Braille*: The story of Louis Braille, who created the system making reading and writing possible for the blind, and who attended the Royal Institute for Blind Youth in Paris. Grades 6–8

- *Franklin Delano Roosevelt*: A recounting of how, despite physical challenges, Roosevelt leads the United States out of the Great Depression and through World War II. Grades 6–8

- *Lincoln: A Photobiography*: A winner of the 1988 Newbery Medal, which is rarely awarded to nonfiction, a testament to the quality and appeal of this biography. *Lincoln* follows the sixteenth president from boyhood to death. Grades 6–8

- *Cowboys of the Wild West*: This is the story of the true American cowboy—who was often a person of color and seldom carried a gun—as opposed to the movie and television stereotype. Grades 6–8

- *The Life and Death of Crazy Horse*: Crazy Horse defeated the U.S. Cavalry at the Battle of Little Bighorn and never signed a single treaty, yet he was not a warlike man. This book contains many quotations and drawings from the past as well as photographs by Amos Bad Heart Bull. Grades 6–8

DON GALLO

Editor Don Gallo has been called "the godfather of young adult short stories," and he has proven successful again and again at reaching his stated goal of publishing "lively, entertaining, insightful" stories that have not been previously published. Don is past president of the Assembly on Literature for Adolescents of the National Council of Teachers of English and vice-chair of the Conference on English Education. He has been a professor of English at Central Connecticut State University (24 years) and at the University of Colorado at Denver, a reading specialist for Jefferson County Schools in Colorado, and is now an adjunct professor at Cleveland State University after his retirement from CCSU. His collections have won numerous awards and he continues to publish new works. He is the founder of Authors4Teens.com, a website and organization providing a wealth of information about young adult literature and authors.

BOOKS

- *Destination Unexpected*: Ten stories about teens venturing into the unfamiliar from Kimberly Willis Holt, David Lubar, Will Weaver, Joyce Sweeney, Richard Peck, Graham Salisbury, Margaret Haddix, Ron Koertge, Ellen Wittlinger, and Alex Flinn. Grades 8–12

- *Join In: Multiethnic Short Stories by Outstanding Writers for Young Adults*: Includes works by Lensey Namioka, Rita Williams-Garcia, Alden R. Carter, T. Ernesto Bethancourt, Linda Crew, and Minfong Ho. Grades 8–12

- *On the Fringe*: Stories about teenage misfits from Jack Gantos, Will Weaver, Angela Johnson, Chris Crutcher, Nancy Werlin, Graham Salisbury, Alden R. Carter, M. E., Kerr, Joan Bauer, and Francess Lantz. Grades 9–12

- *Sixteen: Short Stories by Outstanding Writers for Young Adults*: Stories by Norma Fox and Harry Mazer, M. E. Kerr, Robert Cormier, Bette Greene, Richard Peck, and others. Grades 8–12

- *No Easy Answers: Short Stories about Teens Making Tough Choices*: Sixteen stories about teenagers facing adversity written by top authors, including Louise Plummer, M. E. Kerr, Jack Gantos, Gloria D. Miklowitz, Walter Dean Myers, Monica Hughs, Virginia Euwer Wolff, Will Weaver, Ron Koertge, and Lensey Namioka. Grades 8–12

- *Time Capsule: Short Stories about Teenagers Throughout the Twentieth Century*: A story about each decade of the 20th century from star authors, including Richard Peck, Graham Salisbury, Bruce Brooks, Trudy Krisher, Chris Lynch, Alden Carter, Chris Crutcher, and Will Weaver. Grades 8–12

- *Ultimate Sports*: Sixteen original short stories about different sports, including wrestling, boxing, racquetball, tennis, basketball, football, track and field, distance running, and one "ultimate" sport in the future. Grades 8–10

Jack Gantos

Jack Gantos spends many days of the year on the road visiting with aspiring young writers in schools and helping teachers and librarians make books and writing important in the lives of young people. He never stays away from his home in Boston for too long, however, preferring not to be away from his wife, Anne, and their daughter, Mabel, for more than a few days at a time.

Jack's father was employed in military construction, and Jack's family moved 40 times during his school years, to such places as Barbados, Florida, and Cape Hatteras, North Carolina. His Jack Henry books are inspired by childhood events in these places, and his partial autobiography, *Hole in My Life*, begins in south Florida, where he attended high school. When Jack talks to groups of kids, he not only tells them he started journaling in elementary school, but he brings along his old journals to prove it. In addition to words, the journals contain doodles of his old neighborhoods and the events that happened in them. The sketches are actually amazingly clever cartoon caricatures of everything from alligators to whole neighborhoods. The doodles were the brainstorming from which his stories sprung, a technique he now teaches to young writers all over the country.

Hole in My Life is Jack's account of more than three years of his life, including two years in which he served part of a six-year sentence for trafficking in a controlled substance. With the help of a prison counselor, Jack secured his release from prison and admission to a four-year college. Jack eventually joined the faculty at Emerson College in Boston and developed the masters program in creative writing in children's literature. He has also served as faculty for the Vermont College M.F.A. program in children's literature.

Books

- *Joey Pigza Swallowed the Key*: Joey is the epitome of a child suffering from attention deficit hyperactive disorder, and guess what? His behavior is not too different from his father's and his grandmother's. Joey has enough trouble trying to cope with school while suffering the effects of ADHD, let alone the problems presented by a dysfunctional extended family. The first in the Joey Pigza trilogy. Grades 6–8 (but of interest to readers of any age who have lived in a family with an ADHD child)

- *Jack's Black Book*: A darkly humorous book in which 14-year-old Jack Henry experiences the insanity of adolescence. Among other things, Jack builds a dog coffin in his industrial arts class and uses it for an extremely belated ceremony for BeauBeau, the deceased family pet. Grades 6–9

- *Jack's New Power: Stories From a Caribbean Year*: Jack Henry spends his seventh-grade year in Barbados. Fictionalized autobiography. Grades 6–8

◆ *Hole in My Life*: Jack Gantos tells the story of missing years in his life when he served part of a sentence for drug trafficking. A humorous plot evolves into a nerve-wracking ordeal as Jack survives a time in his life that could have been much worse, if not fatal. A testament to wise choices and the consequences of bad ones. Grades 10 and up (very popular with at-risk youth)

A CONVERSATION WITH JACK GANTOS

Adapted from Blasingame, James. (2003). Interview with Jack Gantos. *Journal of Adolescent and Adult Literacy, 46*(1), 85.

JB: Over the course of your career you have branched out to audiences of different ages but never abandoned your previous readers. You continued to write Rotten Ralph books after you began the Jack Henry stories and did not abandon Ralph or Jack when you started the Joey Pigza books. Your newest works are obviously for an older audience than anything you've written before. How do maintain integrity of voice as you write for these different audiences?

JG: Each age group has its own degrees of separation, and I put a great deal of effort into assuming the voice, heart, and soul of them all. With the Jack Henry and Joey Pigza books, I strive to find just the right voice to carry the age and issues and nuances of the characters.

I'm very mindful to locate the voice of these stories in the mind and body of a young adult. I want my work to be an authentic expression of the experiences I had when I was young. Being genuine is a great part of what I have to offer young adult readers. To condescend to them is the kiss of death.

This is not to say that I condescend to my other, younger audiences. For each audience I try to be spot on for them—Rotten Ralph is rotten; he needs unconditional love, and my primary-age audience understands that. They make mistakes every day and they expect to be forgiven, too. This journey from making a mistake to receiving forgiveness is part of everyday life for a kindergartner.

For my older audience I envision readers who, while they are youthful, are still confronted with adult issues and responsibilities, all the while navigating between finesse and failure on their course toward adulthood.

JB: Your newest works mark an evolution in your writing, yet an intangible similarity still exists among your main characters, from Rotten Ralph to Jack Henry to Joey Pigza to "Muzak for Prozac" and the 19-year-old Jack Gantos in *Hole in My Life*. Are your protagonists somehow related to one other?

JG: Yes, I think they are related. At a reading conference in Atlanta, I just gave a speech titled "From Violation to Redemption" because when I look back over my work from Rotten Ralph to Jack Henry to Joey Pigza to *Hole in My Life*, I clearly make out the cycle from breaking rules to searching for answers to making mistakes and finally to seeking forgiveness and/or finding an answer.

All my characters have a slightly different version of violation and redemption, but overall that is the theme I find overarching in my work. I can only guess that one of the reasons I have had a steady group of readers over the years is that they empathize with this very cycle. Who wouldn't?

With *Hole in My Life*, I suppose readers of my previous work can now say, "Now I know why he wrote those other books. He *is* each of those characters." I think they can make a great case for that argument.

JB: What are you working on now, and what projects do you see in the near future?

JG: I've just finished what I think is the third and final Joey Pigza novel, *What Would Joey Do?*, and now I'm working on a Jack Henry book set in fourth grade. I do have a few novels in mind after that which are middle grade/young adult and then perhaps I'll write some adult novels. I'm one of those writers who won't write about something unless it's interesting to me, so I'm better understood through my interests rather than age.

MEL GLENN

Mel Glenn's family moved to Brooklyn, New York, from Zurich, Switzerland, when he was 3 years old. After high school, he majored in English at New York University, and when he graduated, he joined the Peace Corps and headed for a two-year assignment to Sierra Leone, Africa. After earning an M.A. from Yeshiva University, he began teaching junior high in Brooklyn. Ultimately, he ended up back at his alma mater, Lincoln High School, where he taught for 31 years before retiring from teaching (but not writing) in 2001.

Mel's first book, *Class Dismissed! High School Poems*, was published in 1982 and won the Golden Kite Award, as well as being named to the American Library Association's Best of the Best Books 1970–1982. Since then he has published a dozen hit books.

BOOKS

♦ *Class Dismissed!: High School Poems*: Mel Glenn's collection of his own poems about the tragedies and triumphs of high school. Grades 7–10

♦ *Class Dismissed II: More High School Poems:* From romance to sports, drugs to dances, Mel Glenn's poems cover the range of the high school experience. Grades 7–10

♦ *Foreign Exchange: A Mystery in Poems:* Rather than a foreign country, a group of exchange students from inner-city Tower High School are guests at Hudson Landing, a small lakeshore town. When local sweetheart Kristen Clarke is murdered, Hudson Landing fingers point at Kwame Richards, an African-American student from Tower High. Told in free verse from the viewpoints of those involved. Grades 7–10

♦ *Split Image:* Laura Li is intelligent and appears to be happy, as far as her Tower High School classmates can tell. Laura's life underneath the surface, however, is miserable because of her tyrannical and traditional Chinese mother and a series of unfortunate events that lead her to commit suicide. The story is told in a series of poems from people who interacted with her. Grades 7–10

♦ *Who Killed Mr. Chippendale? A Mystery in Poems:* All of the students who knew Mr. Chippendale, a Tower High School English teacher, express their thoughts and feelings about him in free verse after he is murdered. Grades 7–10

♦ *The Taking of Room 114: A Hostage Drama in Poems:* Mr. Weidemeyer holds his Tower High School history class at gunpoint on the day before graduation. The story is told in free-verse poems from the viewpoints of the characters. Grades 8–11

♦ *Jump Ball: A Basketball Season in Poems:* A Tower High School basketball season unfolds in free verse. Grades 7–10

A CONVERSATION WITH MEL GLENN

From an e-mail interview on November 15, 2004.

JB: Why did you choose the genre of verse to tell your stories?

MG: Frankly, it chose me. My mind works in metaphors and short phrases (literary ADD?). Edgar Lee Master's *Spoon River Anthology*, my creative source, moved me, motivated me to turn my internal camera upon the students I taught every day. I wanted to reflect their lives, while, in essence, trying to understand my own, since I taught in the same high school I went to as a kid.

JB: After a lifelong commitment to high school English teaching, what do you know to be true about your students over the years that you tried to capture in your books?

MG: I know that turbulent worlds lie beneath the surface. Adolescents seek to find pieces of themselves when they are the puzzle. Teens are at war with everything and everyone, years spent in perpetual ache, physical and mental, with sudden bursts of incandescent joy. These split images will, hopefully, coalesce into whole human beings, someday.

JB: Have kids changed over the years?

MG: No, I don't think so. Fashion, music, indeed all of teen culture has changed, convulsively, but human emotion, positive and negative, has always been part of the teenage palette—red love, lost and found, green envy, blue friendship, gray crises of self-confidence, white, unalloyed happiness. I suspect these universals, these feelings, will never change.

JB: What do you think makes for really good young adult literature?

MG: It may be too simple to say, but I think a major key for good young adult literature is one word—identification. Even if the setting is foreign, the characters alien, the plot weird, when a reader can say, "Hey, I feel what that character is going through," a tangible connection has been made between printed word and human recipient, or in other words, What is that character to me or me to that character that I should care so?; the reader and the protagonist intertwine.

VICKI GROVE

Vicki Grove lives with her husband, Mike, a music teacher, in a 100-year-old farmhouse near Ionia, Missouri. She writes most days in a cute little house that her father built for her just for that purpose and just across the hayfield from the main house. Vicki credits her third- and sixth-grade teachers, Mrs. Wise and Mrs. Sanders, with inspiring her to write. She often ends a day of writing by going to the gym for kickboxing or step aerobics or going to sing in a choir.

BOOKS

♦ *Rimwalkers*: Fourteen-year-old Tory and her 13-year-old sister, Sara, leave Milwaukee to spend a summer on the farm. Life on the farm is far from idyllic. Grades 6–9

♦ *Destiny*: Rather than sell potatoes door to door for her stepfather, 12-year-old Destiny finds a job reading to an older woman who is losing her vision. Destiny learns a lot about people and life as the lives of those she knows intertwine. Grades 6–9

♦ *The Crystal Garden*: Eliza and her mother move in with her mother's boyfriend in the small town of Gouge Eye, Missouri. Eliza struggles with popularity and the true meaning of friendship when she is exploited by the in-crowd after abandoning a real friend. Grades 6–9

♦ *Goodbye My Wishing Star*: Like many family farms in the 1980s, the Tucker's place will be sold before the bank forecloses on it. Jennifer Tucker watches her neighbors battle the inevitable until it happens to her own family. Grades 6–9

♦ *Reaching Dustin*: Carly must interview Dustin Groat as an assignment for the sixth-grade newspaper. Dustin's family lives in a compound in the country and is under investigation by the authorities for all kinds of things. Carly must separate the reclusive Dustin from his environment. Grades 6–9

♦ *Starplace*: When 13-year-old Frannie is chosen to sing with Celeste, an African-American student, the civil rights movement has not yet come to 1961 Oklahoma. Grades 6–9

A CONVERSATION WITH VICKI GROVE

From an e-mail interview on January 31, 2005.

JB: You often write about people who live in rural communities or small towns. What draws you to exploring that setting? Do farm kids have additional issues to deal with beyond those of city kids?

VG: I think writing is definitely painting with words, and I think the "colors" each writer uses most often are probably the people and places and situations that person knows best and cares about most. I know, and love, the rural American Midwest. I was born in Illinois and grew up on a farm there, lived in a small Oklahoma town through my teen years, then moved to Missouri to go to college and have lived in farmhouses in the Ozarks ever since (for 30-plus years—yikes!). I feel fortunate to have a certain bone-deep understanding of this area because, frankly, I think when authors search for settings and situations to write about, small towns and rural places are often passed over, perhaps thought of as being unexciting. Nothing could be further from the truth.

JB: You come up with things that your characters do that are both hilarious and a little sad at the same time, like when Eliza shaves her arms in *The Crystal Garden*. Are these things pure inventions of your imagination or do they have some basis in past experience?

VG: Oh, dear—you got me! I have to admit that the nutty things are most often from experience. In fact, I'm going out on a limb here, but based on the 30 or so other writers I know as friends, I believe—how should I put this? Let's just say I think few of us were the most always-in-control, popular, and self-assured kids in the class. No, to put it bluntly, we were more likely the nerds, the chess club gurus, the gawky geeks who were always trying to either fit in or to remain invisible as we scribbled our heartfelt poetry and bit our nails to the nub and told everybody we didn't care about going to any dumb old dance (we said this, of course, because we weren't invited).

In the book you mentioned, Eliza shaves her arms from wrists to shoulders to try and look more like the popular girls she envies so much. In seventh grade, I did exactly that. I also shaved my eyebrows, took a two-inch swath off right through the middle with my dad's hardcore Gillette double-edged razor. I wrote the book having Eliza do that as well, but the publisher nixed it, had me delete it. She said it was over the top and no real girl would ever actually shave her eyebrows! So there you go (*sigh . . .*). My personal opinion is that anyone will do anything to fulfill a certain strong need we all have for something Eliza would call popularity, and that I might, at this point in my life, call acceptance.

I think I often, in fact, have my characters accidentally find acceptance from some unlikely but very fulfilling source while they're doing all sorts of humiliating things in a fruitless quest to be popular. Much in life is a paradox (my favorite word, this decade). It bothers me a little when I'm talking with kids at a school and I'm asked the inevitable question, "Are you famous?" Or the other one, a close second, "Are you rich?" My books are all about kids who discover both those things are false quests, but there are great riches to be had in opening yourself to honest friendships and lasting family relationships, all the non-flashy stuff that turns out to be solid gold. I only write what I believe, and that's it in a nutshell, all I know about life.

JB: You have described your daily writing routine in the miniature house that your father built in the hayfield by your house with great affection. Do you think writers would benefit from a sanctuary for the act of writing?

VG: I'm so spoiled, having this tiny little playhouse to come out to each day. I think what writers need most is silence, honestly, and that's what I treasure most about this little place. There's no phone out here, no radio, no washing machine "thunking" or cat knocking over the plants. I think the world today is much more noisy than the world I grew up in, though that world was plenty noisy, too. My own two children, Mike and Jenny, grew up in a quiet house. Our TV reception was too poor to put up with in this old farmhouse, so we didn't have the television on much. We all read a great deal, and I think maybe the biggest gift we, my husband and I, accidentally gave them was the knack of being quiet with their own thoughts. Now, in their late twenties, both my kids are thinkers. They can look out a window in silence and think about things big and little—music, art, history, pizza choices, what pet to get. They have iPods, but they leave them at home to take long, quiet, contemplative walks. They don't have television sets. I'm afraid lots of people can't function without razzmatazz in the background these days, and this makes me sad. Silence seems to actually scare a lot of people, as if they're frightened of the thoughts they might have if they turned off all the gadgets that fill their lives with sound. There's so much to be gained from silence. In silence, your own splendid ideas have opportunity to come percolating up from deep within your glorious soul, eventually finding their way to exact words that you and only you would use.

To put this another way, if you write something based on your favorite television show, or if you write poetry that's structured or worded like a type of music you listen to, this isn't really writing, at least not as I understand it. Writing has to be original, and the only way I know to be original is to write from the small voice you can hear deep within yourself. You have to be quiet to hear that voice, though. Quiet, and sometimes patient.

That brings me to journaling, my favorite subject, my oxygen, my tool for getting through a hard day, my joy on a great day, my constant addiction! Do it, keep a journal, write those little thoughts and ideas down constantly. When I'm asked for advice by a young writer, that's what I say. Cultivate silence, and keep a journal. If your father builds you a playhouse for writing in some day, don't forget to thank him, frequently.

JB: You seem to love kids. Do you think that is a common trait among authors who write for young adults?

VG: I don't just love kids; kids are breathtaking, and I stand in awe of them on a daily basis. I watch kids obsessively. I sneak around at schools, hide in restroom stalls or behind library stacks, journaling what I hear and what I see as I watch the cavalcade of colorful life seething past and just shake my head, gobsmacked (as they say in England)!

These are challenging times, with everything so fast, with the world so connected, and yet I see young people being so generous, laughing and crying and showing compassion. These very young people with so much life ahead, so much to give and feel, and they seem to feel so connected to and compassionate for young people all over the world. I have so much hope for the future, so much optimism, watching kids. I feel so sorry for the grownups who don't have the opportunity I have to go to schools and see kids in their element, being such wonderful people. They wrench my heart, too, the kids who are trying so hard to find their place, and I think most of them are. (Who isn't?!) I can't understand the few very self-confident kids, the shiny girls like the ones on television, the muscled boys who seem never to have a self-doubt. My heart is with all the others, the kids who are questing, trying and failing, getting back up, finding themselves in the corners of their lives, learning to be good people, kind people, empathetic people.

I agree completely with Dr. Seuss, that adults are merely obsolete children.

I would hope all writers who write for young adults feel the same sense of wonder I do around kids. Once in a while I dread going to teach my fifth-grade Sunday school class, for instance, and every time that happens, that will be the day they save me, say the silly thing that solves my problems, give me the laugh that sends me sailing into the next week. What can I say? Kids are great, period.

VIRGINIA HAMILTON

Virginia Hamilton grew up with her parents, two brothers, and two sisters on a truck farm in Yellow Springs, Ohio, surrounded by the farms of their relatives. In addition to being a farmer, her father was the dining hall manager at nearby Antioch College. Virginia received her education at Antioch College, Ohio State University, and the New School for Social Research.

Virginia and her husband, fellow author and poet Arnold Adoff, moved back to the farm later in life. Virginia is skilled at multiple genres and has won numerous awards. She was the first African American to accomplish a number of things in children's and young adult literature, including winning the Newbery Medal, for *M. C. Higgins, the Great*, in 1974. In 1995 she became the first author of young adult literature to receive a John D. and Catherine T. MacArthur Fellowship.

BOOKS

* *House of Dies Drear*: Thomas Small's father, a professor of history, moves the family to Ohio and a house that was a stop on the Underground Railroad before the Civil War. Thomas struggles with neighbors who try to scare them off, and the ghosts of past occupants. Grades 6–9

* *The Mystery of Drear House: The Conclusion of the Dies Drear Chronicle*: In this sequel, Thomas Small's family decides what to do with the treasure left by the abolitionist Dies Drear, and Thomas struggles with new relationships. Grades 6–9

* *Cousins*: Cammy hates her cousin Patty Ann until something tragic and irreversible changes her perspective. Grades 6–9

* *Sweet Whispers, Brother Rush*: Fourteen-year-old Tree's deceased uncle appears to her, and her bad feelings about being charged with caring for her handicapped brother soon change. Grades 6–9

* *Plain City*: Buhlaire-Marie Sims, a biracial 12-year-old, discovers that her father did not die in Vietnam as she has been told, but is instead a homeless man living in Plain City. Grades 6–9

* *Many Thousand Gone: African Americans From Slavery to Freedom*: Stories of individuals and events that comprise the history of slavery and its end in the United States. Grades 6–9

* *M. C. Higgins, the Great* (Newbery Award winner): As a slag heap creeps towards their home in Appalachian Ohio, 15-year-old M. C. Higgins decides what to do. Grades 6–9

* *The Bells of Christmas*: Jason's family experiences an Ohio Christmas in 1890 with their relatives. An accurate portrayal of African-American lifestyles in the late nineteenth century. Grades 6–9

PETE HAUTMAN

Pete Hautman grew up in St. Louis Park, Minnesota, after moving there from Berkeley, California, at the age of 5. After attending St. Louis Park High School, he attended the University of Minnesota and the Minnesota College of Art and Design. In 1991, after a spin through a variety of occupations, Pete wrote his first novel, *Drawing Dead*, and adopted the full-time occupation of novelist. Pete's career success was highlighted in 2004 with the National Book Award for *Godless*, the story of bored teens who parody religious cults by worshipping the city's water tower.

He and his significant other, mystery writer Mary Logue, met when Pete took a writing class Mary taught at the Loft, a Twin Cities literary organization. They were writing colleagues before their romance flowered. Mary and Pete split their time between Stockholm, Wisconsin, and Golden Valley, Minnesota.

BOOKS

♦ *Sweetblood*: Sixteen-year-old Lucy Szabo has a very difficult time coping with diabetes. She is often on the verge of a coma caused by her sky-high or rock-bottom blood sugar. Lucy has a fascination with vampires and a unique theory about them. She speculates that vampires were actually diabetics before medical science understood their malady. She believes a diabetic experiencing the highs and lows of blood chemistry might in fact manifest bizarre symptoms not unlike the behavior of the undead. Lucy's problems are exacerbated by the bizarre people she is introduced to in a chat room for other vampire aficionados, appropriately called Transylvania. Grades 9–12

♦ *Hole in the Sky*: In the future, Earth's population will be devastated by a deadly flu; only those who have not been exposed, those who survived infection, and those who are naturally immune will be left. In the year 2038, a bizarre cult of infection survivors terrorize Arizona, where Ceej and his remaining family members live. Grades 9–12

♦ *Stone Cold*: Fifteen-year-old Dennis Doyle finds he has a true talent for—but also an obsession with—high-stakes poker. Grades 8–11

♦ *Drawing Dead*: When ex-cop Joe Crow finds himself with gambling debts, he enters the ugly underbelly of Minneapolis, peopled with interesting underworld characters who deal in drugs, loans, gambling, and an illegal rare comic-book black market. Grades 8–11

♦ *Rag Man*: Former clothing company owner and all-around nice guy Mack MacWray finds murdering his double-crossing partner to be quite liberating. Some people just love the new conscience-free Mack, but his true friends want the old Mack back. Grades 8–11

♦ *Godless*: Most adults and even some teens take it too seriously when 15-year-old Jason and his friends create a bogus, tongue-in-cheek religion that worships the local water tower. Grades 7–10

A Conversation With Pete Hautman

Adapted from Blasingame, James. (2005). Interview with Pete Hautman. *Journal of Adolescent and Adult Literacy, 48*(5), 438–439.

JB: In *Sweetblood*, Lucy, the protagonist, theorizes that the mythology of vampirism may have evolved through a misunderstanding of the physical manifestations of diabetes many centuries ago when diagnosis of the condition didn't exist, let alone treatment. Even with the advantages of modern medical science, Lucy doesn't seem able to successfully cope with her own diabetes. Even though it nearly kills her and puts her in situations she would prefer to avoid, she fails to keep track of her blood sugar and insulin levels. Her life is a series of crises and near catastrophes. Why can't she keep it together? Wouldn't life be easier?

PH: Let me answer that in two parts.

Part one: Lucy is one of those characters who, like a lot of teens, drives adults crazy. What teen hasn't heard an exasperated parent say, "Why can't you just . . . ?" or "It would be so much easier if you would only . . . " I know I heard it.

The problem is that when you are 15 years old it's not all that easy to make the "right" decision. Lucy does her best, and frequently fails; however, like most of us, she survives the consequences of her own bad judgment.

Part two: From the outside, insulin-dependent diabetes looks like an easily managed disease. It's just a matter of balancing food, insulin, and exercise, right? Wrong. Managing diabetes is like riding a bike down a treacherous, unfamiliar mountain trail. In the rain. At night. One-handed. With unreliable brakes. Sure, it can be done. But not without a few spills along the way.

JB: I couldn't help but notice the contrast between two of your characters in *Sweetblood*: Wayne, the daytime identity of Draco, whose mystery draws Lucy (a.k.a. Sweetblood in the Transylvania Chat Room) into his circle, and Antoinette, the piercing and tattooing artist, whose tattoos tell the story of a pretty rough life and whose comments bespeak an unexpected wisdom. What is the difference between them, and did you mean them to exist as polar opposites in Lucy's life?

PH: I think of Antoinette and Wayne/Draco not so much as opposites, but as very similar forces in Lucy's life. Both offer wisdom, but Wayne's wisdom comes with a greater price.

Antoinette, incidentally, is another example of someone who has made a lot of bad decisions in her life. Had Lucy encountered her 10 years earlier, their relationship might not have been so benign.

JB: And how about the two polar-opposite young men in her life? Dylan, the alluring, cool new boy at school, versus Mark, the big, athletic but sort of dopey guy whom she's known all her life—which one do you like? Is one of them actually you? Both of them?

PH: The two boys, Dylan and Mark, represent elements of a classic love triangle. Think Rhett, Ashley, and Scarlett from *Gone with the Wind*; or Rick, Victor, and Ilsa from *Casablanca*. Sexy Bad Boy, Noble-but-Boring Boy, and Headstrong Young Beauty.

Neither of the male characters is particularly me. I'm more like Lucy.

JB: One of the things that both Lucy in *Sweetblood* and Jason in *Godless* have in common is parents who think their child is destroying his or her life and so must be relieved of control and autonomy. Lucy loses her computer so that she can't get into the Transylvania Chat Room and is forced to visit an annoying psychiatrist, and Jason (after his cult following hold a midnight mass inside the town water tower) is grounded for life and forced to go to regular religious youth group/brainwashing sessions. Do you think most young people are constantly in jeopardy of their parents taking over, and is this good parenting or bad? Jason's father clearly misunderstands him and substitutes cliché conflicts and moral dilemmas for what's really going on—he doesn't seem to really be helping Jason grow up at all. Is he a typical parent?

PH: A parent's first instinct, always, is to protect. This works out great for everybody during a child's first few years, but when adolescence arrives, everything changes. The child must learn to take on more adult responsibilities, and the parent must learn to let go. This horrendously painful and exciting process usually takes about seven or eight years. Is Jason's father a typical parent? I can't say. But I do know that he is not alone.

I think that Jason's father takes a huge step in the end, when he empowers Jason to find his own answers. In that, at least, he is being as good a parent as he can be.

JB: It's clear that Jason, Henry, Magda and the others don't really believe that the town water tower is a god (the Ten-legged One) and that it's all just a way to entertain themselves, but Shin seems to take it seriously; in fact, he gets pretty weird about it. What is his problem? Does he reflect the mentality of some real kids?

PH: Yes, I think he does. Some teens are very good at taking things to extremes. There is something thrilling and liberating about giving oneself over, 100 percent, to a set of ideas, whether it be video games, goth philosophy, music, sports, religion, etc. Consider the extreme to which some teens take Islamic fundamentalism. *Kaboom!*

JB: Henry is definitely on his own program in life. He acts as he pleases and has an unusual array of interests and behaviors. He is easily feared and fascinating at the same time. How did you arrive at such a character?

PH: I know Henry well. He is modeled on several friends I had between the ages of 12 and 17, all of whom got me in a lot of trouble. Or perhaps I should say, they each helped me get myself in trouble. Thirty-five years later, I've lost track of most of them, but I know at least one is dead, one is a successful businessman, one is a novelist . . . wait a second. That one's me.

KAREN HESSE

Karen Hesse grew up in Baltimore, Maryland, and credits her fifth-grade teacher, Mrs. Datnoff, with starting her on the path to being an author through her support and encouragement. In addition to wanting to be a writer, as a child Karen wanted to be an actor, an archeologist, and an ambassador. She started college at Towson State University, but eloped with a young sailor named Randy Hesse and moved to Norfolk, Virginia, where Randy's ship was based, and waited out the Vietnam War. When Randy was discharged from the navy, the couple enrolled at the University of Maryland, and Karen graduated with a degree in English in 1975.

Karen's writing career would begin years later, after her daughters were born, with her first book, *Wish on a Unicorn* (1991), and continue through many young adult novels and picture books. Karen won one of young adult literature's biggest awards, the Newbery Medal, with her book *Out of the Dust*, the story of a young woman surviving the Great Depression and Dustbowl in Oklahoma in the 1930s, told in verse, and inspired in part by tragic events Karen read about in an old, small-town Kansas, Dustbowl-era newspaper. Karen and her husband live in Battleboro, Vermont.

BOOKS

- *The Music of Dolphins*: Although the premise of this book sounds farfetched, Hesse tells this story so well, readers find their disbelief suspended. When the U.S. Coast Guard discovers that rumors of a girl living with dolphins off the Florida coast is true, they "rescue" the young woman, who is totally unsocialized to human company, and hand her over to scientists studying human development by investigating (imprisoning) young people who have been separated from human contact for years. Told as journal entries from the protagonist Mila's point of view, the text grows more and more sophisticated as her language skills evolve. Grades 5–8

- *Out of the Dust* (Newbery Award winner): Fourteen-year-old Billie Jo narrates this story in free verse, as she and her family try to make a living on a farm in Dustbowl-era Oklahoma. A senseless accident results in the death of Billie Jo's mother and Billie Jo's own crippling injury. As she and her father persevere, a bittersweet victory is won. Grades 6–9

- *Letters From Rifka*: Suggested by events from the lives of Karen Hesse's own ancestors, this book tells how 12-year-old Rifka and her family flee persecution in 1919 Russia and attempt to reach America. Told in letters to her cousin, Rifka's story is moving and inspiring, as she survives typhoid fever, separation from her family, and quarantine at Ellis Island. Grades 6–9

- *Witness*: When the Klu Klux Klan takes root in a 1924 Vermont town, the citizens don't realize the danger posed by racial hatred until it is too late. Told in verse from 11 different voices, this book drives home the contrast between the beautiful Vermont countryside and the ugliness and violence brought by the Klan. Grades 7–9

S. E. HINTON

S. E. Hinton is a lifelong resident of Tulsa, Oklahoma. She burst onto the young literature scene and did a lot to shape it with her first novel, *The Outsiders*, written while she was still in high school. Like other women writing for male as well as female audiences, she chose not to publish under her full name (Susan Eloise) but to use her initials instead: "I figured that most boys would look at the book and think, 'What can a chick know about stuff like that?'" She credits her husband, David, whom she married in 1970, with helping her to conquer writer's block as she attempted her second novel, *That Was Then, This Is Now*, by helping her set a goal of writing two pages each day. Four of her books have been made into major motion pictures: *The Outsiders*, *Tex*, *Rumblefish*, and *That Was Then, This Is Now*.

S. E. Hinton has described herself as being "a very private person," who enjoys horseback riding and competing in dressage and jumping competitions.

After a 19-year rest from publishing, S. E. Hinton came out with *Hawkes Harbor* in 2004, a novel marketed to adults but one that would also appeal to older teens, although some aspects of language and sexual activity might be deemed inappropriate for younger readers.

BOOKS

♦ *The Outsiders*: After their parents are killed in a car accident, Ponyboy and his older brothers attempt to remain a family. As "greasers," wrong-side-of-the-tracks miscreants, they and their friends are at odds with the "socs," the youth from privileged, white-collar families. Ponyboy and his friend, Johnny, hide out in an abandoned church until children caught in a fire inspire them to heroism. Ponyboy's sensitivity and literary talent seem to be leading him toward a better life. Grades 7–9

♦ *That Was Then, This Is Now*: Mark and Byron have grown up together as best friends, but as they grow older, they find themselves growing apart. At age 16, Byron feels he has betrayed Mark when he turns him in to the police for selling drugs. Grades 7–10

♦ *Rumblefish*: Rusty-James wants to be as tough as his older brother, the legendary Motorcycle Boy. Rusty longs for the good old days when gangs were everything and street fighters ruled. The mood and setting of this book make it seem less real and more allegorical than Hinton's other books. Grades 6–8

♦ *Tex*: Fifteen-year-old Tex and his older brother, Mace, are pretty much on their own. Their rodeo rider father hasn't been home in months and the boys are running out of money. Things turn ugly and dangerous as they try to fend for themselves. Grades 7–10

VALERIE HOBBS

Valerie Hobbs moved from Scotch Plains, New Jersey, to Ojai, California, as a teen, not unlike the protagonist in Valerie's first book, *How Far Would You Have Gotten If I Hadn't Called You Back?*, who moves to fictitious Ojala, California, from New Jersey. Although the two sides of the country proved to be cultural opposites, Valerie "thought it was all thrilling at the time."

Valerie's book *Sonny's War*, which tells the story of a teenage girl whose brother returns from Vietnam, was not written solely from her imagination; in fact, her own brother returned from the war and she witnessed the protests that took place on college campuses, including the University of California at Santa Barbara (UCSB), where she was a student. Valerie earned her B.A. at UCSB before going to Kailua, Oahu, in Hawaii, to teach high school English. She returned to UCSB for graduate school. While working on her master's degree, she was a waitress at the John Dory restaurant, an experience that found its way into some of her novels, including *Letting Go of Bobby James, or How I Found My Self of Steam*.

Valerie worked for many years in the writing program at UCSB and is now Professor Emeritus there. She continues to write and visit schools.

BOOKS

+ *Sonny's War*: Fourteen-year-old Cory must cope with the fact that her brother is constantly in harm's way as a soldier in Vietnam. Meanwhile her favorite high school teacher protests the war both legally and illegally. Vietnam-era California is in chaos over the war, adding even more confusion to the angst of adolescence for the female protagonist. Grades 8–10

+ *Letting Go of Bobby James, or How I Found My Self of Steam*: Sixteen-year-old Jody Walker refuses to accept physical abuse from her new husband, the very same treatment she has watched her mother resign herself to. Jody starts a new life in Florida and finds a new, supportive community among the workers and patrons at Thelma's Open 24-Hour Café. Jody stands firm when pressures come to bear on her and those around her to accept a life of abuse and subjugation. Grades 8–10

+ *Carolina Crow Girl*: Eleven-year-old Carolina lives with her mother and sister in a modified school bus that they've driven from the East Coast to California. When they seek refuge on the estate of the wealthy Crouch family, Carolina meets Stefan Crouch, a boy her age confined to a wheelchair. Carolina rescues a wounded crow and nurses it back to health, but she must eventually it set free. Grades 6–9

+ *Tender*: When 15-year-old Liv's grandmother dies, she must go to live with her father, an abalone diver in California. Resentful of his prior abandonment, Liv comes to terms with her hurt when she assumes the role of his "tender," the person who handles his lifeline while he dives. Grades 8–10

- *Get It While It's Hot, or Not*: Four high school juniors, who once swore a lifetime allegiance to one another struggle to cope with the others' problems, including pregnancy and AIDS. Grades 8–10

- *Stefan's Story*: In this sequel to *Carolina Crow Girl*, Stefan Crouch goes to visit his friend Carolina when she moves north to Oregon logging country. Stefan, confined to a wheelchair, struggles with his feelings for Carolina, especially when she is drawn to a young motorcycle hoodlum. As a controversy stirs over proposed logging of old-growth forest, Stefan takes a stand that surprises everyone. Grades 6–9

A CONVERSATION WITH VALERIE HOBBS

Adapted from Blasingame, James. (2004). Interview with Valerie Hobbs. *Journal of Adolescent and Adult Literacy*, 48(2), 176–177.

JB: As *Letting Go of Bobby James, or How I Found My Self of Steam* opens (and after only three months of marriage), Jody's new husband, Bobby James, strikes her across the face, and she realizes that "we have reached some kind of place we can never go back from" [page 7]. Contrary to the advice her mother (a sad story in her own right) gives, and unmoved by Bobby's selfish attempt to coerce her into returning home to Texas toward the book's end, Jody chooses not to return to Purley, Texas, and not to return to her new husband. What is "the place" at which she arrived? Why did she make this choice? How does this decision square with all the romantic memories she has of Bobby when they were dating? Would many young women do the same? How is Jody different from women who remain in abusive relationships?

VH: I hope there are other Jodys out there, girls and women for whom one smack is enough. It took two for me as a young woman, even though I was one of those who scorned battered women, who couldn't understand why anybody with a shred of self-worth would stay in an abusive relationship. I literally saw stars—probably a priceless experience (knowing the place "we can never go back from")—but for a young woman it was frightening and belittling.

Knowing there is the "place we can never go back from" is what saves Jody. I suspect that all abused women know that place; abused children certainly do. The power has shifted absolutely into the hands of the powerful, and the threat, spoken or unspoken, is always there: you do what I want or else. And life becomes a prison. Jody's mother knows "that place," but she's refused to accept it. She's finally beaten down so far she can't even imagine another kind of life. The older I get the more I believe in an inner voice that always tells us the truth, whether we listen or not.

JB: What role do Thelma's 24-Hour Café and Grill and all its inhabitants play in Jody's life story? Is this in any way autobiographical?

VH: "Restaurant people"—not the part-time summer job waitresses, but the "lifers," those who go from restaurant to café to grill, cooking, serving, busing tables, doing the dishes—are a breed apart. Those I've met in all the years I was a part-timer had led such interesting, unusual lives. Many lived on the edge—of addiction, of homelessness, of sanity—but managed to hang on. Often they drew strength from the workplace, from those like themselves who understood that kind of life. They can be among the kindest, most charitable, most tolerant people you can ever know. My father was a lifer. He served or cooked in restaurants all over New Jersey before opening his own restaurant in Ojai, California, where I learned the trade.

JB: Even at the very end, Jody's mother is still attempting to entice Jody back to Texas and a life similar to her own. How did you want the reader to feel about Jody's mother?

VH: Sympathy, I hope. In a loving but unflattering comparison, Jody sees her mother in the same situation as a whipped dog, too beaten down to change her life, or even to know that she can. Jody doesn't tell her what happened in Perdido with Bobby James, so her mother assumes Jody is simply being a wayward wife. In her mother's moral system, such as it is, Jody is disobeying the rules of family and church.

JB: Jody's personal voice is quite distinctive. Her folksy articulation of some thoughts and feelings is often memorable in its wisdom and/or its beauty: "Out here it looks like the end of the world, like God ran clean out of ideas and closed up shop" [page 130]. How do you generate some of these wonderful expressions, like "God ran clean out of ideas and closed up shop"?

VH: I don't understand the creative process, I just do my best to keep up with it. Things pop into my head and I write them down. Cory in *Sonny's War* said something similar about the ocean going by her car window "like it was going on forever and you weren't." I suppose my unconscious has some pretty idiosyncratic ideas about the way the world works. In my loftier moments, I call these kinds of things gifts because that's what they feel like, unearned freebies.

JB: Effaline and Jody are the recipients of a little bit of good fortune in the middle of much misfortune. Is there enough good fortune in most lives to enable us to persevere in the face of adversity?

VH: I certainly believe in good fortune now, though I didn't when I was younger. That's one of Jody's strengths, being able to see the glass as half full when others would see it half empty. I think we tend to value other abilities and skills above the "simple" one of optimism, but that's the one that pulls us through the hard times. It took me too long to learn that. As a teenager I was an awful cynic and saw nothing but the dark side of things. Isn't cynicism just a poor cover-up for a lack of self-esteem? It seems so to me now.

JB: Authors choose incidentals in their novels that sometimes have meaning, subliminal or otherwise. For example, you chose the movie *Misery* (for which Kathy Bates won an Oscar as the love-you-to-death fan of an author played by James Caan) as the movie playing in the theater where Jody spent her nights when she was homeless. You also chose *The Great Gatsby*, a novel about attempting to create the life you really hope for, as the first book she reads in Jackson Beach. As the author, the inventor of Jody's reality, how much attention/intention did you give to background incidentals?

VH: I suppose because I was an English major for so long, and then an English teacher, my favorite novels will always be floating around in my subconscious. I don't plan for them to pop up. It may even be a bit of a stretch for Jody to "get" Gatsby, except that she too has big dreams. But I also love Jody's way of saying what's true, that *Misery* really is about a woman chopping a man's legs off. Forget the deeper meaning.

WILL HOBBS

Will Hobbs grew up in a military family and lived in or near some of the most beautiful and wild places in the world, especially in Alaska and California. After graduating from Stanford, Will moved to Durango, Colorado, where he and his wife, Jean, were teachers for many years before Will became a full-time writer. He and Jean live outside Durango and continue to hike through the San Juan Mountains and raft the rivers of southwestern Colorado.

Will does a lot more than speculate about the possible adventures his protagonists might have in the wild settings in which he places them; he experiences the adventures first (often accompanied by Jean) and then if a good story suggests itself, he writes it. This includes everything from sea kayaking among sea lions and killer whales in Alaska (which led to *Wild Man Island*) to cleaning thousands of pounds of fish as they came flopping over the side of a salmon trolling boat (which led to *Leaving Protection*).

Will Hobbs enjoys writing what he calls "adventure plus," by layering in some plot devices that explore the history of a place, often as part of a mystery that has lain unsolved for hundreds or even thousands of years. Will continues to travel, look for new adventures, and visit schools where he shares his stories and experiences with young readers.

BOOKS

♦ *Downriver*: At-risk youth abandon their Discovery Unlimited adult leader and head down through the Grand Canyon in rubber rafts unescorted and unapproved. These "Hoods in the Woods," as they call themselves, will learn about a lot of things, including the dangers they have let themselves in for. Grades 6–10

♦ *Bearstone*: Cloyd Atcitty, a 14-year-old at-risk youth, winds up under the supervision of an old rancher named Walter. As Cloyd comes to trust the old man, he also learns about bears in the wild and gains an understanding of his Ute heritage. Grades 6–10

♦ *Beardance*: In this sequel to *Bearstone*, Cloyd, still under Walter's care, tries to save the last living grizzly bears in Colorado. Grades 6–10

♦ *Leaving Protection*: Robbie Daniels lands a job on a top salmon boat with Captain Storm Petrel. Petrel knows a secret about Alaska's history, a secret so valuable that he might be willing to kill Robbie rather than share in the wealth it will bring. Grades 6–10

♦ *Wild Man Island*: When 14-year-old Andy Galloway disappears from the sea kayaking group he is touring the Alaskan ABC Islands with, it is only to place a tribute at the site of his father's accidental death. But when the weather shipwrecks Andy on a remote island, he unlocks the anthropological secret his father was investigating and meets an apparent "wild man." Everything is not what it at first seems. Grades 6–10

- *Jason's Gold*: Fifteen-year-old Jason Hawthorne meets a man named Jack London on the trail to the goldfields of the 1890s Klondike. Grades 6–10

- *Far North*: Sixteen-year-old Gabe Rogers and his roommate, Raymond, learn the ways of the Dene people in Canada's Northwest Territories in order to survive the winter after a plane crash. Grades 6–10

- *Ghost Canoe*: Fourteen-year-old Nathan MacAllister pursues a mystery that includes treasure and murder, with the help of the Makah whaling tribe in 1870s Washington state. Grades 6–10

- *Down the Yukon*: In this sequel to *Jason's Gold*, Jason and Jamie, his girlfriend, participate in a $20,000 race to Nome, Alaska, after their hometown, Dawson City, burns. Grades 6–10

- *The Big Wander*: Fourteen-year-old Clay Lancaster learns about wild horses and the Navajo nation as he searches for his lost uncle in the American Southwest. Grades 6–10

- *Crossing Wire*: Fifteen-year-old Victor must cross the border from Mexico into the United States to save his family. Grades 8–10

A CONVERSATION WITH WILL HOBBS

Adapted from Blasingame, James. (2003). Interview with Will Hobbs. *Journal of Adolescent and Adult Literacy, 46*(5), 444–445.

JB: Andy Galloway, the protagonist in your most recent work, *Wild Man Island*, is often in harm's way, from ocean currents, tides, storms, brown bears, wolves, sea lions, cave passages, the weather, you name it. Southeast Alaska's ABC islands, the novel's setting, seem to be both beautiful and dangerous.

WH: The beauty can take your breath away, and so can the 40-degree seawater. Admiralty Island, where the novel is mostly set, is one of the crown jewels of American wilderness. It's over a hundred miles long and very mountainous. Below timberline you're in the forest primeval. In some areas it rains upward of 13 feet a year, and it has the densest population of brown bears (coastal grizzlies) in the world—one per square mile. It's a setting I couldn't resist.

JB: In *Wild Man Island*, you have a kid from the desert country of western Colorado swim ashore onto Admiralty Island. He is certainly "up against it."

WH: Yes, he is—he even loses his boots as he kicks out of his kayak. He's in a whole lot of trouble, and he's going to make a lot of mistakes. Nothing's going to come easy. He's not going to be able to make a fire, for example. I think readers will find all of this very believable, and will identify. But in spite of his difficulties, Andy maintains his sense of humor, calling himself "shoeless and clueless," and gradually discovers his own inner strengths, which will see him through.

JB: During your own sea kayak trips through the ABC islands, did you and your wife, Jean, face any of the dangers that Andy faced? Any close calls?

WH: Our two kayak trips were close together, during the summer of 1998. The first was a six-day trip along the shores of Chichagof Island, with the humpback whales at Point Adolphus being the featured attraction. The second was a three-day trip on Admiralty Island that focused on the brown bears catching salmon at Pack Creek. On the last morning of our first trip we did have an experience that was something of a close call, though it was more exhilarating than scary. A storm was blowing in and our guides agonized over whether we should paddle several miles to the pick-up spot at a protected cove. Finally the guides decided that everyone in our small group was a strong enough paddler that we could go for it. The wind was blowing out onto the Icy Strait, which was all whitecaps. The danger of being swept away and capsizing in the open strait was very real.

JB: This sounds like the same situation that surprises Andy early in the novel.

WH: It's exactly the same; only he's on the coast of Baranof. We had to keep our kayak at an angle and paddle with everything we had. The swells were rising under us and threatening to roll us out to sea. It was spitting rain all the while, with humpback whales breaching repeatedly and seeming to keep us company the whole way.

JB: *Wild Man Island* is about a lot more than sea kayaking and survival. What got you going on the archeological mystery at the heart of this story?

WH: Several years went by after my sea kayaking trips with me not knowing if a story would grow out of those experiences or not. The kayaking, the natural history, and the place didn't seem like enough. I like to write stories that are "adventure plus." I could picture the adventure part, but the "plus" part was lacking. Then one day an article caught my eye about an alternate explanation of who the first Americans might have been. Fabulous new fossil discoveries were being made on Prince of Wales Island in southeast Alaska. It turns out a good portion of this island and others hadn't been under ice during the last ice age, as was previously thought. Animals living on ice-free islands in the northern Pacific could have provided a food source for seafaring people who came to North America by water, hugging the coastlines, *before* the land bridge opened up. I began to picture a kid shipwrecked in a kayak and winding up in a cave that might be hiding evidence of these earlier travelers.

JB: Admiralty Island Man, the ancient skeleton encrusted in gypsum crystals and calcite, is brilliant. How did you think of it?

WH: It grew out of a phone conversation with a U.S. Forest Service archeologist on Prince of Wales Island. The camps of those seafarers, he said, are now under 400 feet of seawater, but there's always the possibility that people climbed the mountains and left things in caves. "Like a burial?" I asked. "Possibly," he replied. That was my first glimmer of Andy's Admiralty Island Man. The photographic detail in my description—the gypsum crystals and the calcite encrusting the fossilized bone—came from my caving experiences and from cave books I had been collecting.

JB: You seem to be meticulous in researching the premises upon which your novels are based. *Far North*, *Ghost Canoe*, and *Jason's Gold* especially come to mind. How important do you believe accuracy is to a story?

WH: I believe that the reader's experience is much richer when I've done my homework. It's that texture of realistic detail that makes the story believable for a reader and all the more enjoyable. The research is great fun because I learn so much along the way. Kids almost always mention how much cool new stuff they learn from reading my books, and the content might account also for the adult appeal that my novels have been enjoying.

JB: Andy is an intriguing character. Where did he come from?

WH: Geographically, of course, he's from western Colorado, not too far from my own home in Durango. His emotional motivation, what made him want to take this Alaska trip, is his devotion to his father, who died there when Andy was about 5. Beyond that, he's a kid like many kids I've known, full of curiosity and determination. He's fascinated by archeology, paleontology, stuff like that. As a longtime teacher, and now as a writer who meets and hears from a lot of kids, I'm convinced that as they get older, they're still as curious and interested as they were when dinosaurs first captured their imaginations. They love to travel in the pages of a book to wild places they've never seen, to imagine being in the Klondike Gold Rush, or to try to solve mysteries like the first Americans. If the content doesn't get in the way of a fast-moving plot, of character and conflict and emotion, then learning something new as you turn the pages makes the reading all the more satisfying. That's the kind of kid Andy is, and I think there are a lot more like him out there, both boys and girls.

JB: Almost all your novels reflect your affinity with wild places. What do you find so appealing about them?

WH: I feel at home. Nature is where we came from, over hundreds of thousands of years. We've only stepped outside it the last couple of minutes, relatively. I've spent a lot of my life stepping back in, and find it incredibly stimulating and invigorating.

Sara Holbrook

Sara Holbrook grew up in the Detroit suburb of Berkley, Michigan, and graduated from Mount Union College in Alliance, Ohio. Sara was a writer for the National Council on Alcohol and Drug Abuse and also worked for a law firm before she turned to full-time poetry in 1993. Her two daughters, Katie and Kelly, were the first audience for her poetry, an audience that has grown to include the thousands of readers who enjoy her books and even those in attendance at the National Slam Poetry Contest. Most of Sara's poetry books are for middle school students, but the autobiographical verse in *Isn't She Ladylike?* is more appropriate for high school or adult readers, especially women, as is *Chicks Up Front*, the title poem of which is about a chance encounter between a young rebel and an older but unrecognized former rebel—herself.

Sara lives in Mentor, Ohio, and has led an Ohio slam poetry team to the national competition, where they placed in the top four. She also earned a top spot herself, as an independent poet. She is a tireless visitor to schools and is a favorite among the students because her delivery of her own poetry is lively, animated, and inspiring. In addition, she is gifted at eliciting the voices of young poets, as well.

Books

♦ *Isn't She Ladylike?*: In this autobiography Sara tells the humorous, sometimes poignant story of growing up. High school and adult

♦ *Chicks Up Front*: These poems are mostly about men and relationships. Cautionary verse for those venturing into new romantic relationships. High school and adult

♦ *The Dog Ate My Homework*: These are funny poems for the benefit of the not-so-serious student. Grades 4–7

♦ *Walking on the Boundaries of Change*: These poems were written specifically for middle school students in sympathy and support for the kinds of unexpected change the world can hand them, including friends who aren't loyal and emotions that can run amok. Grades 6–8

♦ *I Never Said I Wasn't Difficult*: These poems identify with the chaos of emotion and experience that go with early adolescence. Grades 4–8

A Conversation With Sara Holbrook

Adapted from Blasingame, James. (2002). Interview with Sara Holbrook. *Journal of Adolescent and Adult Literacy, 46*(4), 365–366.

JB: Your website, www.saraholbrook.com, has resources for students and teachers interested in reading and writing poetry, including a biography in which you say that you "like to write about two things, mostly—what you know and what you wonder about." Do you recommend these subjects to young poets? Why or why not? Do you have any other advice to aspiring poets?

SH: When I talk to primary-aged kids, I often tell them to lay their fingers alongside their noses and point them this way and that way, and tell them that's where they'll find their poems—right under their noses. It just depends where they point their noses—over here at a teacher, a turtle, a rhino, that chair. The trick is to only point their noses at one thing at a time.

   Kids, even at very tender ages, will want to write about big issues—love, war, the environment, or the seasons. The problem is it's tough to write an eight-line poem about nature, for example, but you might write about how you felt when you saw one dead deer laying beside the road. Poetry is very specific.

   So, yes, I write about what I know and what I wonder about . . . one thing at a time. Poetry is a snapshot; it is not a whole movie. When young people write poetry they are pointing their noses like a still camera, not a video camera.

JB: I just read *Wham! It's a Poetry Jam! Discovering Performance Poetry*, and I am wondering about the young poet who loves to write poetry and would like to share it but has a little trouble with shyness. Can you give any advice on conquering shyness?

SH: I think it helps to practice this poetry performance thing in stages. Stage one is *not* writing a tender poem about the death of your dog and standing up on stage and delivering it with feeling and emotion, making the entire audience weep with you. By the way, I read somewhere that speaking before an audience is the number one fear people have in common—and just to put that in perspective—death was number three.

   So, in order to build self-confidence, I suggest young poets try performing from their seats first (helps with the quivers), performing other people's poems (less risky), and even performing with a friend. When they begin performing their own work, young poets may want to test it out on one other person first. I have found that saying it aloud the first time exposes things I might want to change—both in the performance and in the writing. I also recommend practicing projecting the voice.

The idea that poets can jump immediately into performance poetry with no intermediate steps is a common misperception. The exercises in my book are in a very specific order so that the performer gains crucial skills in voice projection, movement, confidence, etc., before taking to the stage for a solo performance.

JB: In *Isn't She Ladylike?* you address the broad continuum of approaches and attitudes about teaching poetry, from the school administrator who wants to fill the school gym with kids and then march in a poet to the university poet/academic who thinks children should never experience poetry that rhymes. How do you think we should be approaching poetry with our students, especially the young ones (elementary and middle school age)?

SH: We are trying to sell kids on reading and writing, right? Let's think about this like a marketing plan. What is our marketing goal in exposing kids to literature (poetry included)?

I think our goal is to improve students' communication skills so that they will be able to express themselves and understand one another. Now, *some* of our students will take these skills and go on to create the great literature of their generation, but we are not just teaching *some* of the kids. *All* of them need good communication skills. And *none* of them can express themselves creatively in words if they don't have adequate language skills. So I say we start there.

I happen to think that we can teach kids good language lessons through poetry. It teaches us to focus on one thing at a time, to be descriptive (I saw what I saw and it looked like this), to be concise and precise. These are good language lessons.

Kids like patterns and rhyme. We know this. Read any picture book that has been in print for a long period of time (what is it, 50 years for *The Cat in the Hat*?) and at the base of it you will find pattern and rhyme. Pulitzer Prize winner Mary Oliver points out that free verse evolved out of rhyme—and our students are evolving. Our charge as educators is to support them on their paths to finding their own voices (see overall marketing goal), and if they are in a rhyming phase, then we need to find ways to teach them language skills within that context.

Kids know that poetry doesn't have to rhyme—a lot of them just like patterns and rhyme. They *like* it. I don't think we should dismiss that. We don't expect their journalistic writing to sound like it was taken from the editorial section of *The Wall Street Journal*. Why would we want their poems to all read like they were taken from an academic journal? For God's sake, we can barely get *adults* to read academic journals.

And while we are on that topic—in the adult realm, we seem to have accepted that "good" poetry is all in this single, sparse, unemotional voice, and by doing so we have narrowed our vision to such a skinny margin that most adults feel left on the outside. If we do this to kids—we'll never reach our goal (see marketing plan).

JB: Among others, one major theme seems to pop out in *Isn't She Ladylike?* That is "Take a chance, take a risk in life, and follow your heart." Is that your advice to the young and the not so young?

SH: Remember in my story about skinny-dipping, that little toe in the water—it's enough to take your breath away, isn't it? It does mine. The thing is, kids are more prone to taking risks than adults, but they come up short in the judgment department because they lack maturity. No one wants them to take risks on railroad tracks or wind up in solitary confinement. I think poetry helps them as they focus on what is real. Writing about consequences, for instance. We learn to be critical thinkers when we write poetry. To stop, look, and listen. And then do it again. To remember how something made us feel inside—an injustice, a blossoming, a success or loss. These are paths to maturity.

PAUL JANECZKO

aul Janeczko grew up in New Jersey, where as a young boy he hoped to "survive one more year of delivering newspapers without being mauled by Ike," a hideous dog that plagued him on his paper route. Paul taught high school English for 22 years before leaving teaching to travel from school to school as a visiting poet. In addition to composing his own poetry, he has edited numerous poetry anthologies with a variety of collection themes from love to cowboys. Paul lives in Hebron, Maine, with his wife and daughter.

BOOKS

♦ *Blushing: Expressions of Love in Poems and Letters*: Love poetry and letters from some of the best writers of all time, including Shakespeare and Maya Angelou. Grades 7–12

♦ *Seeing the Blue Between: Advice and Inspiration for Young Poets*: Thirty-two poems and advice from some of the best poets, from Nikki Grimes to Ralph Fletcher to Naomi Shihab Nye. Grades 7–12.

♦ *I Feel a Little Jumpy Around You: A Book of Her Poems and His Poems Collected in Pairs* (co-edited with Naomi Shibab Nye): This collection of poems in pairs has the male perspective and the female perspective on each topic. Grades 7–12

♦ *A Poke in the I: A Collection of Concrete Poems*: These poems are ripe with meaning, conveyed both in the words and in their visual representations. Grades 7–12

♦ *Poetry From A to Z: A Guide for Young Writers*: This book is filled with poems and information on writing poems in a variety of forms. Grades 6–9

♦ *Stardust Hotel*: The 15-year-old son of ex-hippies who now runs the Stardust Hotel writes in free verse about the residents, an assemblage of interesting and sometimes eccentric characters. Grades 7–10

♦ *Wherever Home Begins*: These poems are memories of places that were well known to the poet, beautiful or deteriorating, city or country. A great diversity of places with strong descriptions that evoke emotion. Grades 7–10

♦ *Looking for Your Name: A Collection of Contemporary Poems*: The title is a reference to the names on the Vietnam War Memorial. Some of these poems are from Vietnam vets, but the collection covers a range of topics, including gay and lesbian relationships, sports, family violence, and a letter to Ann Landers from Frankenstein's wife. Grades 8–11

ANGELA JOHNSON

Angela Johnson was born in Tuskegee, Alabama, but spent most of her life in Ohio, where she says her heart resides. She was permanently influenced by an elementary school teacher named Wilma Mitchell who read stories to the students over lunch at Maple Grove School. Angela knew as early as third grade, when her teacher read *Harriet the Spy* to the class, that she wanted to be a writer.

Angela has pointed out that as an angry, punk poetry writer in high school, she did not want to write poetry that people would like or understand. She attended Kent State University in Kent, Ohio, where she lives today. Before becoming a full-time writer, Angela worked with children through Volunteers in Service to America (VISTA), at a summer camp, and at a day care center.

BOOKS

♦   *Bird*: Thirteen-year-old Bird runs away from her Cleveland, Ohio, home and follows her stepfather to Alabama in an attempt to bring him home and back into the family. She hides near her stepfather's sister's farm and meets two other teens: Ethan, whose grip on life is tenuous because of health issues, and Jay, who just lost his brother. Grades 7–9

♦   *The First Part Last*: In this prequel to *Heaven*, Bobby and Nia become parents at age 16. When Nia falls into an irreversible coma, Bobby decides to keep their daughter, Feather, and raise her. Bobby's lifestyle of hanging out and tagging (painting graffiti), will need to change, but neither Bobby's middle-class parents nor Nia's upper-class ones provide Bobby with the kind of support he will need. At the book's end he decides to join his brother in Heaven, Ohio, which he believes will provide a better family environment for Feather. Grades 8–10

♦   *Heaven*: Fourteen-year-old Marley is shocked to find out that she is adopted and that her Uncle Jack (who sends her postcards from around the country as he travels) is actually her father. Marley baby-sits a little girl named Feather, whose single-parent father, Bobby, is an artist in this small town of Heaven, Ohio. Grades 8–10

♦   *Toning the Sweep*: Fourteen-year-old Emily, her mother, Diana, and Emily's grandmother, Ola, take turns telling the family story of the past and present. Emily and Ola are unhappy with the fact that Ola must leave her desert home and move nearer to family, who live in Cleveland, because she is dying of cancer. Emily learns that Ola escaped to the desert when her husband was the victim of a lynching. Grades 8–11

♦   *Looking for Red*: Thirteen-year-old Mike (Michaela) loses her older brother at sea and must deal with the ensuing grief. Grades 8–10

Cynthia Kadohata

Cynthia Kadohata loves tacos, and has a personal record of eating six in one setting. Cynthia was born in Chicago and also lived in Georgia and Arkansas as she was growing up (at one time she had a thick southern accent but not anymore). Her very first story, "The One-Legged Ducks," was about a planet populated by ducks with only one leg. The *Atlantic Monthly* rejected it, and Cynthia was officially a writer. In 2005 she would win the Newbery Medal for *Kira-Kira*, a story that was at least partially autobiographical, at least the taco part. Cynthia adopted her son, Sammy, from Kazakhstan in 2004. Her family also includes their Doberman pinscher, Shika Kojika.

Cynthia's father and his family were interned in the Japanese internment camp in Poston, Arizona, on the Colorado River Indian Reservation during World War II, which would become the setting for her novel *Weedflower*, the story of a young Japanese girl interned in the camp and her friendship with a young Mohave boy.

Books

♦ *Kira-Kira*: When the Takeshimas move to 1950s Georgia from the Midwest, their lives change considerably. The harsh conditions of work in a chicken processing plant do not prevent a warm and loving home life for Katie, the narrator, and her older sister and mentor, Lynn. Grades 6–9

♦ *Weedflower*: When Sumiko's family is interned in the Japanese interment camp on the Colorado River Indian Reservation during World War II, an unlikely friendship develops between Sumiko and a young Mohave boy. Grades 6–9

♦ *CRACKER! The Best Dog in Vietnam*: A touching story about a military canine during the Vietnam War. Grades 5–9

M. E. KERR

M. E. Kerr is a native of Auburn, New York, who grew up in a family that strongly valued reading. M. E. Kerr is Marijane Meaker's pseudonym, which she began to use in 1972. Marijane's irrepressible sense of humor resulted in a school suspension while she was at Stuart Hall, a boarding school for girls in Vermont; she decorated a dartboard with the pictures of faculty members from the yearbook and made the dartboard available to dormitory dwellers at Stuart Hall. Needless to say, the discovery of this dormitory pastime did not sit well with school authorities. Eventually, Marijane graduated from Stuart Hall, but "questionable recommendations" did not aid her attempts to enter college. She was eventually accepted to Vermont Junior College and attended the University of Missouri to finish a four-year degree in English.

In 1972, under the pen name of M. E. Kerr, Marijane published her first novel, *Dinky Hocker Shoots Smack*, and her career was off and running. M. E. Kerr broke ground in young adult literature as one of the first authors to write about subjects that were taboo in earlier years, even though they were very much present in the lives of many teens. One of these topics was AIDS, the subject of *Night Kites*, published in 1986.

BOOKS

◆ *Dinky Hocker Shoots Smack*: This book is not really about a heroin addict. Fifteen-year-old Tucker Woolf finds a lost kitten and posts an unusual ad seeking someone to adopt the cat. Enter Dinky (Susan) Hocker, an overweight and strong-willed teenage girl who paints graffiti ("Dinky Hocker Shoots Smack") for people to read as they leave the ceremony during which her mother receives a humanitarian award. Grades 7–10

◆ *Night Kites*: Seventeen-year-old Erick Rudd has more than he can easily deal with between a new relationship with Nicki and his brother Pete's revelation that he has AIDS. Grades 8–12

◆ *Fell*: John Fell, a working-class teen (son of a deceased police officer), accepts a suspicious offer to trade places with a wealthy family's son and meet certain goals at Gardner, an exclusive prep school. Fell agrees but the deal proves the old adage "If something seems too good to be true, it probably is." This book is an enjoyable mystery rather than an expose of the gritty problems of youth, as most of Kerr's books are. Grades 7–10

◆ *Fell Back*: In this sequel to *Fell*, John Fell must get to the bottom of a mysterious death that is not the suicide it first appears. Grades 7–10

◆ *Fell Down*: In this third in the John Fell mystery series, Fell must investigate the death of a friend. What could be spookier than ventriloquism as an added plot device? Grades 7–10

RON KOERTGE

Ron Koertge grew up in western Illinois where he learned to bale hay and do other kinds of farm work. Today Ron and his wife live in South Pasadena, California, where Ron taught for 37 years before devoting himself to full-time writing and other employments. Ron's ideas for characters and plot premises often come from his own life experience; for example, Ben and Colleen in *Stoner & Spaz* were inspired by a young man with whom Ron's wife was working at the time and a young woman whom Ron had in class. An avid racing fan, Ron also uses his familiarity with racetracks to create settings and plot devices in his novels such as *Margaux With an X*. In addition to young adult novels, Ron writes poetry for teens and adults that is admired for its irreverence, humor, and insight by some of the world's most distinguished poets, including U.S. Poet Laureate Billy Collins. Ron was a screenplay writer for a number of episodes of the original *NYPD Blue* television program.

BOOKS

- *Geography of the Forehead*: A collection of poems that poke intelligent fun at almost everything. Grades 10–12

- *Stoner & Spaz*: Ben is a witty young man with cerebral palsy. Colleen is a "stoner" who connects with him by chance one night at a movie. The two will explore the claim that opposites attract. Grades 8–10

- *Margaux With an X*: Margaux Wilcox is gorgeous and popular, and the hip and handsome are lined up to make their pitch to her. A childhood of neglect and abuse have made Margaux Wilcox unapproachable at the soul level until she meets Danny Riley, an unlikely prospect to win Margaux's affections. Danny is as unpretentious as he is kind, and his work at the animal shelter touches Margaux in a new way. Grades 8–10

- *The Brimstone Journals*: This book examines Branston High School (a.k.a. Brimstone) through free-verse poems from the perspective of 15 "Brimstone" seniors. Grades 9–12

- *Confess-O-Rama*: Tony doesn't realize who is listening when he uses an automated hotline to vent his frustrations with his life, his love, and his loss. Grades 7–9

- *Arizona Kid*: Sixteen-year-old Billy leaves Missouri to spend a summer with his gay uncle, Wes, working with racehorses in Tucson, Arizona. Koertge uses humor to deal with some of the serious issues of growing up. Grades 9–12

A Conversation With Ron Koertge

Adapted from Blasingame, James. (2006). Interview with Ron Koertge. *Journal of Adolescent and Adult Literacy, 49*(6), 526–527.

JB: The protagonist of your novel *Margaux With an* X, the movie-star-gorgeous Margaux, seems impossible to impress, yet she feels an attraction to Danny that she can't even explain. The most popular of young men (handsome, rich, confident) not only strike out with her, but also experience the brunt of her cynicism. Danny, on the other hand (whom she acknowledges is not at all good-looking, wears second-hand clothes, and is regarded by the socially elite as "somebody who lives under a bridge" [page 69]), works at the dog pound and seems to accept (even expect) second-class citizen status at school. What does she see in Danny?

RK: My guess is that Danny seems safe to her, and also since he seems to be immune to her charms, something she doesn't entirely understand, she finds him intriguing. It seems likely to me that she's thinking, "What do I not have that he wants?" He must strike her as the polar opposite of the other boys—that is, they're horny and solipsistic; he's diffident and other-centered. Also, he simply thinks about things (or maybe he just thinks!) that her usual pals don't. A short answer to your question might be this: she sees in him a whole other way of being.

JB: As a character, Danny is difficult to explain; he is both extremely logical and extremely unpredictable. He is gentle and calm (he even quotes poetry about trees) but he will fight or get violently emotional at the drop of a hat if he thinks injustice is present. Even in his standing up for what's right he is paradoxical; for example, he very calmly takes on Noah, one of the school elite, when Noah casts an offhand insult Margaux's way at the drive-in. Danny indicates he knows he will lose and accepts the bloody nose as if it were nothing. On the other hand, when an adopted dog is neglected, he goes psychotic and destroys the new owner's car and even turns verbally abusive to Margaux. How and/or where did you come up with such a complex character?

RK: Like a lot of my characters, Danny grew into what he is. I write about nine drafts of a book, and over time, characters step forward and assert themselves. It made sense to me, on a kind of tonal level, to have Danny be paradoxical. In the fight scene at the drive-in, he's just being the kid who, as he says, doesn't want to be known as somebody who chickened out. At the smashing the car scene, he's devolved into his father.

JB: Is Aunt Evie the antithesis of Margaux's father? And if so, does Margaux consciously know it?

RK: Evie is pretty much the opposite of both of Margaux's parents. She's thoughtful and well-read and rather warm-hearted (her pro bono work, for example). But she has also been motivated to be warm-hearted because of her spiritual dilemma—Why am I ill and what can I do about it? In the geometry of the book, Evie is to Margaux's parents as Danny is to other boys. But I needed to be careful and not make Evie a simple paragon of intellect and virtue. I like that she was muscled into virtue out of self-interest.

JB: Inside the tough, calloused shell of Margaux, is there a little girl hoping for a "they lived happily ever after" story? Is it necessary for Margaux to confront her father before she can "live happily ever after"?

RK: I think most of us need to confront our authority figures before we can move on and choose, at least, our unhappiness and not just inherit it. Nothing seems as wasteful to me as living by someone else's rules. I was careful to suggest that Margaux's life after the confrontation with her dad would likely be better but not to insist on it. I think if Margaux follows the examples of Danny and/or Evie, she'll see people who aren't necessarily happy but who are at least protean instead of mummified (another purchase/another wager) anthropoids that pass for her parents.

JB: You are good at creating odd pairs: Stoner and Spaz, Danny and Margaux, even Danny and his Aunt Evelyn. Yet, somehow the pairs work. Can you explain the chemistry of these pairs? What makes them work so well?

RK: I'm not the subtlest writer in the world, so I'm drawn to stark opposites. What I am good at, though, is writing dialogue, so as long as I have characters talking to each other and as long as I'm interested in what they're saying, I'm okay. A metaphor, to answer your question, would probably be the flint/steel one. I'm more likely to get fire banging flint against steel.

JB: There is a short section about Luc, the man at the dog pound who puts the dogs to sleep. Danny actually admires this man (although Luc is a petty thief around work). What is it about Luc or about Luc's job that affects Danny so greatly?

RK: I imagine Danny likes the paradox (there's that concept again) of someone who can mindfully put animals to death and also be a crook. The first part of that seems almost enlightened (doing a terrible job gracefully) while the stealing part seems furtive and petty. Danny wants to grow into the graceful part, and he's interested in how someone with that skill can also be ignoble. He probably wonders what the one has to do with the other.

JB: You are adept at capturing the nuances of life that older teenagers' experience. How did you come upon this ability? Did you work in schools or have teenage kids or spend time around older teenagers in some capacity?

RK: I never had children, but I did teach at a city college for 37 years. I liked to teach the remedial comp course, and once the students learned to trust me, they'd write amazing stories of their adventures and follies. The girl in *Stoner & Spaz* is like a lot of the tough cookies who sat in the back of the room, and lots of them swore in a rather lyrical way that lots of teachers find inappropriate but that struck me as so totally honest it was almost chaste.

JB: Do you have any advice for beginning fiction writers?

RK: Almost no young writer reads enough difficult stuff. I like to always be looking words up and feeling dazzled and puzzled by what I read.

GORDON KORMAN

Gordon Korman grew up in Canada prior to attending college in the United States. His first published novel was *This Can't Be Happening at MacDonald Hall*, a seventh-grade English class assignment that was accepted by Scholastic when Gordon was still in school; he thought that since he was going to send in the Scholastic paperback order, why not send in his book manuscript, too. Gordon's publishing career took off and has never slowed down. At 16, he won the Air Canada Award for the most promising young writer in Canada.

Gordon has published well over 60 books, including popular series like Dive and Everest. Some of his books are primarily humorous, such as *No More Dead Dogs*, but others are primarily adventure and very serious, such as the Dive series.

Gordon, his wife, Michelle, and their two children live in New York.

BOOKS

- *Son of the Mob*: Vince Luca is embarrassed that his father is a mafia kingpin, although his father is known for his honesty. Vince refuses to have any involvement in "the family business." He and Kendra Bightly fall in love, but when her father is an FBI agent placed in charge of surveillance over Vince's dad, the *Romeo and Juliet* parallels begin. The book treats organized crime with humor but does not make crime appealing. Grades 7–9

- *Jake Reinvented*: Jake Garrett is new at Fitzgerald High School, but his beer parties quickly become legendary. Who is this newcomer whose clothes are right out of a fashion magazine and whose past is a little cloudy? This is an intentional updating of The Great Gatsby set in a present-day high school and with parallels for each of Fitzgerald's original characters and plot events. Grades 8–11

- The Island series (Book One: *Shipwreck*; Book Two: *Survival*; Book Three: *Escape*): When six at-risk youth are placed in a character-building program to work aboard a ship, they hate it, but they hate it even more when the ship wrecks and they are forced to survive on their own. The kids witness a murder by drug smugglers and must hide or die, making survival that much harder. Grades 6–8.

- The Dive series (Book One: *The Discovery*; Book Two: *The Deep*; Book Three: *The Danger*): Misfit teenagers are scuba-diving team interns working for the Poseidon Oceanographic Institute. They come to suspect their individual boat's adult crew are not really scientists at all but treasure hunters who will stop at nothing to find a shipwreck containing a lost shipment of gold. Grades 6–8

* The Everest series: Book One: *The Contest*; Book Two: *The Climb*; Book Three: *The Summit*): After 19 teenagers compete for four spots on a climbing expedition to reach the summit of Mount Everest, the four winners make the dangerous climb to become the youngest (13 years old) in history to reach the top. Grades 6–8

A CONVERSATION WITH GORDON KORMAN

Adapted from Blasingame, James. (2004). Interview with Gordon Korman. *Journal of Adolescent and Adult Literacy, 47*(8), 704–705.

JB: You may very well be the most prolific writer on the planet. When did you begin writing, how did you break into the actual publication of your books, and how do you manage to continue writing so many high-quality books given your busy schedule now?

GK: My first book was a seventh-grade language arts assignment. My teacher, who was also the track and field coach, gave us more than four months to write—we were accountable only for a "chapter" each week. My project turned out to be *This Can't Be Happening at McDonald Hall*, my first novel.

My "big break" was fairly fluky. I was our class monitor for the Scholastic book orders (and keeper of the bonus points), so I sent my manuscript to the address on the Arrow forms. Scholastic Canada (I grew up outside Toronto) published the novel when I was in ninth grade. I still work with Scholastic today, 28 years later. They are the publishers of Dive and my other adventure series, as well as a lot of my backlist. My hardcover publisher is Hyperion. I've been quite lucky. Very few writers have the luxury of sticking with only two companies over nearly three decades.

Even with two publishers, the pace is sometimes pretty frenetic. I've been keeping ahead of my deadlines, but I'd be lying if I didn't confess to some close calls. My editors agree with me that quality is far more important than speed. And I'm learning to balance writing with my speaking obligations. I still enjoy doing school visits, and I feel it's important to keep in touch with readers.

JB: Which of your characters do you most identify with?

GK: I've had so many favorite characters over the years, but I'd have to say I personally identify most with Rick Paradis, the narrator of *Jake, Reinvented*. During the writing, I got so wrapped up thinking of that novel as an homage to *The Great Gatsby* that it never really occurred to me how much Rick's views on the pecking order of a high school are exactly my own.

JB: What kind of writing routine do you recommend to aspiring writers? Any other advice?

GK: I try not to become obsessed with routine. Over the course of my career, my work habits have been exactly as good as they needed to be for me to live up to my obligations at that time. Back when I used to publish only one book per year, those projects somehow managed to take that long (of course, I did tons of school visits in those days).

Lately, I've been learning to use time to maximum advantage. Better planning and more detailed outlines result in less wasted work. A lot of the research for my adventure series is pure reading, and that can be done on airplanes and in hotel rooms. I don't love writing while I travel; it's hard to feel inspired. But I can be pretty effective rewriting on the road. So, when I can, I try to tackle each task at a time best suited to doing that particular thing.

JB: The Dive series required not only highly technical knowledge (I suspect you may be a certified diver) but also required that the technical aspects of diving contribute to rather than detract from plot. Diving is very dangerous and the three Dive books communicate that fact so well that it's an important part of both the conflict and the mood. How did you learn all this, what did you want to accomplish, and how did you go about accomplishing it?

GK: Believe it or not, I'm not a certified diver. My diving know-how comes from a combination of very amateur snorkeling and research. (Add to that a fear of sharks that could only come from someone who was 11 years old when *Jaws* was published.)

I never did much research until I wrote Island, the first of my three adventure series. *Shipwreck*, the entire opening novel, took place on a boat, and I was a total landlubber. So I had to immerse myself in that world. It was murder—sailors have their own language for almost everything. But research turned out to be a skill that would get me through the Everest and Dive books.

Son of the Mob was the only one of my humorous books that required a lot of research. Ironically, I had to learn about organized crime in much the same way I learned about sailing, mountain climbing, and scuba diving.

JB: The four protagonists in the three books are all what might be called misfits. Bobby Kaczinski is a teenage hockey player from Canada who can't shake the memory of injuring an opposing player for life; Dante Lewis is an aspiring teenage photographer, who is totally and secretly color blind; Adriana Ballantyne is a wealthy socialite whose parents seem to ignore her; and Star Ling, whose physical disability disappears underwater, is the only skilled diver among the four. Why did you put this ragged group of youngsters together?

GK: One of the things that works well in the adventure series is taking a quirky ensemble cast and putting them into exciting and dangerous situations. The greater the extent to which these characters are "everykids," the more likely it will be that readers will "ride" the adventure right along with them.

In real life, a dive internship would undoubtedly go to highly trained, extraordinarily talented divers. But it's much more thrilling for readers to experience the scrapes and near misses through main characters with whom they can more easily identify.

JB: Some of your works are lighthearted, even when the subject is pretty serious, as in *Son of the Mob*, but in the three Dive books, human lives are at risk, not only from the dangers of deep-sea diving, but also from the murderous intentions of one or more antagonists. Was this new ground for you?

GK: Absolutely. In fact, no one had ever died in one of my books until the Island series. I was apprehensive at first, but I was changing my style in so many ways that I was almost starting over. So here was another thing I had to learn to do. It was probably easier than it would have been to inject a somber storyline into one of my humorous novels.

I think it's benefited my funny books as well. I used to try to knock my readers off their chairs in every paragraph, but I've learned that kids can be patient. They don't need constant payoffs to stay interested. I don't think I could have written *Son of the Mob* and especially *Jake, Reinvented* if the adventure series hadn't come first.

JB: In the Dive series, two stories are actually taking place: the story of our four teenage protagonists and their attempts to locate a sunken treasure in the present, and the story of 13-year-old Samuel Higgins in the year 1665, when he sailed on the privateer ship, the *Griffin*. What were you trying to accomplish with the two stories and how difficult was this to do?

GK: A lot of the research that I did for Dive concerned treasure hunting, and it occurred to me that searching for a sunken cargo has a lot of detective work built into it. Where is the wreck? What events caused this ship to sink? Why did it end up exactly where it is? It got even more complicated because, in Dive, what seems like one wreck is really two. Was there a way to make all that analyzing and deducing more interesting?

It just hit me—why not sprinkle the contemporary plotline of discovering the treasure with a second story of how the treasure got there in the first place, centuries ago. It's a great way to explain the underwater archeology. And it adds a compelling extra dimension to the series.

I thoroughly enjoyed writing the 1665 storyline. I'd always wanted to try historical fiction, and this was kind of "historical fiction lite." The trick was placing those scenes in the modern story so that they shed just enough light on what was going on in the hunt for the treasure—without giving too much away.

JB: How does an author go about creating a series versus just one novel?

GK: I'm not sure Dive counts as a true series, since it really is one larger novel broken into three parts. I'm working on an untitled series now about a brother and sister who become fugitives. And while there is an overarching storyline about their quest to prove that their parents are innocent of treason, each novel has to stand on its own. That's quite a bit different from the experience of my previous adventure trilogies.

I also can't deny that marketing is part of the decision. The Dive series could very well have worked as an individual hardcover novel. It came out as a trilogy because the people I work with at Scholastic are the paperback series people. They do an incredible job getting books into kids' hands. Over the course of Island, Everest, and Dive, more of my novels have reached more kids than at any other time in my career.

Ursula K. Le Guin

Ursula K. Le Guin has described her childhood as "happy," living in Berkeley, California, during the school year and Napa Valley during the summers, with her father, an anthropologist and professor, and her mother, an author. Ursula traveled east to study at Radcliffe College and Columbia University. She and her husband, Charles Le Guin, have lived in Portland, Oregon, since 1958 and are the parents of three children who now have children of their own.

After many years as a successful author, Ursula made her first attempt at a novel for young adults in 1967 with *A Wizard of Earthsea*. Written at the suggestion of an editor at Parnassus Press, she took only six weeks to complete the book, which was published in 1968 and won the Boston Globe–Horn Book Award. Ursula followed with *The Tombs of Atuan*, *The Farthest Shore*, and *Tehanu*, all set in the fantasy world of Earthsea, a place medieval in culture and technology but populated by dragons and wizards who perform magic, both black and white. Much later, she published *The Other Wind* (2001), a sequel to the other books, and *Tales From Earthsea* (2002), a book of short stories about how the Wizards School on the Island of Roke came to be. In addition to science fiction for young adults, many books for older audiences have come from the pen of Ursula K. Le Guin.

BOOKS

- *The Tombs of Atuan*: In this sequel to *A Wizard of Earthsea*, Ged, now a famous young wizard, will need the help of Tenar, a royal priestess, to escape the labyrinthine Tombs of Atuan, where she is imprisoned and where he has come to steal a magical ring. Grades 7–12

- *The Farthest Shore*: In this sequel to *The Tombs of Atuan*, Ged, now the Archmage (head sorcerer), and a young prince travel beyond the land of the living to bring the goodness of magic back to Earthsea. Grades 7–12

- *Tehanu*: Returning from his quest in *The Farthest Shore*, Ged must call upon the goodness of Tenar, the former priestess now living as a simple widowed farmer, to heal. Together they will help an abused little girl who will save the world. Grades 7–12

- *The Other Wind*: Dragon attacks and dreams of loved ones from the land of the dead foretell a disaster that only Alder, a sorcerer from the island of Ea, and Ged (the Archmage of Earthsea), can prevent. Grades 7–12

- *Tales From Earthsea*: This book is a prequel of short stories to the Earthsea series and is all about how the Wizards School on the Island of Roke came to be. Grades 7–12

ROBERT LIPSYTE

Robert Lipsyte was born into a household full of books in New York City. His parents both worked in education, his father as a principal and his mother as a teacher. Robert attended Columbia University, where he earned undergraduate and graduate degrees in journalism. His career in journalism began at *The New York Times* as a copy boy, followed by a notable career as a sports columnist renowned for his perspective on boxing, and especially for chronicling the career of Muhammad Ali. In fact, Ali may have been the inspiration for the first of a series of Robert's successful young adult novels about boxing, *The Contender*. In addition to young adult fiction, Robert has written many nonfiction works about famous sports figures.

BOOKS

- *The Contender*: Alfred Brooks, a high school dropout from Harlem, finds a way out at Donatelli's Gym through boxing. Eventually he learns that boxing is a means but not the end to a better life. Grades 7–9

- *Free to Be Muhammad Ali*: The biography of one of history's greatest heavyweight boxing champions and most charismatic personalities. Grades 7–10

- *One Fat Summer*: Bobby Marks, an obese 14-year-old from New York, spends his summer taking care of a large estate grounds and learns to stand up for himself. Grades 6–8

- *Michael Jordan: A Life Above the Rim*: This biography focuses not just on Michael Jordan's basketball career but also his commercial success and influence. Grades 6–10

- *The Brave*: Sonny Bear leaves the (fictitious) Moscondaga Reservation for New York where he meets Alfred Brooks (protagonist from *The Contender*) in New York, a boxer turned police officer. Sonny's harnessed anger makes him an excellent boxer. Grades 7–9

- *The Chemo Kid*: When his chemotherapy treatment gives him superpowers, Fred takes on the high school bullies and a company dumping toxic waste. Grades 6–8

- *The Chief*: In this sequel to *The Brave*, Sonny Bear becomes a world heavyweight contender as controversy arises over a proposed casino on the Moscondaga Reservation. Grades 7–9

- *Warrior Angel*: Sonny Bear's heavyweight career takes a detour until a teenager suffering from mental illness (the Warrior Angel) comes to help the young boxer. Grades 7–9

A Conversation With Robert Lipsyte

Adapted from Blasingame, James. (2004). Interview with Robert Lipsyte. *Journal of Adolescent and Adult Literacy, 47*(5), 428–429.

JB: You have noted that while adults may sometimes be offended by accurate, if uncomplimentary, portrayals of adult foibles, teenagers accept, perhaps even embrace, accurate portrayals of themselves and their peers with all their warts. What significance does this have for young adult literature and writers of YA lit? How has this influenced your own writing?

RL: I think it puts more pressure on us to be honest with the reader. I've always sensed an implicit trust among YA readers (probably younger kids, too, but I haven't written for that audience). Older readers are either skeptical or don't much care (just entertain me, scrivener) while teenagers are hungry for information about the world and themselves. They seem open. They talk about characters in a novel as if they knew them, too. It's very heady for a writer. So the characters and the stories have to be true, to make sense. I think you can go anywhere with this—sex, death, nuclear disaster, fantasy—that you can go with an adult book, but there has to be a kind of responsibility to logic and the language just because you are older and more experienced than your reader. You have the same responsibility as a teacher does.

JB: Why boxing? Although a relative few may find fame and fortune in boxing, it is not part of the everyday world of most people in the way that football, basketball, and baseball are. You have firsthand knowledge about many sports and have chosen to place *The Contender, The Brave, The Chief,* and now *Warrior Angel* in the ring. What is it about boxing that has caught your imagination?

RL: I was a bleeder, too [in prior correspondence the interviewer had informally shared information about his own unsuccessful boxing experience], and also never really got off slugging people. But boxing was the first sport I covered as a regular beat, and it was an old boxing manager who told me about the stairs in his gym that became the central metaphor for *The Contender.* I also prefer individual to team sports to write about, probably because of the writer's lame conceit that boxers—who go before the world half-naked and alone to be judged—are somehow soul mates. Oddly, I never really enjoyed the fights themselves as much I enjoyed covering the characters and the training camps, the sense of dedication, of craft, of hopeful spirit. Compared, for example, to the thugs who play baseball, boxers are really sensitive souls.

JB: You have written about Michael Jordan, Muhammad Ali, Joe Louis, Jim Thorpe, and Arnold Schwarzenegger. Does Sonny Bear somehow come out of those legendary personalities or is he a wholly new creation?

RL: Sonny is modeled more on the Native Americans I've known, but his story is certainly furnished by all those years covering the likes of Ali et al.

JB: In *Warrior Angel* you seem to deride the entourage that has formed around Sonny Bear, including Red Eagle, the phony medicine man; the action-movie star whose "Sayonara, snotface" signature line seems likely a comic poke at Arnold Schwarzenegger's "Hasta la vista, baby"; and especially Hubbard, the greedy promoter. From your professional experience, does this reflect the plight of many rags-to-riches champion boxers?

RL: Tyson is probably the best current example of a champ nibbled to death by his entourage. Ali had one, too. Now, more and more basketball and football players seem to have marrow-sucking posses. I understand that they need to insulate themselves from the world, and there's something noble about bringing your community along with you, but there's a reason champions go from rags to riches back to rags, and it's not just because they were dumb or wasteful.

JB: You have developed an intriguing and sympathetic character in Starkey and given the reader substantial insight into his psychological makeup. Do you think young readers are more likely to identify with Starkey rather than Sonny Bear?

RL: Readers are more Starkey than Sonny, I guess. It's a good question and I'm not sure I have an answer. From a distance, I wonder now if they aren't two parts of a whole who needed each other for completion. But I can't say I was actively thinking of that while I was writing.

JB: Do you have any advice of young writers or for young athletes?

RL: Same advice. For writers it's *Rewrite* and for athletes it's *Keep going.* I think most people quit and don't give themselves a chance to get better, to find the limits of their talent. It's amazing how much better you can get by practicing, by doing it over. Old men like me can grow muscles, just by numbing repetition. But that means missing parties and TV shows and hanging out. Same thing about piling up pages, then doing them over and over again. I guess it sounds boring, but the secret is that you have to love the process, the chopping wood, because there's no promise of a pay-off, the roaring fire. So, maybe before anyone takes my advice, young writer or athlete, be sure you love the process of creating stories or playing the sport. 'Cause if it isn't fun, it could be a terrible waste of time for writers or for young athletes.

LOIS LOWRY

Lois Lowry grew up in the household of an army dentist and lived all over the world. When she was a sophomore at Brown University, Lois married a U.S. naval officer and continued globe-hopping before landing in Maine, where she raised four children. Today Lois lives in Cambridge, Massachusetts, with respites in Maine in a Revolutionary War–era farmhouse.

Lois's son died in the cockpit of his fighter jet, an event that left Lois with a desire to work for peace. Her novel *The Giver* is one of the most widely ready of young adult novels and can be read at different levels of meaning by adolescents and adults.

BOOKS

♦ *The Giver* (Newbery Award winner): Jonas lives in a seemingly utopian, futuristic world in which all pain has been removed from human existence, and closely knit but totalitarian communities operate within very tightly controlled social parameters. Occupations are chosen for each individual according to ability, and families raise children who are not their own. When Jonas is chosen to take over as the Giver, the one member of the community who experiences emotion and pain and has memories of the past, he finds that the social order in his community is not all good. Grade 8 to adult

♦ *Gathering Blue*: This book is loosely a sequel to *The Giver*. Again, not-so-utopian futuristic societies leave little room for free will among citizens, and fates are determined by societal rules rather than personal preference. Grade 8 to adult

♦ *Messenger*: This sequel to *The Giver* and *Gathering Blue* presents characters from these earlier books as they discover the flaws in a utopian society in the future. Grade 8 to adult

♦ *Number the Stars*: Danes give a Jewish family sanctuary during the Nazi occupation. Very well-written historical fiction. Grades 8–12

♦ *Find a Stranger, Say Goodbye*: Natalie seeks her biological mother out of an irresistible urge to understand why she was abandoned as an infant. Grades 8–12

♦ *The Silent Boy*: In the early 1900s a doctor's daughter attempts to understand the behavior (and language) of a developmentally disabled boy. Grades 8–12

HARRY MAZER

Like his character Jack Raab in *The Last Mission* (1979), Harry Mazer went into the Army Air Corps at age 17 during World War II and became a gunner on a bomber. In real life, Harry's plane was shot down over Czechoslovakia and he parachuted to safety. Also like his protagonist, Harry was a Jewish kid from the Bronx whose mental images of war were not grounded in brutal reality. Harry is married to fellow author Norma Fox Mazer and has teamed up with his wife to co-write books, including *Heartbeat*, *The Solid Gold Kid*, and *Bright Days, Stupid Nights*. The Mazers have four children and live in New York state.

BOOKS

♦ *Snow Bound*: When Tony Laporte steals his mother's car, runs away, and picks up a teenage hitchhiker named Cindy Reichert, things seem pretty cool. But his attempt to show off his driving skills in front of Cindy result in a wrecked car. Stranded in the middle of nowhere in severe winter weather, with the likelihood of rescue seeming less and less likely, they will have to depend upon themselves to survive. Grades 7–9

♦ *A Boy at War: A Novel of Pearl Harbor*: Fourteen-year-old Adam has been forbidden by his father, an officer on the U.S.S. *Arizona*, to associate with Davi, a Japanese American. When Adam defies his father and goes fishing with Davi, they witness the Japanese attack on Pearl Harbor from the sea, including the sinking of his father's ship. Grades 8–12

♦ *A Boy No More*: In this sequel to *A Boy at War*, Adam and his family have moved to California after his father's death aboard the U.S.S. *Arizona* at Pearl Harbor. Adam's Japanese-American friend from Hawaii, Davi, asks Adam to locate Davi's father in an internment camp outside Fresno, California. Adam struggles with his conscience as he defies his mother, as well as his deceased father's wishes. Grades 8–12

♦ *The Last Mission*: Seventeen-year-old Jack Raab joins the Army Air Corps and becomes a gunner on a bomber. War turns out to be far from the glamorous adventure he'd envisioned. Grades 8–12

♦ *Twelve Shots: Outstanding Short Stories About Guns* (editor): Mazer edited this collection of short stories dealing with firearms. Includes stories by Chris Lynch, Nancy Werling, Richard Peck, Rita Williams-Garcia, Rob Thomas, Ron Koertge, and Walter Dean Myers. Grades 8–12

♦ *The Solid Gold Kid* (with Norma Fox Mazer): Extremely wealthy 16-year-old Derek Chapman and four unlucky bystanders are kidnapped for ransom. Grades 7–9

NORMA FOX MAZER

Norma Fox Mazer taught herself to read when she was 4 or 5, growing up in Glens Falls, New York, and she decided to become a writer at the age of 13. She attended both Antioch and Syracuse universities and met her husband, Harry Mazer, when she was 15. The two of them have teamed up to cowrite three books, *Heartbeat*, *The Solid Gold Kid*, and *Bright Days, Stupid Nights*. The Mazers have four children and live in Jamesville, New York.

BOOKS

◆ *Out of Control*: Valerie must come to terms with life after being sexually assaulted by three boys in the halls of her high school. Grades 8–12

◆ *Silver*: Sarabeth Silver has a hard time making friends at first when she changes to a school in an affluent neighborhood in her junior year of high school. She comes to win the friendship and respect of other girls, especially after helping a classmate who is living in a sexually abusive home. Grades 8–12

◆ *Heartbeat* (with Harry Mazer): A convoluted love story in which Amos loves Hilary, and Hilary loves Amos's best friend, Tod, who also loves Hilary. When Amos is dying, Hilary pretends to reciprocate his love. Grades 8–12

◆ *Babyface*: Fourteen-year-old Toni Chessmore finds out an alarming secret about her family when she goes to live with her 28-year-old sister after her father's heart attack. Grades 8–10

◆ *After the Rain*: In this Newbery Honor book, 15-year-old Rachel learns much about life from her disagreeable old grandfather as he approaches death. Grades 8–10

◆ *Good Night, Maman*: Karin and Marc flee from France during World War II and escape the Nazis' efforts to imprison and exterminate all Jews. Unfortunately, their mother (Maman) is too ill to make the trip and stays behind. Unbeknownst to Karin, Maman fails to survive, but from a refugee camp in Oswego, New York, Karin writes a series of letters to her mother about their new life in America. Norma Fox Mazer based the idea on the actual refugee camp at Oswego during the war. Grades 8–12

◆ *Missing Pieces*: Thirteen-year-old Jesse Wells searches for the father who left home one day and never came back. Grades 7–10

◆ *Crazy Fish*: Eleven-year-old Joyce is an outcast at school because she lives with her uncle, who runs the town dump. Mrs. Fish, a school custodian, becomes Joyce's only friend. Grades 7–9

A Conversation With Harry
and Norma Fox Mazer

Adapted from Goodson, Lori Atkins. (2003). A Sea of Stories: A Conversation with 2003 *ALAN* Award Winners, Norma Fox Mazer and Harry Mazer. *The ALAN Review, 31*(1), 48–49.

LAG: Many young people who have said, "I've never read a book I liked," changed their attitudes about reading when they read their first book by Norma Fox Mazer or Harry Mazer. Why do you think that is?

NFM: I don't know. I'm very glad about it, though. Actually, I think boys respond to Harry's books on one level because he's so in touch with the boy in himself and is able to put that out in a story. Okay, maybe the same can be said of the girl in me.

HM: I write because I'm excited about something, a feeling or an idea about things that I'm trying to express. I write about troubled characters trying to find their way in a world they barely know. I write survival stories. In my lexicon, what story is not a survival story? Those are the stories that, once they have engaged the reader, can't easily be put aside.

LAG: Your collective well of good stories never seems to go dry. How do you explain that?

NFM: Luck? Work? Genetics? All of the above?

HM: We live, all of us, in a sea of stories. Stories we're being told. Stories we tell ourselves. Every day—so many moving, touching, god-awful stories. Norma and I toss stories back and forth all the time, at the table, out on the street, in bed at night. Is this one for Norma? For me? For the two of us? We live in those stories. To live without stories, for us, is not to be alive.

LAG: Does censorship of YA lit continue to be a problem or is the situation improving?

NFM: Improving? I doubt it. Without being pessimistic, I think there will always be that core of people who long to press us all into their own small, confined world, and there will always be those of us who resist.

HM: The censors are always out there. I don't know that they will ever go away or even should. It's good to know that there are people who take books so seriously they want to burn them. Resisting censorship is part of the territory for all book lovers, be they publishers, writers, parents, teachers, or librarians. We need to stand our ground. There are more of us than there are of them.

LAG: You have written roughly 60 books separately and 3 or 4 together. How would you characterize the difference between writing together and writing separately?

NFM: When we're writing together, I can't get as lost in the created world as when I'm alone. The dreaming is done more efficiently, if that's not a completely impossible and oxymoronic idea. So that's a loss. But to balance it, there's the fun of working together, although when we were writing our first book together, we snapped and bickered and disagreed a whole lot, and I was exasperated enough at the end to tell at least half a dozen people, "I will never write a book with that man again!" Ten years later, when our second collaboration appeared, those half dozen remembered exactly what I'd said.

HM: Writing for me is a very mixed experience. I love the idea of the story. It's there, bubbling in my head. I love the voice of a character, but then language fails me. The words don't flow easily. I resist writing the words. Are they right? Are they good enough? Rub it out, erase. Start again. Language ensnares me. The words flow or they don't flow. I don't write enough. I write too much. I can't believe I'll ever get the whole thing down on paper. I get it done, but it's not easy.

    When I write with Norma, little of this happens. The process is different. We talk through the book, the characters, even some of the scenes. Then I write the draft and Norma revises it. The best part is when we sit down together to revise again. Sometimes, as it does when I'm working alone, the words are roiling around in my head, and Norma has to encourage me. A little slap on the back, an elbow, and the dam breaks, and I spit out the words, come what may, and she writes them down. The work gets done without the blocks, the hesitations and doubts. In a word, working alone is hell. Collaboration is a joy.

STEPHENIE MEYER

Stephenie Meyer grew up in Scottsdale, Arizona, and attended Brigham Young University in Provo, Utah. She and her husband, Christiaan, have known each other since they were 4, and, once again, reside in Arizona (Phoenix) with their three sons, Gabe, Seth, and Eli. Stephenie wrote her first novel, *Twilight*, while she was a full-time mom and could only write in the quiet times, like after the boys had gone to bed at night. She researched how a writer gets her first novel published and beat the odds by being successful. Her first book was so well received that she was offered contracts for two sequels and sold the movie rights before she had even written the other books.

BOOKS

♦ *Twilight*: When Bella's mother begins to date a professional baseball player, Bella decides to give her mom some space and move from Phoenix to Forks, Washington, to live with her dad for a year. A romantic relationship develops there between Bella and her lab partner, who also happens to be a vampire. But all vampires are not evil, and some are quite good, as Bella finds out. When an bloodthirsty vampire develops a taste for Bella, her newly adopted vampire family must protect her at all costs. Grades 8–10

♦ *New Moon*: In this sequel to *Twilight*, Bella finds that her relationship with Edward constantly puts her and Edward's family in jeopardy. Grades 8–10

A CONVERSATION WITH STEPHENIE MEYER

Adapted from Blasingame, James. (2006). Interview with Stephenie Meyer. *Journal of Adolescent and Adult Literacy* 49(7), 630–632.

Stephenie Meyer visited Arizona State University campus in Tempe, Arizona, on November 29, 2005, to speak to aspiring authors, English and education majors, veteran English teachers, and a few young readers. Questions and answers used here are taken from the transcript of that presentation. Stephenie also has a wonderful website at http://www.stepheniemeyer.com/:.

JB: You have really vaulted into stardom with your very first novel in a figurative wink of an eye. Are you getting used to seeing your name and book on the *New York Times* Best Seller list and having people ask you to appear all over the country?

SM: I am still very new to giving presentations, signing books, and touring as an author, although I like to visit young readers all over the country and talk about books and reading. I still feel mostly like a mom and just "Stephenie" most of the time. In June of

2003 I sat down to write and haven't stopped since, and now with my first book out, I am in the process of doing the editing work on my next two books. My schedule was already full, but now I have the touring and appearances in addition to everything I did before (which I still do).

JB: I see on your website that you are the devoted mother of three very active, healthy, and wonderful boys: Gabe (8), Seth (5), and Eli (3), which even by itself would be a full-time job demanding tons of energy and all your time. When are you able to sneak some writing into your daily schedule?

SM: Mostly after eight o'clock, after the boys are all tucked in. I do most of my writing at night, often at the sacrifice of sleep. I can do some writing during the day, depending on what the boys are doing, but mostly I wind up writing at night (which fits in well with the vampire theme!). Writing done during the day is more likely to be editing rather than the creative kind of effort—it's kind of hard to get into a story when every five seconds you have to get somebody juice or an apple, so anything accomplished during the day was usually rereading and revising. I do want to make one point about writing; even today, if I turned to any page in the story, I could probably find at least five words I would want to change, so actually, you never really finish; you just find a good place in the process to quit.

   While I was writing, no one except my big sister, Emily, knew that I was actually writing what would eventually turn into a book. She is still my biggest fan and loves everything I write. She read each chapter as I finished it, and she was the one who encouraged me to attempt to get the story published. She is my biggest cheerleader and I am very grateful to her.

JB: Where did your inspiration come from for *Twilight?* The characters and story are so wonderfully fleshed out with descriptive detail: Edward, Carlisle, Emmett, Rosalie, Alice, the whole Cullen clan, feel just as real as vampires can feel and all with the brooding angst of people who are always struggling with some invisible, inner battle. You have captured the traditional vampire essence and given it a very modern, very hip updating. Are you well versed in Ann Rice and other authors of vampire fiction? How about movies? Who is the best vampire ever: Gary Oldman, Frank Langella, or maybe Bella Lugosi or even the 1922 *Nosferatu* star Max Shreck?

SM: Actually, I am not really an expert on the subject of vampires. I haven't read many vampire novels—maybe one, but I don't remember its title, and I don't think I have ever seen a vampire movie. I have been asked in interviews, one for Amazon.com, for example, to name my favorite vampire book and favorite vampire movie, and I can't. Some people would like me to be more of a vampire-ophile than I really am for some reason; in fact, one interviewer wrote up the story of my visit saying that I was wearing all black, and nothing could have been farther from the truth (I had on burgundy and white). The goth thing is really not me.

Actually, the *Twilight* premise came to me in a dream. In my dream, the basics of which would become the meadow scene in chapter 13, I can see a young woman in the embrace of a very handsome young man, in a beautiful meadow surrounded by forest, and somehow I know that he is a vampire. In the dream there is a powerful attraction between the two. When I started to write this, I had no idea where it was going; I had no idea at all in the beginning that I was writing a book. I started writing out the scene from my dream and when I got done, I was so interested in the characters that I wanted to see what would happen to them next. And so, I just wrote and let whatever happened happen.

I actually wrote from chapter 13 to the end, and then I went back and wrote the beginning, now having a better idea of where I was going because I knew I had to match up the beginning and the ending. I didn't really know that I was writing a book until I was almost finished. I just started writing the story for fun, and so I was never intimidated by the immensity of writing a novel; I never felt like I had to get this done or had to get that done. I didn't even think I would let anyone else read it, let alone was I thinking that I would try to get it published—it was just for me, for fun, and I never felt any self-imposed pressure.

JB: How did you arrive at the decision of what to do next after writing the manuscript? How did you know or decide to market it as a certain genre and for a certain age group?

SM: Many people have said, including some of the ASU students here tonight, that they weren't typically big into vampire stories, but they got hooked on *Twilight* and couldn't put it down. I guess it's a vampire story that you don't have to be a vampire fanatic to enjoy. I had a hard time deciding what genre it was exactly, and also for what audience it was written—I really didn't have predetermined ideas about these things and I don't think it fits exclusively into only certain categories. I actually sent the manuscript out to agents of both adult fiction and young adult fiction. It just so happened that the first agent to invite me into a working agreement was an agent of young adult literature. I was writing it for my 29-year-old self, and I have a sort of fan club of 30-something friends who love the book, so I would say that it is probably appropriate for adults and teen readers but not too young.

JB: How do you create your characters so well? What techniques do you use to develop them?

SM: I spend a lot of time with my characters outside of the book—just letting them live outside the story. When I am in the car, for example, I am often listening to music with my characters in mind; so, for example, as I hear a song begin, I think "Ooooh, that's an Edward song, or that's a Jacob song. When I watch TV, now, I think of the actors I see in terms of what characters they could play in my books.

I'm really kind of obsessive about my characters; they are the essence of the book for me, and everything that happens springs from who they are. I kind of let them take over; in fact, I am currently writing a science fiction novel for adults and one of my characters started out as just a minor bad guy, but I have let him develop and now he's sort of taken over the whole story. My characters are kind of out of control, which I guess is why they work so well for the story, for the reader.

JB: Did you know Bella's name from the beginning, from the dream even?

SM: No, actually the two characters from the dream were just "he" and "she" for a long time. What happened was that each of my boys, Gabe, Seth, and Eli, would have been named Isabella if they had been girls. This would been my daughter's name, but I thought, since I'm never going to get to use it, I'll use it in the book. At first it didn't really fit for me, but it grew on me. With my other characters, I tend to go by the time period they were born in, and I go by census reports or similar documents from that time. For example, I got the name for Jasper from a roll call for the Texas army for the Confederacy during the Civil War.

JB: Did you research the Native American nations and stories that appear in the book?

SM: Yes, I did. I did quite a bit of research on the Quileutes, the nation that Jacob and Billy belong to. All of the legends in the books are actually part of their tradition, the werewolves, and so on. The only legend that is not a part of the Quileute tradition is the part I devised specifically to fit the Cullens.

JB: Although many of the characters are vampires, and although there is always the knowledge that the Cullens have killed people and that the thirst, although controlled, is always there with Edward in his most intimate moments with Bella—although all of these things are true, you still have managed to tell a very sweet and innocent love story. How is that possible?

SM: The core of the dream that I had was the sense of this innocent and unselfish love that is going on, but with the undercurrent of his natural desire to bite and kill her. I did try an experiment of rewriting the first chapter from the first-person perspective of Edward, and it was a lot more bloodthirsty coming from the vampire's point of view. I am thinking about putting that first chapter from Edward's perspective in the paperback version when it comes out.

JB: What can you tell us about the possibility of a *Twilight* movie?

SM: I can tell you that MTV Films/Paramount/Maverick Films bought the rights to it as a group. I know that they are on their second script revision, so they seem to be fairly serious about making it into a movie although only about 20 percent of books that studios buy the rights to actually make it to the screen. I have great hopes for *Twilight*, however, and I have certain actors who would be my first choices for certain roles, including Henry Cavill for Edward, Emily Browning for Bella, Charlie Hunnam for Carlisle, Rachel Leigh Cook for Alice, Graham Greene for Billy, Cillian Murphy for James, Daniel Cudmore for Emmett. I am also interested in the thoughts and suggestions of others, and so I have an e-mail address just for those suggestions: actorsuggestions@stepheniemeyer.com.

PAT MORA

Pat Mora grew up in El Paso, Texas, the city where her grandparents relocated during the Mexican Revolution. Pat holds a B.A. from Texas Western University and an M.A. from the University of Texas at El Paso. She has been a Distinguished Visiting Professor at the University of New Mexico, and the Kellog National Leadership Fellowship Award, a National Endowment for the Arts Award, the Southwest Book Award, and the Aztláan Literature Award.

Pat has great regard for teachers and schools and provides many resources for them, in addition to her own school visits. Among these resources are her website www.patmora.com, and its information about El Día de los Niños/El Día de los Libros (Children's Day/Book Day), a very special event in the Southwest in celebration of children, books, and reading.

Pat currently splits her year between Santa Fe, New Mexico, and Cincinnati, Ohio, so that she can visit her children.

BOOKS

* *My Own True Name: New and Selected Poems for Young Adults*: This collection of poems emphasizes family, connections between generations, and telling the stories of our culture. Grades 8–12

* *House of Houses*: Pat Mora tells the story of five generations of her family in this poetic memoir. Grades 8–12

* *Aunt Carmen's Book of Practical Saints*: Eighty-year-old Aunt Carmen voices wisdom on everything from men to religion. Told in verse, a wonderful tribute to womanhood and the story of generations of Mexican-American women. Grades 9–12

* *Borders*: Pat Mora explores the borders between people—social, cultural, political, as well as geographical. Grades 9–12

A CONVERSATION WITH PAT MORA

Adapted from Blasingame, James. (2002). Interview with Pat Mora. *Journal of Adolescent and Adult Literacy, 46*(2), 183.

JB: Your website has a wealth of resources for the classroom teacher, including lesson plans that connect literature to various disciplines, from science to cooking to geography and more. Are you a teacher at heart? A child at heart?

PM: From spending so much time visiting schools I have come to believe that all adults involved in the lives of young people serve as teachers and that our society would be much improved if we all recognized how important a role that is. In answer to the second part of that question, I think being a child at heart is helpful if not essential for writers of books for young people, so I probably am both a teacher and a child at heart.

JB: What role does or should literature play in a child's life, or anyone's life for that matter?

PM: Literature plays an important role in our lives in a number of ways, from providing sheer enjoyment of language to liberating and even challenging us. Literature comforts us and makes us feel less alone in the world, but it also should make us uncomfortable at times by asking us to confront parts of ourselves and others that we may have chosen to ignore. We also escape the ordinary through literature, allowing us to travel and dream in ways we otherwise could not.

JB: In the opening letter of *My Own True Name*, you address your readers as fellow writers and encourage them to "Listen to your inside self, your private voice," to respect their "thoughts and feelings and ideas" and to write about their lives (page 1). Do you believe all students can learn to write well enough to tell the stories of their lives?

PM: Absolutely! What concerns me is the number of young people who doubt that. It's quite a challenge for teachers and, I believe, relates to how teachers view their own creativity and identity as writers. Teachers need to see themselves as writers and help their students to think the same way. Middle and high school students are wrestling with this issue of identity every day, and deep self-doubt can cause them to swallow their own voices. Young people need to think about what it is that is unique about their families and themselves. America needs all our stories, without which we won't have this wonderful mosaic that America really is.

JB: The phrase "our family story" appears at different places in your poetry. What does this phrase mean?

PM: I became keenly interested in family stories when I was working on my family memoirs, *House of Houses*. Although I had written individual poems about an aunt or uncle previously, working on our family story increased my curiosity about the stories of other families. And by family, I mean this figuratively as well as literally. Being Mexican American, I come from a culture in which family is very important, and the metaphor of family is very important to me—our family in this country, our family on the planet.

JB: Your poetry embraces all of life, the sad and the joyful, the young and the old, the ugly and the beautiful, but never valuing one over the other. Can you discuss this?

PM: It pleases me for the reader to recognize that I am not writing so as to put more value on one aspect of life over another, such as grief or joy. I ask the reader to confront issues such as those of diversity and gender, and I hope to help him or her to savor all the facets of life. My next work, tentatively entitled *Adobe Odes*, is intended to accomplish just that.

JB: Teachers, librarians, and young people across the nation are celebrating April 30 as El Día de los Niños/El Día de los Libros (Children's Day/Book Day). Can you tell us about this celebration and where resources are available to schools, libraries, and communities that wish to join in the celebration?

PM: The celebration began in 1997 with teachers and librarians all around the country observing April 30 as a day to celebrate the treasures of children, books, and language. Booksellers, museums, schools, and public libraries will be engaging in special activities on this day. Some links to great sources of information are listed on my Web page at www.patmora.com/dia.htm. In addition, the Association for Library Services to Children has information and ideas for libraries and parents and has created a brochure about the celebration that can be obtained through their Web page at www.ala.org/alsc.

WALTER DEAN MYERS

Walter Dean Myers came from West Virginia to live with his foster parents, the Deans, in Harlem at the age of 3, when his mother died and his father was too poor to provide for him. Walter has credited the love he received from his foster parents as serving him throughout his life. Although he could read well, Walter suffered from a speech problem that made it difficult to communicate with students and teachers. A teacher suggested that Walter might be able to compensate for his speech difficulty through writing poems and stories of his own design, thus avoiding words he could not pronounce. Walter became a competent writer but the alienation caused by his speech difficulties continued and at age 15 he dropped out, returned, and dropped out again at 16.

When he was 17, Walter enlisted in the army. Upon leaving the army, Walter did unskilled labor before going to work for the U.S. Postal Service. He continued to write at night and made his first major breakthrough in 1969 with *Where Does the Day Go?* the winning entry in a contest sponsored by the Council on Interracial Books for Children. Since that time, Walter has made his living from his writing and related activities.

Walter explains that "[m]y ideas come largely from my own background. I write a lot about basketball, and I've played basketball for years and years. I was in the army and I wrote *Fallen Angels* [about soldiers in Vietnam]. I lived in Harlem, and I write about Harlem. I'm interested in history, so I write about historical characters in nonfiction."

Walter and his wife, Constance, live in New Jersey. Christopher, one of Walter's four children, is an illustrator and often works on books with his father.

BOOKS

- *Scorpions*: Jamal is torn between his conscience and his loyalty to friends as a member and leader of a gang. Grades 7–10

- *Bad Boy: A Memoir*: Walter Dean Myers writes about growing up in Harlem in the 1940s and 1950s. Grades 7–12

- *Slam!*: Seventeen-year-old Greg "Slam" Harris juggles basketball, academics, love, and life as a streetwise teen in Harlem attending Latimer Arts Magnet School. Grades 7–10

- *Monster*: Sixteen-year-old Steve Harmon is tried as an adult for a robbery shooting. The jury must determine if he was a willing participant or an innocent bystander. The story is told from Steve's perspective as if he is writing a screenplay. Grades 8–10

- *Fallen Angels*: Perry regularly faces death in Vietnam and questions why he and his fellow African-American soldiers get the most dangerous tasks and why the U.S. is in the war in the first place. Grades 8–12

- *Malcolm X: By Any Means Necessary*: This book chronicles the life of Malcolm X, from childhood to his assassination, and his impact on the civil rights movement. Grades 8–12

PHYLLIS REYNOLDS NAYLOR

Phyllis Reynolds Naylor grew up in the Midwest, where she was read to every night from old standbys like Grimm's Fairytales, *The Wind in the Willows*, *Alice in Wonderland*, the works of Mark Twain, and stories from the Bible. Phyllis remembers a teacher's attempts to teach reading with an easel and picture story, and how the connection between the writing on the pages and the story baffled Phyllis at first. The encouraging aspect of this experience was that Phyllis thought the object was to make up a story to go with the picture, at which she became quite adept, publishing her first work in a church magazine by age 16.

Phyllis is a prolific writer and reached her hundredth book mark with *Walker's Crossing* in 1999 and has not slowed down since. Phyllis modestly points out that she has also received 10,337 rejection slips, as well. Her topics for writing are diverse, as is the age range for which she writes—some books are for readers just on the cusp of adolescence and some for older teens. She often researches topics that have a basis in fact, such as *Blizzard's Wake*, which is about a teenager's experience during the blizzard of 1941 in North Dakota, and *Sang Spell*, a supernatural (purely fictitious) speculation on the mysterious Melungeon people of Appalachia.

Phyllis and husband, Rex, a speech pathologist, live in Bethesda, Maryland.

BOOKS

* *Shiloh* (Newbery Medal winner): When Marty Preston finds an abused beagle in the hills near his West Virginia home, he adopts it, knowing full well it has an owner. Marty will need to search his soul to make the right decision. Should he return Shiloh to his rightful owner, a low-life named Judd Travers, or continue to lie to his family? Grades 4–6

* *Shiloh Season*: In this sequel to *Shiloh*, Marty fears that Judd Travers will attempt to reclaim his dog when hunting season comes. Grades 4–6

* *Saving Shiloh*: In this final book in the Shiloh series, Marty Preston doubts that Judd Travers can ever change from the mean, abusive man the Preston family has experienced over the years. Grades 4–6

* *Sang Spell*: Hitchhiking from Massachusetts to Texas, Josh Vardy finds himself out of luck and in need of help deep in Appalachia. The community upon which he stumbles is the magical village of the Melungeons, a mysterious people whom few have actually seen and no one can explain. Josh will have to learn some important lessons before he is free to leave. Grades 7–10

* *The Fear Place*: Twelve-year-old Doug will have to face the narrow Rocky Mountain ledge that scares him so much (despite the taunts of his older brother, Gordon) when a family vacation turns ugly. Grades 4–7

GARTH NIX

Garth Nix grew up in Canberra, Australia, and graduated from the University of Canberra in 1986 with a degree in professional writing. Later he worked in various aspects of publishing, while simultaneously serving in the Australian Army Reserve. Garth says that he writes as if he, were the audience, and he tries to write a book that he would enjoy as an adult *and* as a 13-year-old. He now lives in Sydney, Australia, with his wife, Anna, and their son, Thomas Henry.

BOOKS

♦ *Sabriel*: In this fantasy that includes modern and medieval worlds, 18-year-old Sabriel must leave the modern world and return to the land of her birth, the Old Kingdom, to rescue her father, the Abhorsen (a reverse necromancer who sends resurrected beings back to the land of the dead). Sabriel learns about her past and her talents as she participates in this quest. Grades 7–10

♦ *Shade's Children*: In a world run by the Overlords, human children are harvested at age 14 (their Sad birthday) so that their body parts can be used to create Frankenstein-like warriors. Shade, something of a Frankenstein himself, commands escaped children from an abandoned submarine. Gold-Eye and other children unite against the Overlords and discover Shade's secrets. Grades 7–10

♦ *Mister Monday*: In this first in a series of seven books, nerdish seventh grader Arthur Penhaligon is saved from a nearly fatal asthma attack by a strangely shaped key provided by an even stranger man, Mister Monday. The key is somehow central to saving the world from a horrible plague, and Arthur is quickly engaged in the quest against various and frightening creatures. Grades 7–10

♦ *Grim Tuesday*: Arthur Penhaligon is back to save the world again, this time from the sinister plot of a character named Grim Tuesday and his otherworldly henchmen. Grades 7–10

♦ *Drowned Wednesday*: Once again, Arthur Penhaligon must battle a supernatural nemesis and save his family and the world, this time a gluttonous female named Drowned Wednesday. Grades 7–10

♦ *The Fall* (The Seventh Tower, Book 1): In a world without sunlight, 13-year-old Tal, resident of the gigantic Castle of Seven Towers, must steal a Sunstone to avert disaster for his family. Grades 7–10

♦ *The Violet Keystone* (The Seventh Tower, Book 6): In this finale to the series, Milla leads the attack to conquer the Castle and Tal faces the Hall of Nightmares. Grades 7–10

Joan Lowery Nixon

Joan Lowery Nixon grew up in Texas and California. She had her first publication at age 10 with a poem in a children's magazine and sold her first article to a magazine at age 17. But in fact, she is reported to have begun authoring at age 2, when she sometimes would tell her mother, "Write this down. I have a poem."

Joan majored in journalism at the University of Southern California, which may have helped her with screening details for inclusion in her stories. Her first novel manuscript, *The Mystery of Hurricane Castle*, was rejected 12 times before being accepted for publication by the thirteenth publisher. That book came out in 1964, and by 1994 Joan had published more than 100 books. Her mysteries are especially popular, and she is the only writer ever to have won four Edgar Allan Poe Awards from the Mystery Writers of America.

BOOKS

♦ *A Family Apart*: This is the first of four books in the Orphan Train series, in which the six children in the Kelly family are sent west by their widowed mother in New York City as passengers on the orphan train, a very real part of American history. Orphan trains took hundreds of thousands of children from the overpopulated and impoverished metropolitan Northeast to the Midwest (then called the West). Along the way, as the train made stops, the orphans were lined up and selected by families for adoption. In this first book, Mary Frances Kelly, 13, and her five siblings head for Missouri and new families in 1860. Grades 5–8

♦ *The Other Side of Dark:* When 17-year-old Stacy awakes from a four-year coma, many things have changed, from hairstyles to her own appearance. The victim of a wound and witness to her mother's murder, Stacy knows that somewhere her attacker, her mother's murderer, is watching and waiting to silence her. Grades 7–10

♦ *Don't Scream*: High school junior Jessica is intrigued by the two new boys, Mark and Scott, who move to her small hometown. When scary things begin to happen, Jessica suspects that something is not right about these two. Grades 7–9

♦ *Whispers from the Dead*: A near-death experience leaves 16-year-old Sarah apparently capable of communicating with the dead. A family move and a new home only aggravate Sarah's situation when she detects a murder that occurred there. Grades 7–9

♦ *Murdered, My Sweet*: Fifteen-year-old Jenny Jakes and her famous mystery-writing mother are drawn into murder investigations when the reading of a rich cousin's living will seems to lead to a rash of deaths. Grades 6–8

NAOMI SHIHAB NYE

Naomi Shihab Nye was born in St. Louis, Missouri, to an American mother and Palestinian father. When she was 4 her family moved to Jerusalem for one year before moving on to San Antonio, Texas, where she still lives today. Naomi began writing at age 6, and her genre of choice from the beginning was poetry. As a teen she had her work published in *Seventeen* and continued to submit and publish in other magazines as a college student at Trinity University in San Antonio, Texas, where she earned her B.A.

In an interview on the PBS program *Now with Bill Moyers*, Naomi credited her deceased Palestinian grandmother, Khadra Shihab, who lived to the age of 106, with inspiring her to write poetry for peace and understanding, especially after the attack on the twin towers in New York on September 11, 2001. Naomi not only writes poetry from an Arab-American point of view, but has also written children's books.

BOOKS

◆ *19 Varieties of Gazelle: Poems of the Middle East*: This book contains 60 poems about life in the Middle East and life from an Arab-American perspective, including an introduction and opening poem about the September 11 attack on the World Trade Center. Grades 6–12

◆ *The Space Between Our Footsteps: Poems and Paintings From the Middle East and North Africa*: More than 100 poets and painters from 19 countries contributed to this anthology, compiled by Naomi Shihab Nye. Grades 6–12

◆ *Words Under the Words*: A collection of Naomi's poetry about the Middle East, the American Southwest, Central America, and Asia. Grades 6–12

◆ *Fuel*: Collected poems about topics from her life, from Texas to Jerusalem. Grades 6–12

◆ *Habibi*: Fourteen-year-old Liyana Abboud and her family move from St. Louis to her father's childhood homeland in the Middle East. The reality of life in this conflict-torn part of the world is driven home as they face prejudice and the testing of their own values. Fiction inspired by the author's own experiences. Grades 6–12

◆ *What Have You Lost?*: Nye's collection of over 100 poems by talented poets—with photographs by her husband—deal with the losses of life, from the tangible to the intangible. Grades 7–12

◆ *Never in a Hurry: Essays on People and Places*: Autobiographical pieces on people and places the author has encountered. Grades 7–12

LINDA SUE PARK

Linda Sue Park, winner of the 2002 Newbery Medal for *A Single Shard*, grew up in Illinois, the daughter of Korean immigrants. Linda published her first work, a haiku poem, when she was 9 years old, in *Trailblazer,* a children's magazine, for the payment of one dollar. Linda Sue continued to write and publish works in magazines for young people before she went off to college at Stanford University. She was a gymnast at Stanford and graduated with a degree in English. In addition, Linda Sue has degrees from Trinity College in Dublin, Ireland, and from the University of London. After living for a time in Ireland, in 1990 she and her husband and their two children moved back to the United States. They now make their home in Rochester, New York.

BOOKS

- *A Single Shard* (Newbery Medal winner): In twelfth-century Korea, an orphan (Tree Ear) is apprenticed into the pottery trade. When he is sent on a journey to present the king with a special pot, Tree Ear must cope with tragedy and danger. Grades 7–10

- *The Kite Fighters*: In fifteenth-century Korea, two brothers, Kee-sup and Young-sup, prepare for the annual New Year kite-fighting event. Tradition holds that Young-sup must help his older brother to win, but the brothers have two different sets of talents: one is the master kite craftsman and the other has skill in flying the kite. Grades 7–10

- *When My Name Was Keoko*: When Japan captures Korea during World War II, Koreans are forced to abandon their own customs and assimilate into Japanese culture, including taking Japanese names. Ten-year-old Sun-hee and 13-year-old Tae-yul must find their way in the new order. For Tae-yul, this means enlisting in the Japanese army to protect the family. Grades 8–10

A CONVERSATION WITH LINDA SUE PARK

Adapted from Blasingame, James. (2002). Interview with Linda Sue Park. *Journal of Adolescent and Adult Literacy, 46*(3), 269.

JB: Your character development is masterful. Jade Blossom, Sun-hee (Keoko), Tae-yul, Young-sup, and Tree Ear are fascinating protagonists from times and places long ago and far away. How do you go about developing a character?

LSP: I do a lot of research before I start to write, and much of what I read evinces the considerable differences between daily life in old Korea and in the U.S. today. When I sit down to write, I feel pretty confident about my research, so in the writing itself I concentrate on the characters—on how they might feel when faced with certain problems and, more importantly, how they might act in response.

For example, Young-sup in *The Kite Fighters* is required by the conventions of his society to treat his older brother with a great deal more respect than you would see in most American families today. But wouldn't he have experienced the same feelings of envy and competitiveness and love that younger brothers today feel?

That's one of the things I love about historical fiction: it's a wonderful opportunity to explore what it means to be human. I guess you could say that if my research into the setting and plot point up the differences between people then and now, in my character development I try to examine the similarities.

JB: Can you give any advice to young writers and/or teachers of writing?

LSP: Read! Reading a lot is the key to improving your writing. Read for fun—for entertainment, for pleasure, to lose yourself in a good story. And if you read enough, you absorb important ideas on both the story level and the sentence level. Things like how to keep a story moving, and what makes a wonderful sentence. I don't know *any* good writers who aren't also ferocious readers.

For both young writers and writing teachers, I would say that in addition to assignments that target particular writing skills, it is important to be able to write without "fear of reprisal." By this I mean having or providing the opportunity to write wild stories or heartfelt poems or anything a person wants to write, without worrying about a controlled response, without being graded or having grammar and spelling corrected and so on. Simply to write for the joy of it. I think writers need to find a balance between expressing themselves freely and fine-tuning that expression for communication with others.

JB: You have a beautiful website at www.lindasuepark.com that has considerable resources and interesting links for young people, teachers, and writers of any age. How important is the Internet to you as a source of information?

LSP: Writing is a lonely job. You spend a lot of time with just yourself and your thoughts. Being able to communicate with other writers and with people interested in books through the Internet is such a gift. I've made very good friends through the Internet. And I've been able to get in touch with knowledgeable experts who have helped me with my research.

That's the most important aspect of the Internet for me—contact with others. So I enjoy having a website; I hope readers are getting to know me and my work a little better because of it. As far as actual research goes, I still tend to rely more on printed materials—books and journals—but the Internet is a great place to find out where to start.

JB: How important are stories in your family?

LSP: In one sense, my parents are not storytellers. I did not learn about old Korea from them, nor did they tell many stories about their childhood until I started asking them (while I was working on *When My Name Was Keoko*). We lived far away from most of the extended family, so there weren't grandparents or aunts or uncles around telling stories, either. But my family does love to talk! We're a pretty gabby bunch. We love to cook and eat, too, so when we get together, there's always a lot of eating and talking going on. We talk about funny things that happen to us, or sad things, or things that make us think. So the idea of sharing has always been important in my family. I think my writing is a natural extension of that.

I get interested in something, and I write about it to share it with others. I've been so fortunate that through my books, and because of the Newbery Award, I now get to share with so many more people!

KATHERINE PATERSON

Katherine Paterson was born in Qing Jang, Jiangsu, China, the daughter of Christian missionaries working in China. Her family had moved 18 times by the time Katherine was 18 years old. Just before the start of World War II, the Patersons moved to the U.S., where Katherine attended King College, in Bristol, Tennessee, and graduated with a degree in English. Katherine taught sixth grade for a year in Lovettsville, Virginia, an experience that inspired her Newbery Medal–winning book, *Bridge to Terabithia*.

Katherine studied to be a missionary and served in Japan for four years before returning to the United States to go to graduate school, where she met and married a Presbyterian minister named John Paterson. After Katherine and her husband had adopted two children and had two of their own, a friend started Katherine in a creative writing class, in which she wrote her first published novel.

BOOKS

+ *Bridge to Terabithia* (Newbery Medal winner): Jesse befriends the only fifth grader in his rural Virginia school who can beat him in a footrace, a new girl named Leslie who steals his crown as the fastest runner. They form a grand partnership and share a fantasy about a place in the woods they call Terabithia, a fantasy world only accessible through their imaginations. When Leslie drowns, Jesse must deal with his feelings. Grades 6–8

+ *Jacob Have I Loved* (Newbery Medal winner): Louise resents how people in her small Chesapeake Bay town view her twin sister, Carol, as the pretty one, the smart one, the good one, the lovable one (her grandmother taunts her with the biblical phrase about twins, "Jacob have I loved, but Esau have I hated"). When World War II comes along, Louise takes a man's role as a crabber in the bay. Eventually, Louise finds herself, her value, and her own way in the world. Grades 8–10

+ *The Master Puppeteer*: In this historical fiction novel, a mystery surrounds a Robin Hood–like figure in feudal Japan. Meanwhile, 13-year-old Jiro is apprenticed to Yoshida, the harsh puppet master, but things are not exactly as they seem. Grades 6–8

+ *The Sign of the Chrysanthemum*: In twelfth-century Japan, 13-year-old Muna searches for his father when his mother dies. The only way he will know his samurai father is by his tattoo of a chrysanthemum. Grades 6–8

GARY PAULSEN

Gary Paulsen, one of the most popular authors of literature for young adults, is a big-hearted man with a rough-and-tumble past who found and developed a talent for writing stories of all kinds, although he is best known for his outdoor adventure stories. He claims Thief River Falls, Minnesota, as home—the place where his family settled after his father retired from the military. All memories of Thief River Falls are not pleasant, however; Gary's parents were alcoholics, and he was often left to fend for himself or else lived with relatives in the country in northwestern Minnesota. Gary credits a tough but kindhearted cop named Nuts Meyers with turning his life down the right path, as well as a librarian who gave him his first library card.

A year at Bemidji State University in Minnesota, a hitch in the army, a job in aerospace that proved dreadfully boring, and a turn at magazine editing comprised Gary's career history before he turned to writing his own material. His writing is filled with accurate details from his own adventures, such as racing a dogsled (more than once) in the fabled annual Iditarod race from Anchorage to Nome, Alaska, or sailing alone around Cape Horn. He is married to Ruth Wright Paulsen, an artist who has illustrated several of his books.

BOOKS

- *Hatchet*: One of the most often read books, by choice or requirement, in middle schools. Brian Robeson, at 13 years of age, is stranded in the Canadian wilderness, far from any hope of rescue. He has only a hatchet as a means for providing for his every need. Brian will need ingenuity and courage just to survive. Grades 5–9

- *The River*: Now 15 years of age, Brian Robeson is asked by a psychiatrist to provide data for a government publication about successful survival by going back into the Canadian wilderness he somehow survived two years earlier. Of course, complications arise, making the term *survival* perfectly accurate. Grades 5–9

- *My Life in Dog Years*: Autobiographical. The author tells the stories of the dogs that have been important in his life, including Cookie, a lead sled dog who saved Paulsen's life. Grades 5–10

- *Puppies, Dogs, and Blue Northers*: Autobiographical. The author tells the stories of sled dogs and pets he has loved over the years. Grades 5–10

- *Dogsong*: Fourteen-year-old Russel Susskit leaves his Eskimo village and takes a 1,400-mile dogsled trip to find his "song." Grades 5–10

- *Nightjohn*: Twelve-year-old slave girl Sarny continually risks punishment simply by learning the alphabet. Nightjohn, an escaped slave who returns to captivity to teach slaves to read, faces a punishment far worse. Grades 7–10

- *How Angel Peterson Got His Name*: Growing up in Thief River Falls, Minnesota, Gary and pals found excitement in everything from a quick trip to the army surplus store and then a run at the land speed record, to wrestling bears to going over the waterfall in a barrel. Autobiographical. Grades 8–12

- *The Amazing Life of Birds: The Twenty Day Puberty Journal of Duane Homer Leech.* Duane keeps a record of his thoughts and feelings as he makes a quick jump from childhood to adulthood. Humor and pathos. Grades 8–10

A CONVERSATION WITH GARY PAULSEN

Adapted from Blasingame, James. (2004). Interview with Gary Paulsen. *The Journal of Adolescent and Adult Literacy*, 48(9), 270–271.

JB: For those readers who don't live in the country, would you explain what an electric fence is, and if possible, explain why in the world adolescent boys would be compelled to pee on one. As far as you know, do they still do this?

GP: Electric fences exist, officially, to keep livestock penned in. They are a single wire charged with a high-voltage, pulsing electricity. They've got enough juice to all but obliterate anything organic that touches them. They were called weed burners when I was a boy and they'll put a several-hundred-pound sow on her back if she brushes against it. In reality, electric fences are magnets for young (and not so young, if you didn't get it out of your system in childhood) boys. I wrote about peeing on an electric fence some ten years ago and, since then, countless men have come up to me and sheepishly admitted attempting this experiment. I do not claim to understand this strange pull. Some men climb Everest. Others pee on electric fences.

JB: What can you identify today in terms of modern-day descendants of the "extreme sports" you and your friends first invented back in Thief River Falls, Minnesota, with the help of the army surplus store. What do you suppose the cost/price tag difference is? Was this reckless behavior or just normal adventure seeking?

GP: I can't really see much difference, to be honest, between jumping off a water tower, as we did when we were boys, and base jumping now. Well, I guess the colorful apparel, the television coverage, the endorsement deals, and oh, yes, the lawsuits. We were much less litigious back then. Of course we didn't wear helmets either. So did one thing lead to the other? I don't know. Personally I have never found the line that separates "reckless" from "adventurous." Of course, I never really looked that hard for it, and as I write this, I sit surrounded by 23 sled dogs having just mailed my entry fee for the 2005 Iditarod.

JB: Are times and kids different today than when you were growing up? What remains the same?

GP: Kids haven't changed at all. They're more technically savvy and have access to more information than we did when I was young, but I think the essence of kids—they are like sponges when it comes to learning, they need the unflagging support of parents, teachers, librarians, booksellers, and maybe even authors, they're smarter than you think, and they know how to have fun in a way that adults seem to have forgotten—remains unchanged. The times, however, are different, sadly, tragically different, but I tend to think that adults have more trouble with that fact than kids do. Young people flex and adapt. They don't miss what they never had and they live, wonderfully, in the moment.

JB: In a recent public reading of the towing/skiing sequence in which Angel Peterson gets his nickname by breaking the land speed record for snow skiing by being pulled behind a hotrod at 90-plus miles per hour, an audience of 40 was spellbound by the story. What makes writing that powerful? Are you conscious of what makes good writing as you are working on a story like this?

GP: Powerful writing is very real, even when it isn't. The line between fiction and nonfiction, truth and fantasy, what really happened and what could happen, blurs if the writing is strong enough. Good writing should immerse the reader in the story to the point where they look up hours later and are surprised to find themselves in a chair in the living room or under the sheets with a flashlight. All I ever try to do when I write is show the reader what I see in my head or what I remember from my own experiences. If I can get all the details down and do it quickly, then I think I am approaching what you may call good writing. I don't think about the writing when I'm doing it, though. I think about the story. I work everything out in my head beforehand so that I can see it and then I just do my best to transcribe the image.

JB: What "extreme sports" do you still do today at your age? Have you put away those thrill-seeking activities?

GP: As I said, I've recently put together a kennel of 23 sled dogs and I'm training and preparing to run the Iditarod again. I thought I'd gotten dogs out of my system some 14 years ago, but all it took was one ride on a friend's sled to realize that the dogs were in my blood and I had to get back to them. For ten years, I tried to distract myself from wanting to be with them again with sailboats. I bought and restored a few old clunker sailboats and was planning to single-hand around Cape Horn. I had a great time and sailed to Mexico, Hawaii, the Inland Passage, Alaska, and all the way to Fiji. I loved the boats and being on the sea but my heart, truly, belongs to and with the dogs in the brush on the back of a sled. And I'll be there until I die.

JB: Who do you read for entertainment in the way that other people read Gary Paulsen?

GP: William Manchester and Patrick O'Brien are two authors I have studied very closely. Mostly, though, the adventure I seek is in the form of personal inspection at zero altitude. I have to be there, have to get my hands dirty, my bones broken, my face dragged through the snow, my head whacked with the beam of a sailboat to really savor the experience. It would be easier if I found my adventures in the pages of a book, but I'm a slow learner, I guess, and I'm out there finding out things for myself.

RICHARD PECK

Richard Peck grew up in Decatur, Illinois, before attending college in Indiana and England and later serving as a chaplain's assistant in the army. Decatur would become the inspiration for Bluff City, the setting for his paranormal stories involving teen protagonists Blossom Culp and Alexander Armsworth.

While Richard was a junior high school English teacher, he was also submitting and publishing articles in the *Chicago Tribune* and *The New York Times*. Richard notes that he wrote his first line of fiction on May 24, 1971, right after school on the day he quit his job as a teacher to become a full-time writer.

BOOKS

♦ *Something for Joey*: The true story of 1972 Heisman Trophy winner John Cappelletti and his relationship with his younger brother, Joey, who was dying of leukemia as John was becoming the best college football player in America. Grades 8–10

♦ *A Long Way From Chicago*: Joey and Mary Alice leave Chicago to spend summers visiting Grandma Dowdel during the Depression in downstate Illinois. Grandma Dowdel has courage, spirit, and ingenuity, all of which she employs in righting wrongs among the citizenry of her small town and the surrounding countryside. Grades 7–10

♦ *A Year Down Yonder* (Newbery Medal winner): In this sequel to *A Long Way From Chicago*, Mary Alice, now 15 years of age, must go to live with Grandma Dowdel in her small Illinois town when Joey and Mary Alice's father loses his job. Despite being regarded as a rich girl from Chicago, Mary Alice gradually assumes the character traits of Grandma Dowdel and learns to live, prosper, and be happy in small-town America. Grades 7–10

♦ *The Ghost Belonged to Me*: This book begins the Blossom Culp books, set in Bluff City, with Alexander Armsworth and Blossom Culp working to solve the mystery of Alexander's haunted barn. Grades 6–9

♦ *Ghosts I Have Been*: In Bluff City, Blossom Culp uses the power of second sight to communicate with the ghost of a boy killed on the Titanic and travels back in time to attempt his rescue. Grades 6–9

RODMAN PHILBRICK

Rodman Philbrick was the oldest of four brothers who grew up in the Philbrick family in Rye, New Hampshire. Rodman hid the fact that he was a writer when he was a teen, including the fact that he completed a novel at age 16, and although he acknowledges that it didn't merit publishing, he was not dissuaded from writing.

Although Rodman dropped out of the University of New Hampshire, he banged out nine novels while working as a carpenter and boat builder before his first book was published by St. Martin's Press in 1978. His first published works were mystery/detective novels for adults (and Rodman has long been a member of the Mystery Writers of America). An editor asked Rodman to take a crack at a young adult novel, and the result was the huge hit—which would eventually become the basis for a major motion picture—*Freak the Mighty*. Many award-winning young adult novels later, Rodman, who lives with his wife, splits his time between Maine and the Florida Keys.

BOOKS

♦ *Freak the Mighty*: Freak is a genius who must wear leg braces and use crutches. Max is a self-proclaimed "butthead goon," who towers over his classmates. Unlikely friends, they become a team, Freak the Mighty, when Freak rides on Max's shoulders. The boys are in danger when Max's father is paroled (he murdered Max's mother). Grades 6–9

♦ *Last Book in the Universe*: In this futuristic story the world is a shambles (no one reads or writes anymore) and is divided into the crumbling cities, ruled by gangs and violence, and the sanctuaries populated by "proovs," genetically improved people who live an idyllic existence. When Spaz, an epileptic outcast, learns that his former foster sister, Bean, is dying, he sets off to save her. He hooks up with an old geezer named Ryter, who teaches him the power of writing and books. Grades 8–10

♦ *REM World*: When teenaged Arthur orders a helmet device to help him lose weight, he finds himself in REM World, and later unleashes a horrible monster. Grades 7–9

♦ *The Young Man and the Sea*: Skiff attempts to follow in his father's footsteps as a man of the sea. The only problem is that his father can't climb off the couch where he and a perpetual can of beer have established residence since Skiff's mother died. Skiff will go in quest of a giant bluefin tuna to raise money to repair the family fishing boat. Grades 6–9

A Conversation With Rodman Philbrick

Adapted from Blasingame, James. (2004). Interview with Rodman Philbrick. *Journal of Adolescent and Adult Literacy, 47*(6), 518–519.

JB: In *The Young Man and the Sea* 12-year-old Skiff Beaman's battle with a gigantic bluefin tuna closely parallels the battle against a huge marlin fought by Santiago in Hemingway's novella of almost the same name. Just as winning the battle of strength with the fish was only the beginning of Santiago's challenge, so it is also for Skiff, who finds himself 30 miles out at sea with no gas for the motor and a 900-pound monster fish dragging behind the boat. Readers will discover, however, that this story is much more than just a retelling of Hemingway's classic; in what ways did you intend Skiff's story to be very different from Santiago's?

RP: I haven't read the Hemingway story since I was in high school, but obviously it made a big impression. I have a younger brother who was a commercial fisherman and worked on a harpoon boat going after bluefins, and recalled his stories about the giant fish. At the height of the bluefin craze, when one fish could bring ten thousand dollars or more, all sorts of folks went out in ill-equipped small boats, and I thought it would be interesting to see the wild scene through the eyes of a 12-year old. So I guess the essential difference in the characters of Santiago and Skiff is one of age. A beginning rather than an ending. Santiago must come to terms with his age, his mortality, his declining strength, and the disappointments of life—in essence, he's a philosopher, commenting on the human condition. In contrast, Skiff is a boy who is absolutely determined to save his father and make them a family again, which is why he's so fixated on resurrecting the family boat. He refuses to give up on life, because to do so would be to defile his late mother's memory. I try not to be corny, but the driving force of the narrative is a very old-fashioned notion about overcoming adversity, about not giving up when life overwhelms you. Also, despite the white beard and an avid interest in fishing, I'm not an innovative stylist like Mr. Hemingway, nor do I share his particular interest in the theme of what constitutes physical courage. I'm simply a storyteller.

JB: Skiff loves the smell of planed cedar and the magic of Mr. Woodwell's boat shop, where his dad (Big Skiff) also spent time as a young man. The events that surround the raising and repairing of the *Mary Rose* seem lovingly written to share what boat builders feel for their work. Is there something magical, or at least very special, about wooden boats and their construction (and reconstruction)?

RP: There is for me! As many of my readers already know, before I was able to write for a living I worked with my hands, and most of the work had to do with boats. It started in repairs on my own boats, which were invariably old, made of wood, and had a tendency to leak. Eventually I learned to build wooden boats, built quite a few in my own shop, and later was a toolmaker—or mold builder—in several fiberglass boat shops. Amos Woodwell was heavily based on a real person. In reality he was a retired teacher of Latin who owned an ancient Friendship sloop, and rebuilt it from the keel up. When I sailed with him he was eighty-something, and I was in my early twenties. I took what I remember of his gentle, keenly intelligent personality and put him in the shoes of a local, legendary builder whose shop I was familiar with—and that's where we get that lovely scent of planed cedar!

JB: Skiff faces adversity in many ways, including the rotten tricks played upon him by Tyler Croft, the son of his father's former friend, Jack Croft. Skiff rises above this by facing challenges more appropriate to a man than a boy. But why do you think young people (as often and accurately portrayed in your books) are so often cruel to their peers?

RP: I wish I knew the answer to the mystery of human cruelty. If so, maybe I could do something about it! I vividly recall being bullied when I was a certain age, and to my shame I also recall bullying a few weaker kids myself. That part of childhood has not changed in the intervening 40 years, and I fear it will always be part of how kids sort each other out—not that we adults should ever condone or tolerate such cruel behavior. As for Skiff having to behave more like a grown-up, my own father struggled desperately with alcoholism, and as the oldest of four brothers I simply had to grow up fast, and make adult decisions when I was quite young. I think I'm a better person for it, too. It's no coincidence that Skiff's last name is Beaman, as in "be a man." By the way, my late father was sober for the last few decades of his life, and devoted himself to helping others beat that terrible disease. So I have witnessed the overcoming of adversity, and know how important it is not to give up hope.

JB: This book seems to acknowledge a code that exists among the men who make their living at sea. Although it is unspoken and only indirectly described, it is readily apparent in the story when men like Mr. Woodwell and Captain Keelson get together. Does this code still exist in New England, and is it an endangered species? What keeps it alive?

RP: I'm happy to say this kind of quiet code of honor and obligation still exists here among Maine waterman, who do indeed look out for each other. It stays alive by example, and out of necessity, and I wanted to show how important that kind of thoughtful kindness can be when adults act as mentors to kids.

JB: You once indicated that telling a good story may sometimes be more important to a writer's success than focusing purely on the literary qualities of a piece. Can you explain what you mean by that and how it has played out in your own career?

RP: I started out wanting to be a literary innovator, much more concerned with the style and complexity of the prose than with the story itself. Eventually I discovered that readers of all levels seem to respond to narrative first of all, and that an overly developed style—which calls attention to the author—can actually detract from the power of the narrative, and thereby diminish the story. And I do believe in the general rule that a good story indifferently written will trump a poor story well written. All of which is not to say that I don't spend many hours rewriting my prose, trying to get it just right. In my case that means taking out all the extra words.

JB: You have sometimes collaborated with your wife on book projects. How do two people go about writing a novel together? It seems like a special relationship would be necessary and/or the relationship might be tested in the process.

RP: Believe me, a special relationship is necessary, and it certainly does get tested—which may explain why Lynn and I haven't collaborated on a project in several years now. In our case the only reason it worked (and I think it worked rather well) is because Lynn did most of the heavy lifting. I outlined and pontificated and rather grandly criticized the results, while she did most of the grunt work of writing the prose. Good deal if you can get it.

JB: You (and your wife) have had great success at novels for adults, as well as novels for adolescents. How are the two efforts different, and how are the payoffs different?

RP: To my way of thinking, the efforts are identical. For the writer the difficulty level is exactly the same—struggling to make every word count, and every character come vividly to life. The only thing I do differently when writing a story intended for a younger audience is leave out the swear words. But I must say, the payoffs really are quite different, because young readers are so much more enthusiastic than adult readers. Sometimes one of my books is the first book a kid has ever read, and that's never true of adult readers.

JB: What advice would you like to give to young writers?

RP: Write something every day. When it's finished, write it again. And you must read. If you're not intoxicated by books, and by the power of words, it's unlikely you'll ever be a good writer.

ANN RINALDI

Ann Rinaldi was born in New York City and her mother died a short time later. Ann's father, a newspaperman, discouraged Ann from writing or even going to college, delaying her pursuit of her dreams. Ann began work as a secretary, eventually marrying Ron Rinaldi and leaving the business world to raise a family. After the birth of her second child, Ann began writing, first completing four unpublished novels, then becoming a newspaper columnist with regular columns in two papers. Ann wrote a story entitled "Term Paper," which was not intended specifically for young adults but which was published as a novel soon after its completion, followed by the sequel, *Promises Are for Keeping*.

Ann had not yet become a historical novelist, however. It was not until her son, Ron, began participating in Revolutionary War reenactments that Ann developed an interest in fictionalizing history. Ann's intention is to present historical events without using the myths or the stereotypes of well-known figures, but instead to present the event from the bottom up.

Ann keeps a very large personal library, in which she starts to research her novels' topics before moving on to public and university libraries. Ann is known for her historical research and her young women protagonists. She lives in Somerville, New Jersey.

BOOKS

♦ *Time Enough for Drums*: In Trenton, New Jersey, 16-year-old Jemima Emerson must survive a family and citizenry torn by many differing loyalties during the Revolutionary War. Grades 7–10

♦ *Coffin Quilt*: Fanny McCoy suffers through the tragedy of the famous feud between the Hatfields and McCoys in 1880s Appalachia. Grades 7–10

♦ *Cast Two Shadows*: During the Revolutionary War, 14-year-old Caroline Whitaker is the daughter of a plantation owner and—she comes to discover—a slave she has never met. As the war comes to their home, Caroline and her family members' loyalties are torn apart, and Caroline's mixed ethnic heritage becomes more of an issue than ever before. Grades 7–10

♦ *Wolf by the Ears*: Nineteen-year-old Harriet Hemings is a black servant in Thomas Jefferson's plantation home of Monticello, but her red hair and light skin suggest she may also be Jefferson's daughter. This story is based on the true story of Sally Hemings after DNA testing proved she was the mother of a child fathered by one of the Jeffersons, possibly Thomas Jefferson himself. Grades 7–10

LOIS RUBY

Lois Ruby grew up in and around San Francisco, with a brief stint in the Dominican Republic. Lois loved reading so much as a child that she would walk 12 blocks to the local public library every Saturday morning. Lois identifies the start of her writing career with a satirical piece she wrote about a popular girl in school, which was published in *Teen* magazine.

After graduating with a major in English and a minor in criminology, Lois imagined supporting the family as a probations officer while her husband went to graduate school, but settled for library work instead. She managed to balance work and family, having three children and getting an M.A. in library science from San Jose State University in California. Now Lois and her husband, Tom, live in Albuquerque, New Mexico.

Lois has done some interesting research for her books, including interviewing neo-Nazi skinheads face to face in Denver.

BOOKS

♦   *Miriam's Well*: When Miriam and Adam are paired for a high school English project, Adam is disinterested, but when Miriam collapses with cancer and her fundamentalist parents refuse her medical care, Adam leaps to action. The conflict heightens when Adam's father, an attorney, decides to defend Miriam's parents against the state in a battle for Miriam's custody. Grades 7–10

♦   *Skin Deep*: Dan Penner finds the perfect way to express his anger at losing his place on the swim team and being denied a job because of racial quotas when he meets two skinheads and joins their group. As Dan's involvement with the skinhead culture grows, so does the frustration of his girlfriend, whose family includes two minority children. Grades 8–11

♦   *Steal Away Home*: When Dana pulls away the wallpaper in their old home, she finds a boarded-up human skeleton from 1856—when their house was a station on the Underground Railroad. Grades 7–10

♦   *Soon to Be Free*: In this sequel to *Steal Away Home*, Dana is disturbed by the Burks, two guests who come to their old house, now turned into a bed and breakfast, and appear to be covertly searching for something. A second story unfolds, that of James Baylor Weaver, a 13-year-old Quaker in 1857 who was leading four slaves to freedom. A secret document from the past is hidden in the house, and Dana must find it before the Burks do. Grades 7–10

LOUIS SACHAR

Louis Sachar moved from East Meadow, New York (where his father's office was in the Empire State Building), to pre-suburban Orange County in California when he was 9 years old. Louis started college at Antioch College in Ohio but had to drop out because his family needed him after his father's death. After a short stint as a Fuller Brush salesman, he finished his degree at the University of California at Berkeley, where he graduated in 1976 with a degree in economics.

Louis's interest in literature for children and young adults began at the University of California when he enrolled in a college internship at Hillside, an elementary school, and became "Louis the Yard Teacher." None of the books the kids were reading impressed him very much, and he decided to write some of his own; Hillside School became the fictitious Wayside School in his successful Wayside School series, which actually uses the names of kids he knew when he was supervising noon recess at Hillside.

Louis went on to study law while continuing to write, acquiring his law degree in 1980 and passing the bar exam. He would need to practice for the next nine years to finance his writing habit before his royalties grew large enough to support his family.

Louis lives with his wife, Carla, and their daughter, Sherre, in Austin, Texas. Louis is a dog lover, and his two dogs are the only family members allowed to join him in the office when he is writing a new book.

Louis's books are mostly for an audience that ends at middle school, such as the Wayside School series, the Marvin Redpost series, *Sixth Grade Secrets*, and *There's a Boy in the Girls' Bathroom*.

BOOKS

+ *Holes*: Stanley Yelnats, whose name is a palindrome, comes from a long line of cursed Stanley Yelnats, all the way back to his great-great-grandfather who crossed a gypsy named Madame Zeroni. When Stanley goes to detention camp after being wrongly convicted of stealing a valuable item from a celebrity charity auction, the curse seems to have worsened. Stanley and his newfound friends at Camp Greenlake (there is no lake) are made to dig, supposedly as punishment but in truth to help the corrupt warden search for buried treasure. In the end, all seemingly unrelated events from past and present tie together as Stanley and his family shed the curse. Grades 6–9

GRAHAM SALISBURY

Graham Salisbury grew up in Hawaii and might have continued in the 100-year-old tradition laid down by the men in his family of working for the *Honolulu Advertiser*, a local newspaper. But Graham was destined for another kind of writing. As a youngster he surfed and fished on the Big Island and attended prep school before heading off to California State University at Northridge. At Cal State Northridge he failed English twice before getting an A the third time around. He received an M.F.A. from Vermont College of Norwich University. Graham has been a member of a rock band, worked on a glass-bottom boat and a deep-sea fishing boat, and taught elementary school. He and his family now live in Portland, Oregon.

BOOKS

♦ *Lord of the Deep*: Thirteen-year-old Mikey Donovan admires Bill, his fishing boat captain stepfather, above other men until Bill lets himself be manipulated into cheating on a fishing record by two unscrupulous tourists. Grades 6–9

♦ *Under the Blood-Red Sun*: Thirteen-year-old Japanese American Tomi Nakaji is buffeted by the storm of World War II, especially the Japanese attack on Pearl Harbor that he and a friend witness. What happens to Tomi's family after Pearl Harbor makes it difficult for him, but he accepts the burden of carrying his family's honor bravely after his father and grandfather are arrested. Grades 6–10

♦ *Blue Skin of the Sea*: Through a series of related short stories, the author follows the trials and adventures of Sonny Mendoza as he grows up in a small fishing village. Grades 6–9

♦ *Jungle Dogs*: Twelve-year-old Regis must brave fierce dogs as well as gangs as he grows up in Hawaii. Grades 6–9

♦ *Island Boyz*: Ten stories and one poem capture the essence of growing up in Hawaii. Grades 6–9

♦ *Eyes of the Emperor*. Young Japanese American soldiers stationed in Hawaii, their place of birth, find themselves treated as the enemy after the bombing of Pearl Harbor. The author based this book on the true story of a bizarre attempt to train dogs to find Japanese guerillas, as told to him by the Japanese American veterans who experienced it. Grades 7–10

WILLIAM SLEATOR

William Sleator began writing at age 6 with a story about a fat cat, although he points out the story needed heavy editing. He grew up in St. Louis, Missouri, and graduated from Harvard with degrees in both English and music. His early creations in school may have been a little unusual, such as the musical piece "Guillotines in the Springtime," which indicated an interest in the "grotesque and macabre," according to William.

At Harvard, William composed music and continued to write stories, as well as maintain a journal. While working as a pianist at the Royal Ballet School in England, William lived in an old cottage in a forest, a place that had been a quarantine house for smallpox victims, which led to his first book for young adults, *Blackbriar*. William eventually turned to full-time writing and left his work with music behind. His science fiction works often reveal an interest and knowledge of real scientific principles. He lives part of the year in Boston and part of the year in Thailand.

BOOKS

♦ *Interstellar Pig*: Sixteen-year-old Barney loves to play a new and exotic board game with the three strangers renting the seaside cottage next door, but he soon comes to suspect that they are actually dangerous and deadly aliens disguised as human beings and that their game is not only very real but threatens the planet Earth. Grades 5–9

♦ *Parasite Pig*: In this sequel to *Interstellar Pig*, Barney is once more drawn into the weird game that has lethal penalties for losing. A new wrinkle is thrown in as parasites and life cycles of bizarre creatures become a factor in the game. Grades 5–9

♦ *The Boxes*: When 15-year-old Annie opens the boxes left in her care by her mysterious Uncle Marco, she finds telepathic creatures that can affect the passage of time. Grades 5–9

♦ *The Last Universe*: Fourteen-year-old Susan must push her dying, wheelchair-bound brother, Gary, through a mysterious park-like garden in their backyard, complete with pond and hedge maze. When the garden begins to behave strangely, as if quantum physics rule there, strange, new things happen every day. Grades 7–9

♦ *Oddballs*: William Sleator writes in fiction format about the funny and strange adventures of his family as he was growing up. Grades 6–9

GARY SOTO

Gary Soto, whose grandparents came to California from Mexico during the Depression, was born and grew up in Fresno, California, and still visits there on an almost monthly basis. His family worked on the farms around Fresno and in raisin-packing plants; tragically, Gary's father was killed in a factory accident at one of these packing plants. Gary was not a dedicated student in high school but was beginning to develop an interest in literature, an interest that would further develop at Fresno City College and blossom at Fresno State University. A few of his favorite writers include Pablo Neruda, Gabriel Garcia Marquez, Carson McCullers, William Faulkner, William Shakespeare, and Walter Mosely.

Gary carries the title of Young People Ambassador for California Rural Legal Assistance (CRLA) and for the United Farm Workers of America (UFW). He provides information and support of many kinds to CRLA, an organization that provides legal help to the rural poor in California. Soto is active in UFW, as well.

Gary and his wife, Carolyn, live in Berkeley, California, and have a daughter, Mariko, who is a veterinarian.

BOOKS

♦ *Baseball in April and Other Stories*: Eleven short stories chronicle the ups and downs of growing up in central California. Grades 7–9

♦ *Buried Onions*: Life in Fresno, California, can be discouraging, and 19-year-old Eddie finds it nearly impossible to succeed there, especially after the senseless murder of his cousin Chuy. Grades 9–12

♦ *The Afterlife*: This sequel to *Buried Onions* tells the story of 17-year-old Chuy's life as he reflects back after his death. Grades 9–10

♦ *Local News: Stories*. Thirteen short stories about life as a teenager in central California, this book comes after *Baseball in April* and continues in that vein. Grades 6–9

♦ *Taking Sides*: Lincoln Mendoza finds himself playing against his old basketball team and his former best friends when his family moves to the suburbs after being robbed in their former neighborhood. Grades 7–9

♦ *Summer Life*: In a series of essays, Gary Soto paints vivid pictures of life growing up in Fresno, California. Grades 7–12

♦ *Living Up the Street*: Narratives that tell the story of Gary Soto's life growing up in Fresno, California. Grades 7–12

A Conversation With Gary Soto

Adapted from Blasingame, James. (2003). Interview with Gary Soto. *Journal of Adolescent and Adult Literacy, 47*(3), 286–287.

JB: It's almost impossible to talk about *The Afterlife* without also talking about *Buried Onions*, recognized since its publication in 1997 as one of the best works in YA fiction. *The Afterlife* and *Buried Onions* have the same characters and begin with the same event. In the earlier book we follow Eddie for several days as he attempts to deal with the death of his cousin Chuy. He must cope with his aunt, Chuy's mother, who insists that he extract revenge with a gun, and with the hopelessness of life for him and his friends in Fresno, California. Is it fair to say that *The Afterlife*, told from the murdered Chuy's point of view, is much more optimistic than *Buried Onions*? Did you feel that there was more of the story of life in Fresno that needed to be told?

GS: *The Afterlife* is indeed more optimistic than *Buried Onions*. These two YA novels are companion books that evoke, I hope, your basic Fresno chaos and young people's responses to this chaos. In *Buried Onions* we have Eddie, age 19, trying to skirt his aunt's anger and her mind-set of "Let's seek revenge." So Eddie is fearful of extended family, and rightly so. I mean, his aunt wants the young man who killed her son hunted down and put down for good. In *The Afterlife* we have Jesus—a.k.a. Chuy—who wakes up dead from what can only be described as a senseless killing. He wakes and discovers that he is a ghost of sorts, one with limited powers of mobility (even social!) and a limited number of days on this dirty planet. In spite of the brevity of his life, Chuy feels whole because he finds love in the form of another teenager, this one who has killed herself. You have to be optimistic when you search *and* find love.

JB: In *Buried Onions*, Eddie observes: "*Respect.* That word got more people buried than the word *love*. One snide look, an arc of spit, a little shoulder bump, and it was '¿Y que?' And you were laid low as a shadow" (page 9). In the first book, the inference might be made that Chuy's life was often at risk because he ran with a rough crowd, but in *The Afterlife* we find out that his death was totally unpredictable. If death can be so unexpected, what does this say about life?

GS: The death scene in *The Afterlife* occurs in a dirty bathroom in a dirty dance hall and it's all because the protagonist, Chuy, says to the guy standing at the basin next to him that he likes his shoes. The shoes, as the reader discovers, are yellow and out of line with the kinds of shoes most young people wear. It's an innocent remark, one uttered because he's happy. Still, the remark gets Chuy killed. He was a young man and brought down before he even got to voting age. Life, then, can be seen not as a given but something that can be taken away without warning or reason.

JB: In both books, southeast Fresno seems to be a place where Fate never gives anybody a break. Even José, the tough marine in *Buried Onions*, is nearly murdered by younger boys when he is home on leave. In *The Afterlife*, however, Chuy seems to have gained an understanding of the people and the place, and to accept things rather than judge them. Does this reflect an understanding of your own about your hometown?

GS: I understand some of Fresno's social milieu and yet am at a loss at other aspects. I love Fresno. We have bad air and bad water, and we're ranked fourth as the city with most cars stolen. If you're visiting Fresno, make sure it's not in a Honda. Yet, this is where literature happens—we have more poets and writers, successful ones, than a lot of larger cities. However, I would not risk saying that I really know Fresno. The city has changed; it's gotten bigger and there are streets I would not travel on—the "nice" ones with SUVs in the driveways. Too scary for me.

JB: After his death, Chuy comes to a much better understanding and appreciation for who he was. Do you think many young people need something to wake them up to the value of who they are?

GS: I remember reading a little aphorism that says, "Wake up as much as you can." I suppose young and old must wake up as much as possible. Sleep helps. Good music and theater help. Friends help. Home cooking helps. Literature helps. I believe that there can be a powerful literary experience for young people when they encounter, as if for the first time, a novel that stares *them* in the eyes.

    Usually the reader is asked to stare at the characters as they scurry across the page. But sometimes I have the feeling when I'm reading a wonderful novel that the characters stop and stare at me, the reader. The characters are asking, "Hey, are you with me? Keep following and we'll see you at the end."

JB: Crystal, the attractive cheerleader/champion athlete/most popular girl in school, seems to have little in common with Chuy, but in death (Crystal has committed suicide) the two of them seem to be soul mates. Why did you choose to create Crystal as you did?

GS: Crystal represents a young man's desire. She is a dream and, in fact, since she is a ghost, has the qualities of a dream—all bodiless sensations. Crystal is much different from Chuy, and that's OK because at the heart of this book is a love story. Chuy falls in love with someone who is better-looking and seemingly with a social standing a cut above his standing as a regular C+ student. In some regards presenting characters different from the other is a contrived device. I mean, look at the great books—ah, *Romeo and Juliet*—and you'll discover characters that are really opposite in looks, temperament, family connections, ambition, social standing, etc.

    Another point: At the time of his death Chuy is game for life; he has a date for the evening and a chance to swap tongues in the parking lot. Life is good. However, for

Crystal, who the reader would think has her act together, her confidence has all but disappeared. A sensitive person—possibly over-sensitive—she feels like a failure and one option is suicide—or so she believes.

JB: One of *The Afterlife*'s most powerful moments happens when Eddie hands the gun back over to Chuy's mom. Chuy is greatly relieved: "I turned and saw my *primo* Eddie shoving something large and heavy [the gun] into my mom's hands. My mom tried to give it back, but Eddie—bless him—wouldn't have it. It was back in my mom's care. The world was safer, quieter" (page 133). Why are Chuy and Eddie so opposed to doing what Chuy's mom explains in the first book is only justice, a justice that the police won't even attempt?

GS: Chuy and Eddie, closer in age, have lived a street life. They know their surroundings and know the damage guns and violence bring on. Chuy's mother is removed from the daily romps of these two young men. Sure, she may hear a gunshot at night and a car window being smashed. Perhaps she's had stuff stolen from her front porch or garage. She most likely has bars over her bedroom window. But she doesn't know street life like Eddie or Chuy, and when she finds out that her son (Chuy) has been killed, she wants to take action. She goes to her nephew and begs for revenge. She herself would not know how to kill another person, but since Eddie is young, thus emotionally pliable, she believes that he could do it.

JB: What hope is there for young people growing up in such an environment?

GS: Is there hope for figures like Eddie and Chuy, two brown teenagers living in southeast Fresno? Sure. Sometimes people are scared of a rundown neighborhood—and southeast Fresno has plenty of that—and judge as they drive through an area that it's better to stay away. But that's all surface response. It's like good manners or dress; we may be fooled into thinking that someone who dresses well may in fact be a better person. But we know that not to be true. Look at Sam Waksal of ImClone, a guy who dressed well, drove a nice car, at the snap of his fingers had jets at his disposal, lived in houses on the coast and in the woods. This seemingly successful person got caught with the money bag. And what is doing now? Seven-plus years in prison? Then, we may have people out in southeast Fresno who have little more than a roof over their heads and cars ready for the junkyard. But the content of character, as Dr. Martin Luther King Jr. spoke of it, is what distinguishes a person, not dress or possessions.

    The Afterlife is dedicated to two health providers, Mark Lasher and Channah Cossman, two remarkable individuals who work in possibly the most dilapidated areas of Fresno—the west side. They don't blink an eye when they serve this area. They go to work and care for people because that's what serves the world and, at heart, serves them as great human beings. Yes, there is a chance of greatness for people like Eddie and Chuy, and even cheerleader Crystal.

JERRY SPINELLI

Jerry Spinelli began writing at age 16 when he wrote a poem about his team's amazing football victory, a poem that was published in the local newspaper. A native of Norristown, Pennsylvania (he lives in Phoenixville, Pennsylvania, now), Jerry loved sports and imagined playing shortstop for the Yankees. He went to Gettysburg College and was editor of the literary magazine there.

He began his professional career as a magazine editor before becoming a full-time author. Jerry's first successful novel, *Space Station Seventh Grade*, followed four unsuccessful novels for adults. *Space Station Seventh Grade* was inspired by one of his children raiding the refrigerator of the fried chicken Jerry was planning to eat the next day. Jerry is married to children's book writer Eileen Spinelli (*Sophie's Masterpiece*, *Three Pebbles and a Song*), and they have six children and many more grandchildren.

BOOKS

♦ *Maniac Magee* (Newbery Medal winner): Jeffrey Lionel "Maniac" Magee, an orphan with a variety of homes, from the zoo to the racist McNabs' house, has mythical athletic prowess in this tall tale about crossing the boundaries of race. Grades 6–9

♦ *Knots in My Yo-Yo String*: Jerry Spinelli tells the story of growing up in Norristown, Pennsylvania, with humor and pathos. Grades 6–9

♦ *Milkweed*: In 1939 Warsaw, Poland, an orphan (nameless, he is tagged "Misha" by his older-brother figure, Uri) is taken in by a Jewish family and experiences the horror of the Nazi persecution of the Jews. Grades 8–10

♦ *Crash:* Athletic superstar Crash Coogan narrates this story about how he came to realize that being the star and harassing people who are different from him (like mild-mannered Quaker Penn Ward) does not make his life worthwhile. Grades 7–8

♦ *There's a Girl in My Hammerlock*: Because of Title IX gender equity legislation for schools, Maisie Potter cannot be barred from joining her school's eighth-grade wrestling team. Maisie will have to wrestle with more than boys on the mat, however, as social pressure and media attention put some holds of their own on her. Grades 6–8

♦ *Stargirl:* Stargirl (a.k.a. Susan) shows up for the first time at Micah High School in Micah, Arizona, as a junior whose home-schooling has left her as free of spirit and mind as she is of peer pressure and the normal teenage obsession with conformity. The students don't know how to take her and vacillate between adoration and ostracism. Ultimately, Stargirl is unaffected and may just be the only one at Micah High who retains integrity. Grades 6–10

JANET TASHJIAN

Janet Tashjian grew up in Providence, Rhode Island, and loved to read as a youngster, especially mysteries such as Nancy Drew and Encyclopedia Brown. Janet graduated from the University of Rhode Island with majors in both philosophy and journalism and went immediately into marketing and sales. It wasn't until later that she realized that her heart was not in business. After reading *The Things They Carried* by Tim O'Brien, she realized that she had a deep-seated need to be a writer. This inspired her to enroll in the M.F.A. program at Emerson College, where she was the student of award-winning author Jack Gantos, a teacher whom Janet credits, along with James Carroll, with helping her find her true purpose in life, writing books for young people. Janet and her husband, Doug, live in Boston, Massachusetts.

BOOKS

♦ *The Gospel According to Larry*: Seventeen-year-old Josh Swensen is secretly the Internet cult figure Larry, whose Gospel According to Larry sermons against our consumer-crazy society are widely read and wildly popular. The girl he loves (who prefers a less-than-brainy athlete as a boyfriend) greatly admires Larry, forcing Josh to agonize over whether or not to reveal his secret identity. Grades 7–10

♦ *Vote for Larry*: In this sequel to *The Gospel According to Larry*, Josh Swensen (Internet identity: Larry) runs for president against George Bush and John Kerry. Larry uses his wildly popular website to disseminate information. But the first thing Josh/Larry will have to do is inspire Congress to pass a law lowering the required age for the presidency. Grades 7–10

♦ *Faultline*: Seventeen-year-old standup comic Becky Martin must come to terms with the fact that she is in an abusive relationship with her darling but cruel boyfriend, Kip Costello. Grades 7–10

♦ *Multiple Choice*: Fourteen-year-old Monica Devon seems to be obsessive-compulsive, except for the fact that she recognizes her need to be perfect and devises a coping mechanism to thwart her compulsions, a multiple-choice game. Whenever Monica faces a decision, she invents a series of multiple-choice decisions, only one of which she would normally do. Grades 7–10

A CONVERSATION WITH JANET TASHJIAN

Adapted from Blasingame, James. (2004/2005). Interview with Janet Tashjian. *Journal of Adolescent and Adult Literacy, 48*(4), 350–351.

JB: In both of the Larry books you open and close with you, Janet Tashjian, the author, meeting with Larry, your protagonist, as if he were real (I'm not saying he isn't, by the way), which is a neat trick for helping the reader into the story. How did you come upon that technique? Do you and Larry truly meet somehow in your psyche? How much of Larry is you?

JT: I like to push the narrative envelope with each of my books. I'm interested in the form as well as the content of a novel. With *Gospel*, I knew I wanted to use several postmodern techniques, mainly blurring the line between fiction and nonfiction. So I put myself in the book, then other real people, like Bono. Both books were so much fun to write. Larry is one of my favorite characters to hang out with. We are a lot alike—very hyperactive and hyper-focused—but I can't hold a candle to his idealism and discipline!

JB: You people your books with a lot of socially conscious characters: Bono and U2; the whole mass of people at Larry-Fest; Janine, who impresses Larry when they first meet in the used record store where she refuses to talk on Mondays "to combat the barrage of words that assault us each day"; Beth and Simon, who have a whole three-ring binder of accomplishments; the new Peter in *Vote*, who wears an earring and paints houses instead of working in advertising. So many of your characters refuse to live "the unexamined life." Do you typically hang out with people who try to live their lives with intention rather than living according to the whims of the powers that be, overt or covert?

JT: Most of the people I know live their lives with great intention and purpose. They are all very active in politics and social change; two of my friends and I made an ad for moveon.org that came in as a runner-up in their Internet ad campaign. It might be because we grew up in the sixties or it might be that we're witnessing another wave of activism. Most of the teens I know are also politically active; they're much more interesting kids than those concerned only with their own lives.

JB: One important plot premise in both books is the idea that a person shouldn't be owned by his or her possessions, so Josh/Larry proposes getting your worldly possessions down to 75. How many possessions do you have?

JT: I don't know how many possessions I have, but it's more than 75. That being said, I've been an anti-materialist for years. I don't own a lot of "stuff" and I hate going shopping (except for books or music!). I'm embarrassed by our consumer culture; it's so bereft of any kind of meaning. I love that so many kids are fighting branding in their schools and refusing to be treated as a consumer first, a human second. We have so much more to offer the world than our spending power.

JB: When Beth and Simon fling their challenge at Larry and he is considering getting back into the "changing-the-world business," Larry wonders, "Was this my destiny, my vocation? Or was I just trying to impress a girl?" (pages 30–31) This is a funny line, but it also seems to represent how teenagers vacillate between idealism and practicality. Is this something you have experienced/observed firsthand?

JT: I think we all vacillate between idealism and pragmatism. Everyone wants the world to be a better place; the difficult part is doing something about it. I'm always interested in the opposing forces at work in people; we all have ulterior motives. As a novelist, it's fun to explore them through a character's choices.

JB: How do you address such serious issues and yet do it in such a humorous way?

JT: I like to deal with serious subjects in my novels—consumerism, dating violence, special needs, voting—but without humor, they'd just be didactic, not entertaining. Tucking those issues into an interesting story line with strong characters makes for much more enjoyable reading. I'm big on humor in the books I read, too; I love black comedies and satire. I devoured Vonnegut growing up. Funny is big for me. And sitting at my desk alone, making myself laugh? It is, hands down, the best part of the job.

JB: Beth and Josh's love strays away from the platonic in the second book. What did that decision involve (on your part, not theirs)?

JT: When I did school visits for *Gospel*, everyone wanted to know about Josh and Beth's relationship. Many readers considered the book a love story. I knew Beth would figure prominently in the sequel and after all the interest in their relationship, I decided to take it to the next level. (Besides, after all those years of being in love, I thought Josh deserved a break.) But I had to throw in Janine, too; I didn't want to make it too easy for him.

JB: Do you have any advice for young writers?

JT: Yes. Write every day, even for a few minutes. Write what matters to you, not what you have to do for school. Find other people who like to write and form a group—that will give you deadlines (bring five pages next Monday) and feedback (only constructive and gentle criticism allowed). Read good books and study what the writer was trying to achieve. And don't give up! As I tell Larry in *Gospel*, "The best person to tell your story is you." It's a line I stand behind completely.

MILDRED TAYLOR

Although Mildred Taylor was born in Jackson, Mississippi, her father moved the family to Toledo, Ohio, when Mildred was 3 months old to escape racial segregation and prejudice in the 1940s South. Mildred attended the University of Toledo, often the only African American in her classes, and entered the Peace Corps upon graduation, headed for Ethiopia. After two years of teaching in Ethiopia and on the Navajo Reservation in Arizona, Mildred earned a master's degree at the University of Colorado. Mildred was active in the Black Student Alliance at the University of Colorado and helped to implement a black studies program there. Mildred Taylor still lives in Colorado.

Mildred's fiction has basis in fact, rooted in the stories she heard her parents and other relatives telling at family get-togethers, especially on visits to Mississippi. As a student in high school, Mildred was dismayed by the lack of information, especially accurate, positive portrayals of African Americans and their history, which ran counter to the accounts she heard from relatives who had been living the experience or who had received the oral account passed down over the years. Many of these true narratives wound up as the basis for whole books, such as *The Land*, the story of how Mildred's great-grandfather acquired prime land in Mississippi despite a lifetime of setbacks and the bad wishes of other men. This book acted as a prequel to Mildred's very successful books centered on the Logan family from rural Mississippi, most often with Cassie Logan as the protagonist. Cassie Logan and her family succeed in life due to family ties, persistence, faith, and strong values.

BOOKS

♦ *Song of the Trees*: This is the first book in the Logan family saga. Cassie Logan and her family face adversity in Depression-era Mississippi when greedy white loggers attempt to force Cassie's family to let them cut down the trees on Logan land. Grades 6–10

♦ *Roll of Thunder, Hear My Cry* (Newbery Medal winner): This is the second book in the saga of the Logans, a close-knit African-American family who survive in Depression-era Mississippi through family values and integrity. Nine-year-old Cassie Logan is at the story's center. Grades 6–11

♦ *Let the Circle Be Unbroken*: In this third book in the Logan saga, Cassie and her family struggle but maintain their faith in right and wrong as their friend is subjected to an unfair trial for murder. Grades 6–10

♦ *The Road to Memphis*: As World War II begins, Cassie Logan is in her last year of high school, and the Logan family struggles with many adverse events. Grades 6–10

Vivian Vande Velde

Vivian Vande Velde grew up in Rochester, New York, and still lives there with her husband, Jim. As an eighth grader, Vivian already knew that she wanted to be a writer, but it was reading T. H. White's *The Once and Future King* that revealed to her what kind of writing she wanted to do. As a teenager she liked fantasies that mixed interesting characters with elements that were out of place in time, but she also liked Edgar Allan Poe, Sir Arthur Conan Doyle, J. D. Salinger, J. R. R. Tolkien, Mary Renault, John Steinbeck, and Charles Dickens. Vivian especially liked fairy tales but she didn't believe the archetypes were etched in stone (i.e., that princesses must be beautiful and princes must be fearless).

When her daughter, Beth, was born, Vivian quit her job as a secretary and became a full-time mom, which she says put her in a situation where she had to "either take housework more seriously or come up with a good excuse" not to. And so she wrote her first novel, *Hidden Magic*. Vivian enjoys writing fantasies that address universal themes, and so she replaces the bad boy in the "bad boys attract nice girls" scenario with a vampire in *Companions of the Night*. Among other things, her fantasies may take old fairy tales down new paths, or put a new spin on an old story, such as the Arthurian legend.

BOOKS

* *Heir Apparent*: CPOC (Citizens to Protect Our Children) are picketing the Virtual Reality Arcade, but they will not prevent 14-year-old Giannine Bellisario from using the gift certificate her father gave her for her birthday. Her virtual reality game of choice is Heir Apparent, a game that takes her back to a medieval fantasy world where she must battle barbarians, dragons, and more to become king and win the game. When the CPOC demonstrators damage the machine while Giannine is playing, the consequence is that she can only escape the virtual reality by winning the game. Grades 7–9

* *Companions of the Night*: When 16-year-old Kerri Nowicki interrupts a group of vigilantes about to kill a handsome young man named Ethan, she has no idea that she is about to get involved with a vampire (Ethan) or that her actions will endanger her family. Grades 7–10

* *Hidden Magic*: A less than beautiful princess, Jennifer; her rejected suitor, the vain Prince Alexander; a lovable young sorcerer; and an evil witch are the characters in this parody of conventional fairy tales. Grades 7–10

* *Being Dead*: Seven horror stories with teen protagonists. Grades 7–10

Cynthia Voigt

Cynthia Voigt was born in Boston and, as a youngster, loved to read Nancy Drew, Cherry Ames, *The Black Stallion*, and *The Secret Garden* (this last book she discovered at her grandmother's house). She graduated from Smith College and spent a short time working at an ad agency in New York. She attended St. Michael's College in Santa Fe, New Mexico, and went on to teach in Maryland at the Key School, where she was also English Department chair. She loves teaching and has said repeatedly that she hopes to continue, regardless of how successful her writing career is. Cynthia is married to Walter Voigt, also a teacher, and they have two children, Jessica and Peter. Cynthia now makes her home in Deer Isle, Maine.

Books

♦ *Dicey's Song* (Newbery Medal winner): With their mother in a psychiatric ward, the Tillerman children wind up in the care of their grandmother on her farm on Chesapeake Bay. Dicey Tillerman and her grandmother have a lot in common (they are both too reserved), and both learn to change. Grades 7–9

♦ *Homecoming*: The Tillerman children must fend for themselves and find a new home when their mother abandons them as they sit in the car in a mall parking lot. Grades 7–9

♦ *A Solitary Blue*: Abandoned by his mother at age 7, Jeff Greene lives with his father, an aloof man whom he calls "Professor." Jeff learns to fend for himself to such an extent that he is suspicious of the care afforded by his mother when she reenters his life. He learns the difference between real and feigned parental love. Grades 7–9

♦ *Come a Stranger*: Mina loves to dance, and she is devastated when she is rejected by her dance camp (because of her ethnicity, or because she is getting older?). Mina comes to love Tamer Shipp, a young pastor who helps her through a hard time. Grades 7–9

♦ *The Runner*: "Bullet" Tillerman must cope with an abusive father, a mother close to a nervous breakdown, and a new (African American) member on his beloved track team. Grades 8–10

M. JERRY WEISS

M. Jerry Weiss has given a lifetime of service to young adult literature and shows no signs of slowing down. Among other awards, he has won the prestigious Assembly on Literature for Adolescents of the National Council of Teachers of English's Ted Hipple Service Award, the A. B. Herr Award, the International Reading Association's Special Service Award, the NCTE Intellectual Freedom Award, and the International Reading Association (IRA) Arbuthnot Award, just to name a few, and he has at least one award named after him—the New Jersey Reading Association M. Jerry Weiss Award.

Jerry is Professor Emeritus at Jersey City State College, and has also taught classes on young adult literature at Montclair State College, among others. In addition, he and his wife, Helen, have worked together to edit many volumes of short story collections and plays. They make their home in Montclair, New Jersey.

BOOKS

(Collections edited by M. Jerry Weiss.)

- *Big City Cool: Short Stories About Urban Youth* (co-edited with Helen S. Weiss): Short stories Walter Dean Myers, Sharon Dennis Wyeth, Paul Many, Joseph Geha, and more. Grades 8–12

- *From One Experience to Another* (co-edited with Helen S. Weiss): Fifteen top writers of young adult literature share personal narratives from their teen years, including Joan Bauer, Walter Dean Myers, Avi, Richard Peck, Gordon Korman, and more. Grades 7–10

- *Lost & Found* (co-edited with Helen S. Weiss): David Lubar, Jerry Spinelli, Paul Zindel, Jon Scieszka, Tamora Pierce, Mary Ann McGuigan, Mel Glenn, and other top young adult authors look back on the pain and joy of their own adolescence. Grades 8–12

- *The Signet Book of Short Plays*: Short plays from famous and favorite playwrights from Thornton Wilder to William Saroyan to Tennessee Williams to Shel Silverstein. Grades 9–12

- *Books I Read When I Was Young: The Favorite Books of Famous People*: Some of the world's most famous people share the titles of the books that inspired them. Grades 8 to adult

- *Dreams & Visions: Fourteen Flights of Fantasy*: Fourteen top fantasy writers contributed short stories to this collection. Grades 8–12

A Conversation With M. Jerry Weiss

Adapted from Blasingame, Jim. (2003). A Love of Young Adult Literature: ALAN 2003 Ted Hipple Service Award winner, M. Jerry Weiss. *The ALAN Review, 31*(1), 51–52.

JB: You have worked with a multitude of young people and famous authors as you collected information, stories, and poems for such works as *Books I Read When I Was Young: The Favorite Books of Famous People, Lost & Found,* and *Big City Cool: Short Stories About Urban Youth,* among others. What were some of the most memorable moments and what were some of the most surprising?

JW: *Books I Read When I Was Young* was a great project that originated with the Commission on Literature. It was published by Avon Books and donated to NCTE for its members. I was impressed that my letters to performers, politicians, sports figures, authors, etc., could generate such an avalanche of good stories and suggestions. An interesting answer came from Mrs. Kennedy Onassis who indicated she was too busy to respond. So I wrote her another letter, pointing out that since at that time she was working as an editor at a publishing house, didn't she think it was important to take just a few minutes to respond to students' requests to know what books had made an impression on her when she was young? She then wrote a lovely note by hand, and it was published in this book.

In 2001, Hyperion published *The Best Loved Poems of Jacqueline Kennedy Onassis,* compiled by her daughter Caroline. In the final section of the book, "In Her Own Words," Caroline refers to *Books I Read When I Was Young* and includes the text of the letter her mother sent to me. It's nice that this happened.

In developing our anthologies *From One Experience to Another* and *Lost & Found,* Helen and I had often heard teachers report that when they asked students to write personal essays, the students would complain, "We don't have anything to write about." Well, we contacted award-winning authors representing a wide range of literary genres and asked each author to write a brief essay, describing a true personal experience and then to write a short story based on that experience. We wanted to show students that there can be a story in even the simplest experience.

We thought a writer well known for fantasy would write us a fantasy story, a mystery writer, etc., but it didn't turn out that way. We received wonderful stories, with some authors exploring new fields for them. This confirmed our belief that we have to let each writer find the genre that is best for him or her rather than say everyone has to write a story or a poem or whatever.

Big City Cool came about through a friend who told us of an editor who wanted a collection of stories about growing up in urban America. This was an interesting project. We did many searches for stories that take place in different cities. However, it was important that the city be identified by its name or the mention of a prominent landmark. Of course, the characters had to appeal to contemporary young adult readers. We needed stories from a good variety of urban settings. While New York and California were no problem, the rest of the country was not as easy. After extensive research, we concluded there just weren't any contemporary tales about growing up in America that identified the location.

Up to now, we had been using stories already published, but at this point, our gracious and intelligent editor worked with us in contacting authors to develop original stories. We were thrilled with the result and are very grateful to those authors who developed new stories for us as well as those who gave us permission to use previously published materials.

JB: You and Helen have worked on so many big projects together. Does the conversation in the Weiss household often turn to young adult books and their authors?

JW: Fairly often. Of course, when we are putting together an anthology, there is a great deal of conversation about young adult literature and authors. Also, when we are preparing our talks, there is much discussion about authors. We always attend sessions at NCTE and IRA to hear authors new and old, and it's always exciting to see our old friends and meet new ones.

JACQUELINE WOODSON

Jacqueline Woodson was born in Columbus, Ohio, but grew up mostly in Greenville, South Carolina, and Brooklyn, New York. Jacqueline began her career in literature as the editor of her fifth-grade magazine. A milestone for her was discovering that good literature was not limited to white authors or William Shakespeare, as she discovered the writing of Toni Morrison, Rosa Guy, and Louise Meriweather. Although she had a hard time sitting still in class, she received praise from her fifth-grade teacher when the class began to write. Woodson, the author, was on her way. Jacqueline's novels for young adults typically avoid stereotypical characters or settings and address all the ways there are to be human through diverse characters and lifestyles.

Jacqueline has a B.A. in English and worked as a drama therapist with homeless and runaway children before becoming a full-time writer. She was awarded the prestigious ALAN Award in 2004 from the Assembly on Literature for Adolescents of the National Council of Teachers of English. She lives in Brooklyn, New York.

BOOKS

♦ *Miracle's Boys*: When their widowed mother dies, Ty'ree, Charlie, and Lafayette must fend for themselves. Ty'ree will postpone his dreams of a college education to take care of his younger brothers, Charlie can't seem to stay out of trouble with the law, and Lafayette can't understand why life seems to be set against them. Nonetheless, the boys hold onto hope for a better time. Grades 8–11

♦ *I Hadn't Meant to Tell You This*: Twelve-year-old Marie is one of the popular girls in her school and neighborhood in a prosperous black suburb in Ohio. When Marie wanders into a friendship with Lena, a white girl with a painful secret, she learns something about her new friend that she must decide to keep secret or divulge in Lena's best interest. Grades 9–11

♦ *If You Come Softly*: Ellie and Jeremiah, both the children of successful parents, are students at an exclusive New York City prep school. When their attraction to each other turns into an interracial romance, the world turns cruel. Grades 8–10

♦ *The Dear One*: When 12-year-old Feni's executive mother shares their home with Rebecca, a 15-year-old pregnant girl from Harlem, Feni is angry. As she comes to know Rebecca, however, her attitude changes and a friendship develops between the two of them. Grades 8–11

LAURENCE YEP

Laurence Yep's diverse childhood experience—growing up in a primarily African-American neighborhood in a Chinese-American family and attending a primarily white high school—instructed him in the role of outsider. Even among his fellow Chinese-American students in Chinatown, he was a minority, due to his inability to speak Chinese. Laurence attended Marquette University and the University of California at Santa Cruz before earning a doctorate at the State University of New York at Buffalo.

Laurence's Golden Mountain Chronicles series of eight books follows generations of a family from China to California from 1849 to 1995.

BOOKS

♦ *Dragon's Gate* (Golden Mountain Chronicles: 1867): Fourteen-year-old Otter travels from China to the Land of the Golden Mountain—California. Grades 8–10

♦ *The Serpent's Children* (Golden Mountain Chronicles: 1849): In this prequel to *Dragon's Gate*, a small girl named Cassia attempts to keep her impoverished family together in nineteenth-century China. Grades 8–10

♦ *Thief of Hearts* (Golden Mountain Chronicles Series: 1995): The last book in the Golden Mountain Chronicles series. Stacy does not think of herself as Chinese, but simply American. Her father is Caucasian and her mother is Chinese American. When Stacy is asked to befriend a Chinese immigrant, the two girls will become enemies before they become friends, and Stacy will come to understand more of her own heritage. Grades 8–10

♦ *The Journal of Wong Ming-Chung: A Chinese Miner, California, 1852*: Laurence Yep's volume in the My Name Is America series of books written by renowned authors of young adult fiction and nonfiction. After escaping famine and violence in China, 10-year-old Wong Ming-Chung joins relatives in California looking for gold. When the "Golden Mountain" in California proves mostly myth, Wong and his family find other, ingenious ways to make money. Grades 5–8

PAUL ZINDEL

Although Paul Zindel is best known around the world for his Pulitzer Prize–winning play *The Effects of Gamma Rays on Man-in-the-Moon Marigolds*, the truth is, he has devoted much of his time and energy to writing young adult literature—and his work was recognized in that arena as well.

Paul Zindel grew up in New York without a father and with a mother who worked at unglamorous jobs to support her two children, including being a hotdog vendor and boarding the terminally ill. There were no books in the Zindel home as Paul grew up, and he depended on his own imagination for entertainment.

Paul discovered his talent for writing, especially playwriting, in high school, when his peers asked him to write a funny sketch for a fundraising assembly. Although he was a chemistry major and would begin his career after college as a technical writer for Allied Chemical, Paul's mentor at Wagner College was the playwright Edward Albee.

Paul did not enjoy the corporate world and quickly left to start ten years as a high school chemistry teacher, during which time he continued to write—plays, in particular. When Paul left teaching he started writing novels, believing that the young adult novels he was seeing published were not peopled by teenagers like the ones he knew from his years in the classroom. Later in his career Paul switched from writing realistic fiction about quirky teens to writing horror fiction, attempting a new genre.

Paul, who died in 2003, was very well liked by the young adult literature community, a fact summed up by the "godfather of young adult literature," Don Gallo, who said: "We've lost a giant in the field of books for teens. An incredibly talented person. A nutty, fun-loving, kid-loving guy. A brilliant thinker."

BOOKS

♦ *The Pigman*: Although they sometimes go astray, John and Lorraine learn about good will from a lonely man, Mr. Pignati, who dies before they can thank him. Grades 7–10

♦ *Pardon Me, You're Stepping on My Eyeball*: High school misfits Edna and "Marsh" Mellow meet in the school psychiatrist's office, and a relationship grows. Grades 7–10

♦ *Loch*: Loch and his sister follow their marine biologist father to remote locations pursuing legendary beasts. When they really do find a Plesiosaur in a Vermont lake, the brother and sister try to save it. Grades 6–8

♦ *Reef of Death*: Seventeen-year-old P. C. McPhee answers an emergency call for help from his uncle in Australia. Hidden treasure, a dangerous reef, a man-eating beast, and a mystery that needs solving await him. Grades 7–10

References

Abdullah, M. H. (2002). *Bibliotherapy* (ERIC Clearinghouse on Reading, English, and Communication Digest no. 177).

American Academy of Child and Adolescent Psychiatry. (1997). *Normal adolescent development: Middle and high school years* (Facts for Families, no. 57). Retrieved November 10, 2004, from http://www.aacap.org/ publications/factsfam/develop.htm

Anderson, L. H. (2005). Loving the young adult reader even when you want to strangle him (or her)! *The ALAN Review, 32*(2), 53–58.

Anderson, M. T. (2002, November). *Young adult science fiction literature.* Paper presented at the Assembly on Literature for Adolescents Workshop, National Council of Teachers of English, Atlanta, GA.

Applebee, A. , Langer, J.A., Nystrand, M., & Gamoran, A. (2003). Discussion-based approaches to developing understanding: Classroom instruction and student performance in middle and high school English. *American Education Research Journal, 40*, 685–730.

Associated Press. (2005, April 25). Girls are abusing steroids, too, experts say. *MSNBC.* Retrieved August 20, 2005, from http://www.msnbc.msn.com/id/7633384/

Avi. (2004). *About Avi.* Retrieved November 10, 2004, from http://www.avi-writer.com/aboutAvi.html

Barenblat, R. (2004). Interview with Naomi Shihab Nye. *Pif Magazine.* Retrieved December 22, 2004, from http://www.pifmagazine.com/SID/240/

Bauer, J. (2003). *Biography.* Retrieved October 30, 2004, from http://www.joanbauer.com/jbbio.html

Bean, T. W. (2004). Making reading relevant for adolescents. In R. Robinson (Ed.), *Readings in reading instruction: Its history, theory and development* (pp. 263–268). Boston: Allyn & Bacon.

Bland, G. (2001) Out with the old and in with the (not so) new. *English Journal, 90*(3), 20–21.

Blasingame, J. (1998). *The Writing Conference presents: Karen Hesse.* Ottawa, KS: The Writing Conference.

Blasingame, J. (2003). Interview with Richie Partington. *Journal of Adolescent and Adult Literacy, 47*(2), 186-187.

Blasingame, J., & Bushman, J. H. (2000). In T. Hipple & S. Creech (Eds.), *Writers for young aults, supplement 1.* New York: Charles Scribners Sons.

Bloom, S. P., & Mercier, C. M. (1997). *Presenting Avi.* New York: Twayne Publishers.

Blume, J. (2004). *Questions on writing.* Retrieved November 1, 2004, from http://www.judyblume.com/ writing–jb.html

Blume, J. (2002, November 19) New York Public Library online chat. Retrieved November 1, 2004, from http:// www.judyblume.com/articles/NYPL_online_chat_11-24.02.html

Bush, G. W. (n.d.) Freedom and accountability: Summary of proposals. In *No child left behind.* Retrieved August 3, 2004, from http://www.whitehouse.gov/news/reports/no-child-left-behind.html#2

Bushman, J. H. (1998). *The Writing Conference presents: Robert Cormier.* Ottawa, KS. The Writing Conference.

Cart, M. (2004). Email interview, November 12, 2004.

Cart, M. (2004). What a wonderful world: Notes on the evolution of GLBTQ literature for young adults. *The ALAN Review, 31*(2), 46–52.

Casey, C. (n.d.). *Carried by creative currents.* Retrieved October 2, 2004, from Children's Literature Web site: http://www.childrenslit.com/f_hesse.html

Castellitto, L. M. (2004). Setting sail with Nancy Farmer on a new adventure. *Bookpage.* Retrieved December 28, 2004, from http://www.bookpage.com/0410bp/nancy_farmer.html

Children's Book Council. (2004). Meet the author/ illustrator: Paul B. Janeczko. CBC *Magazine.* Retrieved September 21, 2004, from http://cbcbooks.org/ cbcmagazine/meet/pauljaneczko.html

Children's Literature. (n.d.). *Meet authors and illustrators: Russell Freedman.* Retrieved November 8, 2004, from http://www.childrenslit.com/f_freedman.html

Cisneros, S. (2003). *Biography.* Retrieved November 2, 2004, from http://www.sandracisneros.com/html/about/ bio.html

Comer, M. (2005). Life with Ted: A Hipplite speaks out. *The ALAN Review, 32*(2), 19–21.

Courtot, M. (n.d.) *Meet authors and illustrators: Paula Danziger.* Retrieved November 5, 2004, from Children's Literature Web site: http://www.childrenslit.com/ f_danziger.html

Coville, B. (n.d.). *Bruce Coville: An illustrated biography.* Retrieved January 5, 2004, from http://www.brucecoville. com/bio.asp

Crowe, C. (2001). *Mildred D. Taylor.* Retrieved December 26, 2004, from University of Mississippi, the Mississippi Writers Page Web site: http://www.olemiss.edu/mwp/dir/ taylor_mildred/

Crowe, C. (2003). *Biography.* Retrieved January 26, 2005, from http://www.chriscrowe.com/about/biography.html

Crutcher, C. (1992). Healing through literature. In D. Gallo (Ed.), *Author's insights: Turning teenagers into* readers and writers. (pp. 33–40). Portsmouth, NH: Boynton Cook.

Crutcher, C. (2003). *King of the mild frontier*. New York: Greenwillow Books.

Danielson, A. M. (2003). *Author profile: Norma Fox Mazer*. Retrieved November 13, 2004 from teenreads.com: http://www.teenreads.com/authors/au-mazer-norma.asp

Davis, B. (n.d.). *Block Party: An interview with Francesca Lia Block*. Retrieved October 31, 2004, from amazon.com: http://www.amazon.com/exec/obidos/tg/feature/–/12106

Dedeo, C. (2000). *ClassicNotes: Mildred Taylor*. Retrieved December, 26, 2004, from GradeSaver: http://www.gradesaver.com/ClassicNotes/Authors/about_mildred_taylor.html

Donelson, K. L., & Nilsen, A. P. (2005). *Literature for today's young adults*. Boston: Pearson Education.

Draper, S. (2004). *Sharon Draper's bio*. Retrieved October 10, 2004, from http://sharondraper.com/bio.asp

Duncan, L. *Biography*. (n.d.). Retrieved November 7, 2004, from http://loisduncan.arquettes.com/Biography3.htm

Emery, D. (2004). *M.E. Kerr*. Retrieved December 29, 2004, from Rhode Island College, the Alliance for the Study and Teaching of Adolescent Literature Web site: http://www.ric.edu/astal/authors/mekerr.html

EPA's top 100 authors: Spinelli, Jerry. (1984). Retrieved December 26, 2004, from http://www.edupaperback.org/showauth.cfm?authid=74

EPA's top 100 authors: Taylor, Mildred. (1999). Retrieved December 26, 2004, from http://www.edupaperback.org/showauth.cfm?authid=75

EPA's top 100 authors: Voigt, Cynthia. (1999.) Retrieved December 26, 2004, from http://www.edupaperback.org/showauth.cfm?authid=109

EPA's top 100 authors: Zindel, Paul. (1999.) Retrieved August 23, 2004, from http://www.edupaperback.org/showauth.cfm?authid=86

Erikson, E. H. (1968). *Identity: Youth and crisis*. New York: Norton.

Farmer, N. (2003, November). *Writing young adult literature*. Paper presented at the Assembly on Literature for Adolescents of the National Council of Teachers of English, San Francisco.

Federal Interagency Forum on Child and Family Statistics. (2005). *Family Structure and Adolescent's Living Arrangements*. Retrieved August 20, 2005, from http://childstats.ed.gov/americaschildren/pop6.asp

Fletcher-Spear, K., Jenson-Benjamin, M., & Copeland, T. (2005). The truth about graphic novels: A format, not a genre. *The ALAN Review 32*(2), 37–44.

Gallo, D. (2001). How classics create and alliterate society. *English Journal, 90*(3), 33–35.

Gallo, D. (2003). Remembering Paul Zindel. *The ALAN Review 30*(3), 27.

Gantos, J. (2003). *Hole in my life*. Boston: Farrar, Straus, and Giroux.

Gardyn, R. (2001, November 1). A market kept in the closet. *American Demographics*. Retrieved August 21, 2005, from http://www.adage.com/search.cms

Glenn, M. (n.d.). *About Mel*. Retrieved November 8, 2004, from http://www.melglenn.com/

Goldsmith, F. (June, 2004). Ursula major. *School Library Journal*, 52.

Gonzalez, G. L. (2001). *History of the national poetry slam*. Retrieved September 10, 2004, from A Little Bit Louder Web site: http://www.geocities.com/loudpoet/resources/NPS_History.htm

Goodson, L. A. (2004a). Finish that chapter, the lights out: A reader becomes a writer. A visit with Vivian Vande Velde. *The ALAN Review, 32*(1), 21–24.

Goodson, L. A. (2004b). Singlehanding: Interview with Gary Paulsen. *The Alan Review, 31*(2), 53–59.

Goodson. L. A., & Blasingame, J. (1999). A conversation with Christopher Paul Curtis. *The Writers' Slate, 15*(1), 1–9.

Greenblatt, J. (2000, March). *Patterns of alcohol use among adolescents and associations with emotional and behavioral problems* (OAS Working Paper) Rockville, MD: Substance Abuse and Mental Health Services Administration. Retrieved July 28, 2005, from www.oas.samhsa.gov/NHSDA/TeenAlc/teenalc

Halls, K. M. (2002). *Bruce Coville follows his vision*. Retrieved October 10, 2004, from SmartWriters.com: http://www.smartwriters.com/content/view/117/16/

Hautman, P. *Personal*. Retrieved November 8, 2004, from http://www.petehautman.com/personal.html

Hayn, J., & Patrizi, B. (2005). *Deceit, rejection and despair: Connecting* Speak *and* The Scarlet Letter. Retrieved August 20, 2005, from Web site of Laurie Halse Anderson: http://www.writerlady.com/Deceitdespair.html

Herz, S. K., & Gallo, D.R. (2005). *From Hinton to Hamlet: Building bridges between young adult literature and the classics*. Westport, CT: Greenwood Press.

Hinton, S. E. (n.d). *Bio*. Retrieved November 9, 2004, from http://www.sehinton.com/bio/index.html

Hobbs, V. (n.d.). *About the author*. Retrieved November 9, 2004, from http://www.valeriehobbs.com/about_hobb.html

Hobbs, W., & Hobbs, J. (2004). *Meet Will Hobbs*. Retrieved October 10, 2004, from http://www.willhobbsauthor.com/meet.html

Holbrook, S. (2002). *Isn't she ladylike?* Huron, OH: Collinwood Press.

Holbrook, S. (2004). *About Sara Holbrook.* Retrieved October 1, 2004, from http://www.saraholbrook.com/bio2.htm

Howe, M. (1999). *Naomi Shihab Nye.* Retrieved December 22, 2004, from University of Minnesota, VG: Voices From the Gaps Web site: http://voices.cla.umn.edu/vg/Bios/entries/nye_naomi_shihab.html

Hurst, C. (1998, January). Featured author: Katherine Paterson. *Carol Hurst's Children's Literature Newsletter.* Retrieved December 22, 2004, from http://www.carolhurst.com/newsletters/31dnewsletters.html.

Hurst, C. (n.d.). *Featured author: Richard Peck.* Retrieved December 23, 2004, from Carol Hurst's Children's Literature Web site: http://www.carolhurst.com/authors/rpeck.html

Johnston, L. D., O'Malley, P. M., Bachman, J. G., & Schulenberg, J. E. (2004, December 21). *Overall teen drug use continues gradual decline; but use of inhalants rises.* Retrieved July 28, 2005, from Monitoring the Future Web site: http://www.monitoringthefuture.org/pressreleases/04drugpr.pdf

Karolides, N. J. (1992). The transactional theory of literature . In N. J. Karolides (Ed.), *Reader response in the classroom.* White Plains, NY: Longman.

Kerby, M. (n.d.). *The author corner: Robert Lipsyte.* Retrieved November 13, 2004 from Carroll County, MD, Web site, Mona Kerby's The Author Corner Web site: http://www.carr.org/mae/lipsyte/lipsyte.htm

Koh, M. (2004). *Biography of M.E. Kerr.* Retrieved October 3, 2004, from http://www.mekerr.com/

Krashen, S. (1993). *The power of reading.* Englewood, CO: Libraries Unlimited.

Krathwohl, D. R. (2001). A revision of Bloom's taxonomy: An overview. *Theory Into Practice, 41*(4), 214.

Korman, G. (2003). *No more dead dogs.* A presentation for the 2003 Arizona English Teachers' Association Convention, Avondale, AZ

Korman, G. (n.d.). *Gordon Korman Biography.* Retrieved November 11, 2004, from http://gordonkorman.com/

Lamb, W. (2000, July–August). Christopher Paul Curtis. Retrieved October 11, 2006, from http://www.hbook.com/publications/magazine/articles/jul00_lamb.asp

Latrobe, K., & Hutcherson, T. (2002, Summer–Autumn) An introduction to ten outstanding young-adult authors in the United States. *World Literature Today,* 75–76.

Le Guin, U. (2003). *Frequently asked questions.* Retrieved November 11, 2004, from http://www.ursulakleguin.com/FAQ_Questionnaire5_01.html#Childhood

Lesesne, T. (2003). *Making the match: The right book for the right reader at the right time.* York, ME: Stenhouse.

Levy, E. (2005). Remembering Paula Danziger. *The ALAN Review, 32*(2).

Lowry, L. (2002). *Biography.* Retrieved September 4, 2004, from http://www.loislowry.com/bio.html

Moyers, B. (2002, October 11). Naomi Shihab Nye: A Bill Moyers Interview. *PBS: Now with Bill Moyers.* Retrieved December 22, 2004, from http://www.pbs.org/now/transcript/transcript_nye.html

Myers, W. D. (1994). Margaret A. Edwards Award acceptance speech. *Journal of Youth Services in Libraries, 8*(2), 129–133.

National Endowment for the Arts. (2004) *Reading at Risk: A survey of literary reading in America* (Research Division Report No. 46.). Washington, DC: National Endowment for the Arts.

National Institute on Drug Abuse for Teens. (n.d.). *Anabolic steroids.* Retrieved July 10, 2005 from http://teens.drugabuse.gov/facts/facts_ster1.asp#used

National Mental Health Association. (2001). *Mental Illness and the family.* Retrieved August 1, 2005, from http://www.nmha.org/infoctr/factsheets/15.cfm

Nilsen, A. (1997). *Presenting M. E. Kerr.* New York: Twayne Publishers.

Nixon, J. L. (2001). *Mystery writing: My biography.* Retrieved December 21, 2003, from Scholastic: http://teacher.scholastic.com/writewit/mystery/bio.htm

Olendorf, D. (Ed.) (1992). *Something about the author: Robert Lipsyte* (Vol. 113, pp. 99–104). New York: Gale Research.

Park, L. S. (2004). *Bio.* Retrieved December 2, 2004, from http://www.lspark.com/bio.html

Paterson, K. (2004). *About Katherine Paterson.* Retrieved December 22, 2004, from http://www.terabithia.com/about.html

Penguin Putnam. (2000). *William Sleator.* Retrieved December 23, 2004, from http://www.penguinputnam.com/nf/Author/AuthorPage/0,,1000030218,00.html

Philbrick, R. (2004). *My biography.* Retrieved December 2, 2004, from Scholastic Books Web site: http://teacher.scholastic.com/writewit/bookrev/bio.htm

Probst, R. E. (1984). *Adolescent literature: Response and analysis.* Columbus, OH. Merrill.

Psychiatry and Reuter's Health. (2005). *More kids getting multiple drugs for mental ills.* Retrieved August 5, 2005, from the National Institutes of Health, National Library of Medicine Web site: http://www.medicineonline.com/news/12/1263/More-Kids-Getting-Multiple-Drugs-for-mental-ills.html

Reichard, S. (1998). *Eve Bunting and Ann Rinaldi.* Retrieved December 23, 2004, from Suite 101.com: http://www.suite101.com/article.cfm/childrens_writing/6008

Reid, A. H. (2004). *Meet the writers: Nancy Farmer.* Retrieved December 28, 2004, from the Barnes and Noble Web site: http://www.barnesandnoble.com/writers/writerdetails.asp?userid=Ft1LFAfAXD&cid=1033958#bio

Rinaldi, A. (2002). *Biography.* Retrieved December 23, 2004, from http://www.annrinaldi.com/docs/Rinaldi_bio.html

Robinson, J. D. (1997). *Rod Philbrick: Portrait of a writer.* Retrieved October 3, 2004, from SeacoastNH.com: http://www.seacoastnh.com/artists/philbrick/index.html

Rosenblatt, L. (1938). *Literature as exploration.* New York: Appleton Century.

Ruby, L. (2004). *About Lois.* Retrieved September 28, 2004, from http://www.loisruby.com/about/aboutlois.html

Sachar, L. (2002). *Author Bio.* Retrieved November 13, 2004, from http://www.louissachar.com/Bio.htm

Salisbury, G. (2004). *About me.* Retrieved December 23, 2004, from http://www.grahamsalisbury.com/biography.html

Sanchez, A. (2004). Crossing two bridges: Coming out and the power of images in YA literature. *The ALAN Review, 32*(1), 56–60.

Santucci, V. (n.d.). *Gary Soto: A Teacher Resource File.* Retrieved December 24, 2004, from James Madison University, Internet School Library Center Web site: http://falcon.jmu.edu/~ramseyil/soto.htm

Schütz, R. (2004). *Vygotsky & language acquisition.* Retrieved December 5, 2004, from English Made in Brazil Web site: http://www.sk.com.br/sk-vygot.html

Shanower, E. (2005). The art of the graphic novel. *The ALAN Review 32*(2), 32–36.

Smith, C. L. (2000). *Interview with children's/YA author Graham Salisbury.* Retrieved December 23, 2004, from http://www.cynthialeitichsmith.com/lit_resources/authors/interviews/GrahamSalisbury.html

Smith, C. L. (2004). *Interview with children's/YA author Linda Sue Park.* Retrieved December 2, 2004, from http://www.cynthialeitichsmith.com/lit_resources/authors/interviews/LindaSuePark.html

Soto, G. (n.d.). *The official Gary Soto Website.* Retrieved December 24, 2004, http://www.garysoto.com/

Spinelli, J. (2003). *Jerry Spinelli.* Retrieved December 26, 2004, from http://www.jerryspinelli.com/newbery_008.htm

Substance Abuse and Mental Health Services Administration. (2004). *Results from the 2002 National Survey on Drug Use and Health: National Findings.* Retrieved July 1, 2005, http://www.oas.samhsa.gov/nhsda/2k2nsduh/Results/2k2results.htm#fig2.3

Tashjian, J. (n.d.). *Bio.* Retrieved December 26, 2004, from http://www.janettashjian.com/bio.html

Teenreads.com. (2003). *Author profile: Lois Duncan.* Retrieved November 7, 2004, from http://www.teenreads.com/authors/au-duncan-lois.asp

Texeira, E. (2005, August 19). U.S. minorities are becoming majority war of words: As populations change, groups debate the meanings of terms they have been using for years. *Salt Lake Tribune.* Retrieved August 19, 2005, from http://www.sltrib.com/nationworld/ci_2955262

Trelease, J. (2004). *Author profile: Gary Paulsen.* Retrieved December 22, 2004, from http://www.trelease-on-reading.com/paulsen.html

U.S. Census Bureau. (2005, June 9). *Hispanic population passes 40 million, Census Bureau reports.* Retrieved August 6, 2005, from http://www.census.gov/Press-Release/www/releases/archives/population/005164.html

U.S. Census Bureau. (2005, August 11). *Texas becomes nation's newest "majority-minority" state, census bureau announces.* Retrieved August 21, 2005, from http://www.census.gov/Press-Release/www/releases/archives/population/005514.html

Vande Velde, V. (n.d.). *Background.* Retrieved December 26, 2004, from http://www.vivianvandevelde.com/background.cfm

Vygotsky, L. S. (1978). *Mind in society: The development of higher psychological processes.* Cambridge, MA: Harvard University Press.

Walsh, J. (n.d.). *Unusual writing of Pat Mora.* Retrieved September 12, 2004, from Cary Academy Web site: http://project1.caryacademy.org/echoes/poet_Pat_Mora/DefaultMora.htm

Weiss, M. J. (2005). The publisher's connection. *The ALAN Review, 32*(2), 92–94.

Williams, R. (2003). *William Sleator Links.* Retrieved December 23, 2004, from The Green Futures of Tycho Web site: http://www.tycho.org/sleator.shtml

Woodson, J. (2002). *Biography.* Retrieved December 26, 2004, from http://www.jacquelinewoodson.com/bio.shtml

Zindel, P. (n.d.). *Paul Zindel's biography.* Retrieved August 23, 2004, from Scholastic Books Web site: http://www2.scholastic.com/teachers/authorsandbooks/authorstudies/authorhome.jhtml?authorID=217&collateralID=5312&displayName=Biography

Index